THE HUMILIATED CHRIST
IN MODERN RUSSIAN THOUGHT

THE HUMILIATED CHRIST IN MODERN RUSSIAN THOUGHT

BY

NADEJDA GORODETZKY *(Mrs)*

B.LITT. (OXON.)

LONDON

SOCIETY FOR PROMOTING
CHRISTIAN KNOWLEDGE

NEW YORK: THE MACMILLAN COMPANY

1938

Made in Great Britain

CONTENTS

INTRODUCTION

THE title of the present work, *The Humiliated Christ in Modern Russian Thought,* may seem rather vague. It nevertheless expresses our purpose. We keep in mind the theological meaning of the term " the (self) humiliation of Christ " but we intend to approach it first on non-theological ground. Indeed, long before Russian thought was mature enough to face the doctrine of kenosis, the attention of the Russian people was struck by the evangelical call to meekness, poverty, humility and obedience. The popularity of a type representing these qualities, whether in history, literature or devotion, seemed to us fair matter for our investigation. This emphasis, moreover, far from vanishing with time, grew and developed parallel with the development of national thought and character.

We are not concerned with the question whether there was any similar current of thought in the West or elsewhere. We do not take this subject as a "Russian" as opposed to a "non-Russian" one. Neither do we want to present it as exclusively Russian. General characterization of Russian national or religious character would seem to us too rash, as Russia was always a very complex body, ethnographically, historically, socially and religiously.

It is far from our intention to present the doctrine of kenosis, or the "kenotic" character, as the sole religious inspiration of Russian people. We have no desire to belittle the importance of other currents which have been many and various. Thus it has become a commonplace to say that the Russians have always laid special stress upon the resurrection. Very noticeable, too, is their feeling for the cosmic meaning of the incarnation, their hope of transfiguration, their eschatological expectation and their conception of the catholicity,

" sobornost," of the Church. The mere enumeration of these different aspects of religious thought certainly is not exhaustive. Yet the figure of the humiliation of Christ, unconsciously felt and expressed in the accounts of some historical lives, in folk-lore and in secular literature, and finding its final expression in theology, is among the most constant features. We shall therefore examine these documents without forcing all the phenomena of life or art into the scheme. We are fully aware both of the manifold riches of Russian life and thought and of the unavoidable onesidedness of any doctrine considered in isolation. We are not deterred by our inability to explain the Person of Christ by the particular doctrine we deal with. We gladly accept the fact that human understanding cannot hope to comprehend within its categories Him who is the Life and the Truth. Our task is not to prove the doctrine of kenosis to be the only way of approaching Jesus of Nazareth. We set ourselves only to show how He was apprehended by those Russians whose works we shall examine. We have to notice the fact that in the case of Russia the " kenotic " type of life, thought and character, far from being a result of intellectual investigation, preceded it.

It even seems to us that the main importance of Russian " kenoticism " lies precisely in the fact that there was no " doctrine " about it. The Christian intuition and experience rather discovered in the Gospels " the mind of Christ Jesus " than sought to discuss *how* He took upon Himself the form of a servant. If an individual experience of God is precious to us, no less so is the spectacle of a nation trying to find the way to its Saviour and to reflect His likeness. This consideration encourages us to approach a subject which, on its theological side, has already been treated by qualified thinkers. In a way, the present survey is much more an account of a devotional attitude, of life lived in a " kenotic " frame of mind, than an account of the doctrine itself, though we shall endeavour, in the second part of the work, to give some picture of Russian theological thought on the question.

We have already used the expression " kenotic mind." We

shall express by " kenotic mind, or mood, or character " the features which correspond to the " mind of Christ " as defined in the second chapter of the Epistle of St. Paul to the Philippians, vv. 5—11, and in 2 Corinthians viii. 9. Hence, meekness, self-abasement, voluntary poverty, humility, obedience, " non-resistance," acceptance of suffering and death would be the expression of the " kenotic mood." It may also include, though not without reserve, a critical attitude towards human reason or towards civilization. The materials which we have in view apply these characteristics both to individuals and groups. Taken in its direct meaning, this mood should be the following of Christ—as in the case of some saints. On the purely human level, the emphasis on the " kenotic " features may seem morbid. Yet taken in its scriptural fullness, the kenosis brings in a triumphant note. The glory of Christ radiates upon men filling them with hope. We shall see this in the writings of St. Tykhon and of the Metropolitan Filaret. But we shall also come across and mention cases when this " kenotic mood " becomes detached from its scriptural context and hardly claims a Christian origin. This applies to certain political leaders.

" The mind of Christ " of the Epistle to Philippians is also generally known under the term " humiliation." It embraces usually not only the moral qualities of Jesus Christ but also the earthly existence of Jesus of Nazareth, His birth in a manger, His humble human conditions. It refers to the Person of Christ taken in its subjection to the laws of human nature : His growth and development, His human mode of asking questions or expressing ignorance of some facts, His temptation, prayer, His agony and death. We reserve this term more particularly for those among the Russian theologians who mentioned all these features in moral or devotional contexts.

Finally, in the case of the theologians who deal with the christological doctrine, we shall refer to the technical terms of kenosis or the self-emptying of Christ.

As for our method, there arise three questions : (a) Why start from the nineteenth century? (b) To what extent can secular literature be taken into account as an illustration of a religious idea? and (c) How far can we trust the accuracy of novelists in picturing life and character?

The first question is answered by M. Baring: "For all students of literature, and especially for the foreign student, Russian literature . . . begins with the nineteenth century." [1] But the epoch we have chosen is of more than merely literary value for our purpose. "Russian thought became original and creative only in the nineteenth century." [2] It was then that Russians began to meditate upon their national task, upon their place in the European family, and upon the historical and spiritual destiny of Russia. It was during this period that Russia was exhorted to become "the most Christian of all human societies." As for the writers themselves, the nineteenth century first gave definition to the writers' task. Pushkin (1799—1837) found no better words to describe his calling and duty as a poet than those of Isaiah vi. which inspired the prophet. For Lermontov (1814–41), too, the poet was a prophet. The tragedy of Gogol's life (1809–52) was that he felt himself the oracle of God. And—to mention only the most obvious examples—Dostoevsky (1821–81) and L. Tolstoy (1828—1910) fully shared this point of view.

If the cultural expressions of different nations may often be traced back to some religious origin, this is certainly so in the case of Russia. It was not only a religious but a Christian background from which Russian literature originated. A nation possessing no heritage of previous culture received the Gospels and the liturgy in a language closely akin to its own and from them learned to think. Without entering into the domain of history, we may mention the fact that, by the time we are concerned with, literature had become almost the only means of self-expression. Owing to this and to the lofty claim of the writers, "the basic idea of Russian literature was a

---

[1] M. Baring, *Introduction to the Oxford book of Russian verse*, (Oxford, 1924), p. xv.
[2] N. Berdyaeff, *The Russian religious thought of the nineteenth century* in *Sovremennija Zapissky* (Contemporaneous Annals) (Paris, 1930), N. xlii, pp. 309–43, 311.

religious and a moral one; it was based on the conception of the sanctity of human personality and human life in general." [3] This was true of both prose works and of poetry.

But, we may ask, did Russian writers explicitly point to Jesus Christ? Many of them did not. Yet we persist in seeking a theological meaning in their works. We have to keep in mind that political and religious censorship were often an obstacle to the free mention of the Person of Christ; that the influence of rationalism or of a worldly life was too strong with some to leave them in conscious relationship to Christ; while with others, on the contrary, it may have been excessive awe which prevented them from speaking freely of Christ. But Christ was still present in the background of any Russian mind and " all the Russian literature of the nineteenth century was wounded by the theme of Christianity. It even tended to surpass the regions of art and was seeking a religious action." [4] We do not hesitate, accordingly, to illustrate our thesis from the work of secular writers.

It might be objected that fiction is no exact expression of life or character. We have already said that we do not want to prove that the " kenotic character " was the Russian character. If we want to be accurate, we have only the right to show how this character was represented in the materials which we examine. But it may be not inappropriate to add that even from the point of view of one who is interested in definition of the national religious type, our materials could be trusted, especially at this particular epoch. Describing Pushkin's Russia, I. S. Aksakov (1823–95) says: " In the artistic interpretation of life there reigned the demand for simplicity and truth." [5] This was again applied to either prose or poetry. The historians of literature generally admit that " the 'forties in literature was the epoch of a decisive

---

[3] E. Soloviev-Andreevich, *Outlines of the history of Russian literature of the nineteenth century* (SPB. 1902), p. iv—definition valuable as coming from an agnostic historian of literature. On poetry in M. Baring, *op. cit.*, p. xxxix.
[4] N. Berdyaeff, *ibid.*, p. 334.
[5] I. S. Aksakov, *Biography of Tyutchev* (M. 1886), p. 59.

break: the artistic conscientiousness of Pushkin laid the foundation of a realism which became a constant feature of our literature," though at times to the detriment of the formal side of artistic creativity.[6] Nowadays many would agree with N. A. Berdyaeff that the realism of Russian writers was deeper than this exterior definition: " Russian literature became realistic in the sense of religious, ontological realism, in the sense of the contemplation of the deepest realities of existence and of life." [7]

A few words must be added as to our use of our sources. We are obviously limited to the materials which are available in the libraries where we have been able to work: the Bodleian and the Taylorian Libraries, Oxford, and the British Museum; some books were accessible to us owing to the kindness of the Institute of Orthodox Theology in Paris, the Turgenev Society Library, and the Slavonic Library of the Jesuits in Paris. As much of the material we have to deal with is not translated into English, we shall have to give considerable space to quotations. This work, originally a B.Litt. thesis, contained a Bibliography, consisting mainly of Russian books, which is omitted in this present work. We are conscious that at times we introduce information which is not strictly relevant to our subject and which seems to make the presentation of the subject more confusing. Yet we did not avoid this difficulty, thinking that a foreign reader may want to see the place of the kenotic stream in the context of a movement or of the general system of a writer.

The purpose of this study being rather religious than literary, we shall at times have to concentrate not on the greatest writers but on those most representative from this special point of view. Some great writers or thinkers of both the secular and the ecclesiastical world will thus find a very cursory treatment in the present survey.

The nineteenth century, or more exactly the period from

---

[6] A. N. Puypin, *History of Russian ethnography* (SPB. 1890–2), 4 vols., t. II, p. I, cp. p. 349.
[7] N. Berdyaeff, *ibid.*, p. 336.

1836 onwards, is the field we intend to cover. Yet we do not exclude *fin de siècle* writers whose activity continues into the new century. The first edition of Tareev's *The Temptation of the Godman,* for example, is dated 1892, but his thought finds final expression only in his book on *The Foundations of Christianity,* 1908–10. The Rev. S. N. Bulgakov's *The Lamb of God* was published only in 1933.

The author's most sincere thanks are due to the Rev. Dr. L. W. Grensted and to Professors S. A. Konovalov and G. P. Fedotov; also to members of the staff of the College of the Ascension, Selly Oak, Birmingham, and of the Society of Oxford Home Students, as well as to many friends who made it materially possible to write this book. In all cases, there was more than material help or technical advice or criticism— this work owes very much to the affection, trust and general encouragement of all.

ABBREVIATIONS USED IN THE NOTES

M.   =   Moscow
SPB. =   St. Petersburg (now Leningrad)
t.   =   tome (volume)

CHAPTER I

ACCEPTANCE OF HUMILIATION AS A NATIONAL IDEAL

THE nineteenth century in Russia is marked by the rapidity of the general development of the country. It is common to speak of a " ten-year-rhythm," each decade showing a change in the governing ideas.

The beginning of the century was coloured by the " meeting with the West," a result of the war and of the victory over Napoleon. Russian politics, thought and religion were confronted with those of the Western nations. There was something universalistic in this " epoch of Alexander I " (1801–25). At the same time, one was faced with the question as to what Russia is, and what is her place among and relation to the other nations. But this epoch was " an awakening of heart, not yet the awakening of thought," [1] and the problem of Russia remained almost untouched up to the 'thirties. None could better personify this period of " aesthetic culture of the heart," of religious disquietude and political and religious universalism than the Emperor himself. Alexander I died suddenly, and the masses refused to believe the news of his death. A legend spread among the people which we must notice for its " kenotic " tenor. The Tsar was said to have fled to Siberia disguised as a soldier, and to be living there a humble life in a peasant hut, " saving his soul " under the name of the hermit Feodor Kuzmich. [2]

The romantic and utopistic generation of the 'thirties was confined by the political restrictions of the reign of Nicolas I (1825–55) to a life of dreamy inactivity, the origin in Russian life and literature of the type of " the unwanted man." But the creative power of the nation could not be hindered by any censorship. At this period, poetry was the voice of Russia. It still echoed the triumphant motives of recent victory.

---

[1] G. V. Florovsky, *The ways of Russian Theology* (Paris, 1937), p. 128.
[2] A historic personage ; many believe in the historicity of the fact.

It was new when, in his poem " My native Country "
(1841), M. Y. Lermontov wrote :

" I love my land but with a strange affection."

It was not military glory that attracted him, but rather the
picture of sad villages piercing the night with their dim, scattered lights; or else the noise and dance of drunken peasants
on a feast-day. Such scenery and such heroes were not
naturally congenial to a Byronic poet. But this was the
picture which fascinated the Russian writers of the nineteenth
century.[3]

The problem of Russia rose in all its importance before the
generation of the 'forties. The Slavophils and the Westernisers
discussed it at length. The controversy gave an impulse to the
activities of the following decade and inspiration to further
generations. The Slavophils inspired research in folk-lore,
history, ethnography; the peasant became a hero in literature.
The question of the peasantry was central for both the Slavophils and the Westernisers, the former trying to give a definition of the national and religious character of Russia, the latter
concerned with the political situation of their country, both
eager to see the emancipation of the peasants.

The " period of great reforms," the 'sixties (the abolition of
serfdom was proclaimed on February 19th, 1861), coincided
with the progress of positive science which dominated thought
and was almost raised by the young, the " Thinking Realists "
or " the Nihilists " of this period, to the status of a religion.

The 'seventies brought forward the type of " conscience-
stricken noblemen " who wished to " go down among the
people " and to pay what they conceived as the debt of their
civilization. This compassionate " kenotic " current in the
revolutionary-minded youth was opposed within the group
itself by political extremists of materialistic outlook, and by
the active propaganda of anarchy.

The end of the century, after the assassination of Alexander

[3] We regret that it is not possible to give a separate place in this study
to poetry, the more so in view of the lofty and " prophetic " character
of Russian poetry and the place of honour which it always occupied.
Wherever possible, we shall notice poetical works of influence, in connection with our subject.

II (1855–81), was known as "the period of reaction" under Alexander III (1881–94). Two interests characterize this period: Marxism on the one hand and, on the other, a new investigation of religious problems. It is enough to mention the influence of Tolstoy, Soloviev and Dostoevsky.

The twentieth century began with the reaction which S. N. Bulgakov characterized in the title of his book *From Marxism to Idealism*. In fact, there was here more than idealism: it was a return of the intelligentsia into the Church. The problem of the Church and its nature raised by the Slavophils again attracted thinkers. There was an endeavour to weigh the possibilities of an "Orthodox culture." "Kenotic" ideas did not disappear either. They were now, indeed, more precise: in poetry, Russia was still spoken of as "a fool in Christ"; and the theologians spoke directly of the Person of Christ in terms of kenotic doctrine.

THE SLAVOPHILS AND THE WESTERNISERS

The discussions about Russian destinies and character may seem irrelevant to our subject. The controversy between the Slavophils and the Westernisers, it may seem at first sight, concerned some particular events of Russian history and their interpretation. In fact, it was deeper: it touched the very vocation of Russia.

All educated men of the first half of the nineteenth century were, in a way, Westernisers. Ivan V. Kireevsky (1806–56) called his first review *The European* (Europe always meaning Western Europe). The Slavophils did not deny their link with the West. In fact, they received from the West, Slavonic and Germanic, the idea of the nation as the unity of consciousness, their interest in folk-lore, their distinction between reason and intelligence or the juxtaposition of thesis and antithesis. Only, what remained for people in the West in the domain of ideas, became for the Slavophils a reality embodied in Russia. Ivan Kireevsky found the content of the consciousness of the Russian people to be Christianity—the Orthodox faith. He trusted this collective experience of his nation, and so did the other Slavophils. This is why we must carefully examine the whole East-and-West controversy. It will show us how the men who meditated upon Russia conceived her vocation as a Christian country, and what features of Christianity they emphasized. We shall see that the idea of humiliation will find in them convinced supporters.

The Slavophil movement was a religious conception of the world rather than a nationalistic current of thought. The misleading nickname rose out of their sympathy for the oppressed Slavonic nations and the expectation that, once freed from the Turkish or German yoke, the Slavonic brethren, under the moral leadership of Russia, would utter " a new word." It was also thought that Russia, in her silent and suffering history, had grown in understanding and, however backward in civilization, could solve the problems tormenting the West. The task of Russia as the Orthodox country being intimately connected for the Slavophils with Christianity, they were logically drawn to universalism. That Russia should rightly understand her task and destiny seemed of vital importance, not only for the country itself, but for the whole world. The idea of the nation as a Christian entity freed them from national exclusiveness, " offering new possibilities of universal relationship." [4] In spite of such intentions and in spite of their austere criticism of Russia, the Slavophils who collected numerous examples of national Russian humility did not wholly escape from national pride and, at times, blindness with regard to the actual state of their country. Khomyakov was to recall that neither the country nor even its Church answered completely at any moment of history to its potential holiness. This mixture of mystical worship of Russia and ruthless criticism coloured the whole of Russian literature of the nineteenth century linking the patriotic and the " accusatory " writers.[5]

[4] Y. F. Samarin (M. 1900), 8 vols., t. I, p. 221, Notes on an article of S. Soloviev, 1857. C. N. Leontiev, *Works* (M. 1912), 9 vols., t. V, p.19, protesting against the idea of Russia being a purely Slavonic country: " Such a content would be too poor for her universal spirit." V. S. Soloviev, *Works* (SPB. 1896), 10 vols., t. III, p. 196 : " Truth can only be universal." All know Dostoevsky's " a Russian has two native lands, Russia and Western Europe " as well as his speech on Pushkin, whose chief merit he saw in the creation of the " universal " Russian man.

[5] The paradox of national pride and humility was vigorously exposed by V. S. Soloviev after his break with the group in 1881, especially in

The discussions of the problem of Russia took more definite character after the publication of the *Philosophical Letters* (1836) of Peter Y. Chaadaev (1793—1856). The position of the Slavophils and the Westernisers was thenceforward clear. They continued their discussions but remained friends until 1845, when those who wanted to follow Western ways were accused by the poet N. M. Yazykov (1803–46) of treason. This was the data of formal break.

It would be vain to expect definite and elaborate systems of thought coming from any among the Slavophils, whose works were mostly unfinished and fragmentary. As a group, they were pioneers in many fields. They had to work and to think in unfavourable conditions. The pressure of the censorship prevented Ivan V. Kireevsky from developing his philosophical gifts. Suspicion weighed upon A. S. Khomyakov (1804–60) and it took time before the ecclesiastical world recognized the value of his theological writings.[6]   Y. F. Samarin's (1819–76) theological works are of no great interest; he did more as a lawyer and magistrate working for emancipation. Peter V. Kireevsky (1808–56) did the work of gathering and classification of folk-lore. C. S. Aksakov's (1818–60) historical writings are only fragments, valuable for his ideas on community. I. S. Aksakov (1823–95), more than any of the Slavophils, actually helped the Slavs and fought, as a journalist, for their cause. He wrote copiously on the situation of the Church in Russia

On the national problem in Russia, t. V, p. 30.   The paradox of imperialism and humility in the early Slavophils, in Dostoevsky and also in Soloviev, is noticed by M. M. Tareev, *Foundations of Christianity* (M. 1908), t. IV, pp. 295 and 367.   Among many examples of criticism of Russia made by the Slavophils, note I. S. Aksakov's articles on Church and State.   C. S. Aksakov spoke of his nation as sinful though always longing for repentance.   Khomyakov in his poem " To Russia " (1854) says "heavy upon thee presses the yoke of slavery; thou art filled with godless and devastating lies," etc.

[6] F. Smirnov, " Theological ideas of the Slavophils," in the *Orthodox Observer,* 1883 and 1884, refers to this misunderstanding.   Some of the ecclesiastical world (so, for a time, Filaret of Moscow) approved of him, but he could not publish his works and had to write some of them in foreign languages and printed them outside Russia.   After his death, Samarin edited his works in Prague, though in the Russian language. Besides his own writings, Khomyakov translated the Epistles to the Galatians and to the Ephesians and wrote a page of commentary on Philippians, giving to ii. 6 a kenotic interpretation.

and exposed the shortcomings of his time; he pleaded for freedom of conscience and demanded separation between Church and State. The probity of the life and thought of the Slavophils was recognized even by their opponents. We note in our particular investigation their contribution as a group of lay theologians and faithful interpreters of the " kenotic " inspiration of early Russia.

The intuition of a poet expressed better than any systematic teaching the true tendency of the movement. Feodor I. Tyutchev (1803–73) took a position of a convinced Slavophil. His political articles like *Russia and revolution* (1848) or *Papacy and the Roman Problem* (1849) and all his poems of political inspiration illustrated his hope in the future of Russia and his faith in special divine protection reserved to his land, even though it was a " dark land of an unawakened nation." He considered Russia as in the service of Christ, and therefore he expressed hopes of the great day to come, " the universal and Orthodox day " (" Day-break," 1850). In 1854, he wrote "Now is no time for verse" : the war for him was not a political menace but one directed against the " Russian word," against the life and enlightenment of future times. He exhorted his readers " to be faithful and to become justified before God." To the question, what was this mysterious " new word," Tyutchev, and with him all the Slavophils, would answer :

> " Russia cannot be grasped by reason
> Nor measured by a common gauge;
> Her way is different from others—
> Russia is a matter of belief."

This faith in Russia was not of a nationalistic type, neither was it connected with high estimation of either culture, or civilization, or history. In fact, Russia at this time had hardly any civilization and no great culture. And even if historical imperfections could be overcome, even if freedom and happiness should prevail in the country, what of the old wounds, the traces of violence, what of the emptiness and corruption of souls? " Who will heal, who will cover them?—thou, pure garment of Christ " (" Over the dark crowd "). Tyutchev himself knew doubts and passions. The unknown forces of the chaotic nocturnal world were at once frightening and dear to him : " let me experience annihilation, blend myself with the sleeping world " (" Twilight "). He felt the corruption of the spirit and the dissociation of personality. The way from this dark world was clear to him. It was in the Gospels and in the Person of the Saviour (" Lines sent with a New Testament "). Whatever passions may trouble him, " the soul is prepared, like Mary, to cling to the feet of Christ " (" O, my prophetic soul "). Personally, Tyutchev could not always remain faithful to Christ. But he believed profoundly that his nation and, most particularly, the peasants did not fail Christ. This contact of the national soul with Christ was for him a matter of faith, even more : a fact, though perhaps it was not realized by all. Here, in prose form, is the poem " Those poor villages."

> " Those poor villages,
> That featureless nature. . . .
> Land of patient fortitude,
> Land of the Russian folk.

> " The proud glance of a stranger
> Will not notice or understand
> The radiance which transpires
> Thy naked poverty.

> " Laden with the burden of the cross,
> All through thee, my native land,
> In the form of a servant, the King of heav'n
> Went about, bestowing his blessing." [7]

This poem reveals the very heart of Slavophilism. It makes it clear that the " new word " is meant to be essentially Christian, and that it is most likely to be uttered by those silent men whose form the King of heaven assumed. Therefore the attention of the nineteenth century was to be directed henceforward towards the peasantry. It is much more than the attitude of social compassion : it is readiness to learn. " We must learn from the people to become intellectually

[7] This poem was universally known and quoted almost to excess. Dostoevsky takes it as laying bare the basis of Russian character and destiny. Tareev mentions it when speaking, as a theologian interested in

humble; we must realize that in the peasant's conception of the world there is more truth than in ours." [8] To those anxious about the lack of education among the Russian peasantry, Dostoevsky gave the emphatic reply:

> " I affirm that our (' people ') peasants were already enlightened a long time ago, by accepting Christ and His teaching. . . . The man of the people knows everything, though he would not pass an examination in the Catechism. He learned in the Churches where during centuries he heard prayers and songs which are better than any sermons . . . and he knows by heart *O Lord and Master of my life:* [9] all the *essence* of Christianity is contained in this prayer. But his chief school of Christianity was the ages of endless suffering he endured in the course of history when, abandoned by all, oppressed by all, working for all, he remained all alone with Christ, the Comforter, whom he received then in his soul and who saved this soul from despair." [10]

This identification of the peasantry with the vision of the humiliated Christ was extended to the rest of the nation. This is the foundation of the belief in " Holy Russia." The rediscovery of popular songs and folk-lore further showed what treasures lay hidden in the depth of remote villages.[11] The historical and spiritual past revealed through the folk-lore

secular literature, of the humiliation of Christ. Indeed, this poem could serve as epigraph to any work connected with the second chapter of the Epistle to the Philippians. At the same time Tyutchev remains a poet of the elite; the popularity of this particular poem is therefore to be ascribed to its content rather than to the fame of the author.

[8] C. N. Leontiev, t. VIII, p. 110.

[9] A prayer of St. Ephraim the Syrian: "O Lord and Master of my life, give me not a spirit of sloth, of despondency, of lust or of vain talking; but bestow on me Thy servant the spirit of chastity, of humility, of patience and love. Yea, O Lord and King, grant to me to see my own errors and not to judge my brother, for blessed art Thou unto ages of ages." This prayer was a turning point in the life of the revolutionary A. K. Malikov (see below).

[10] F. M. Dostoevsky, *Works* (SPB. 1905–6), 14 vols., Speech on Pushkin, t. XII, pp. 438, 439.

[11] All the Slavophils, especially Yazykov, collected all they could for P. Kireevsky. He organized expeditions in different parts of the country. He died before the publication of his life work. Some of the Southern songs were sent by Gogol. See also the bibliographical and archæological works of Metropolitan Evgeny Bolokhvitinov (1767—1837). One should specially remember the so-called spiritual songs. See G. P. Fedotov, *Spiritual Songs* (Paris, 1935).

inspired confidence to the Slavophils with regard to the future of their country.

The religious approach coloured the whole system of the Slavophils. They underlined the fact that the word *krestianin* (peasant) had the same sound and the same connotation as *christian*. They all trusted "the people's instincts and beliefs" rather than any books, because of the "self-forgetfulness and self-sacrifice which seem to be the basis of their moral nature."[12] Their personal conversions were sometimes due to this contact with, or at least this belief in, the Christian Orthodox soul of the peasants.[13]

The interpretation of Russian history, chief point of disagreement with the Westernisers, is interesting for us. It shows that the main peculiarities of Russian history which appealed to the Slavophils fall into the definition of "kenotic" features. The peaceful character of ancient Russia and the calling of the Varangian rulers (Rurik, 879) seemed to the Slavophils a true expression of the Christian spirit : "There is no stain of conquest on our early history. Blood and enmity did not serve as the foundation of the Russian state. . . . The Church, having limited the field of her activity, never lost the purity of her inward life and did not preach to her children injustice and violence."[14] The nation developed the system of community organization and elected their prince, which was also "a voluntary self-limitation of each individual."[15] This spirit was believed to run through the whole history of Russia and to apply alike to the Varangians and to the case of Michael Romanov[16] (reigned 1613–45). To this exaltation of the love of peace, humility and self-limitation the Westernisers would reply that this very "summoning of a prince from over the

[12] F. I. Tyutchev, *Works,* ed. P. Bikov (SPB. 1912), p. 468, Russia and revolution.
[13] The conversion of I. Kireevsky, due to his discovery of orthodoxy in peasants and also to the influence of his wife, had important consequences not only for himself. He met the monks of Optina and became their helper in the translation and publishing of the early ascetic Fathers. Ever since, Optina has been connected with the literary world.
[14] A. S. Khomyakov, *Works* (M. 1906–11), 4th ed., 8 vols., t. III, p. 28.
[15] Y. F. Samarin, t. I, p. 52, On the opinion of the *Sovremennik,* 1847.
[16] C. S. Aksakov, *Works* (M. 1861–80), 3 vols., t. I, p. 8, Historical writings.

sea is an irregularity, an abnormality "; as for humility, it is " slavish, as Russian pride is slavish." [17]   Even more bitter controversy was provoked by the figure of Peter the Great and by his reforms (reigned 1682—1725). The Slavophils accused him not so much of forcing foreign ideas and ways upon the nation as of breaking with its peaceful character and introducing a schism between government and nation.[18] Ever since, the growing empire, according to them, had gone astray from the national Christian ideals, and the spirit of the State suppressed the brotherly spirit of the village-community.   This community-principle of early Russia was referred to by the Westernisers also but for political ends.   It was not the return to the idyllic past that the Slavophils desired, but the possibility for the country to develop in the Christian spirit of her past.[19]

Even in their political constructions, the Slavophils, at their best, claimed to be ready for sacrifices and self-impoverishment.   No less than the liberal Westernisers, the Slavophils, though themselves landowners, worked for the abolition of serfdom, Khomyakov writing : " the one who is offended can forgive; the offender never forgives; from his crime sprouts hatred. A Christian can be a serf but must not be a slaveowner." [20] Even before emancipation, I. Aksakov went further and proposed that " nobility as a class " should disappear.[21] In external politics, pleading for the liberation of the Slavs, Samarin connected this problem with the question of Poland and advised that Russia should give up Poland " willingly and following her own inner promptings . . . for the sake of the pacification of Europe, which is now turned against us." [22]

---

[17] I. S. Turgenev, *Smoke,* tr. C. Garnett (1896), pp. 45, 52. Fiction expresses here both the author's view and the position of the Westernisers.

[18] G. Florovsky, *The Ways of Russian Theology,* p. 83 : " It was not so much a schism between government and nation as one between government and the Church."

[19] The attitude of the Slavophils with regard to the State was on the whole negative.   C. S. Aksakov speaks of it as a " compromise," " living human Christian conscience being higher than any rightful order " in I. S. Aksakov, *Works* (M. 1886), 7 vols., t. I, p. 679. V. Y. Bogucharsky, *The Active Populism of the Seventies* (M. 1912), p. 21, notices Aksakov's influence on Bakunin and anarchism in Russia.

[20] A. Khomyakov, t. II, p. 97, *Theological writings.*

[21] I. S. Aksakov, t. V, p. 28, from *Day* of 6/1/1861.

[22] Y. Samarin, t. I, p. 343, *Modern content of the Polish problem.*

Even N. Y. Danilevsky (1822–85), a scientist, economist and a partisan of practical policy, would acknowledge, together with C. Leontiev that " Russia has a peculiar political destiny. . . Her interests bear a *moral* character, that of the support of the feeble and injured." [23]   However much Russia might need at the moment political influence in the Balkans, the Slavophils were not interested in these practical matters, but saw the whole Slavonic problem in terms of defending Christian faith, " the universe of orthodoxy." [24]   I. S. Aksakov reported many examples of peasants ready to offer their service and lives for the cause of the " brethren." [25]   For them Russia was the representative " of the principles sought by the Slavs; she must hold aloft in strict purity the political and spiritual banner of Slavism, not in a sense of any ambitious design but . . . as a symbol pointing the way." [26]   This way, like the cultural vocation of the country, must be understood " not as a false privilege but as a real duty; not as dominion but as service." [27]   And Dostoevsky would conclude saying that " all the power of Russia lies in sacrificial disinterestedness—all her personality, so to say, and the whole future destiny of Russia." Moreover, it is not enough to be " longing to serve humanity. . . . Whosoever would be great in the Kingdom of God, let him be the servant of all.   That is how I understand the Russian destiny in its *ideal*." [28]

The Slavophils had the intuition of universal history as the growth of the Kingdom of God.   It was of great importance to them that Russia should feel her real task and place in this process, as this process was felt as an organic one.   We can only mention here the great contribution of the Slavophils to the idea of unity and integrity.   It was worked out in the theological writings of Khomyakov as the definition of *sobor-*

[23] C. Leontiev, t. V, p. 29 (in 1873), cp. N. Y. Danilevsky, *Russia and Europe* (SPB. 1869, 1895), p. 436.
[24] F. Dostoevsky, ed. Berlin 1922, *The Journal of the writer* (1876), p. 561.
[25] I. Aksakov, t. I, pp. 223 and 273, Speech on 24/10/1876.
[26] *Ibid.*, t. I, p. 50, " Slavonic problem " (in *Day*, 1865).
[27] V. Soloviev, t. IV, p. 7, " The great controversy and Christian politics."
[28] F. Dostoevsky, *The Journal*, p. 289.

nost.[29]   In the sphere of thought I. Kireevsky hoped to create
an integral philosophy which would reconcile faith and reason
—a task continued by V. S. Soloviev (1853—1900), with his
philosophy of history as a " god-manly process." Within the
country, they all hoped that " faith, this highest intelligence
endowing reason with life "[30] would help the nation " to
illuminate the popular community-principle by the principle
of the Church."[31] " The new word," the message of Orthodoxy to the rest of mankind, should be a Christian message.
The Russian people and the Orthodox Church were thought
of as the synthesis of the opposed Roman and Protestant
worlds. The task of Russia was understood as the reconciliation of these two worlds, the reunion of divided Christendom.[32]

The claim of Russia in this universal revelation of the
Kingdom of God was defined by Khomyakov when he boldly
said :

> " The only task acceptable to Russia is to be a society
> based upon the highest moral principles. . . . All that has
> for basis self-denial and self-sacrifice is included in one
> word : Christianity. Only one task is possible for Russia :
> to become the most Christian of human societies. That
> is why she has always remained and will remain indiffer-
> ent to all that is petty, conventional and accidental."[33]

Soloviev, though his confessional ideas altered with time, still
believed that " the lofty power which the Russian nation has
to reveal to humanity is a power not of this world, and exterior
wealth or order in relation to it have no value whatever. . . .

---

[29] Term used in the Creed for " Catholic " ; expresses also " the sym-
phonic nature of Catholic consciousness or Catholicism, a spirit in which
all work together and to which all contribute,"—definition from
Sobornost, the journal of the Fellowship of St. Alban and St. Sergius.

[30] I. Kireevsky, *Works,* (M. 1856), 2 vols., t. I, p. 249, on new principles in philosophy.

[31] Samarin, t. I, p. 63, on the opinion of the *Sovremennik.*

[32] *Ibid.,* t. I, p. 116, on nationality in science. The thesis presented by
him at Moscow University in 1844 (on Stephen Yavorsky and Theophan
Prokopovich) defended the same idea. Published posthumously in 1880.

[33] A. Khomyakov, t. III, p. 335. Among his poems the most representative of his idea of the Christian and " kenotic " country: " Isle,"
1836 ; " To Russia," 1839 ; " To Russia," 1854 ; " To the repentant
Russia," 1854 ; " If the doubts in your soul," 1859.

It is a religious vocation." [34]   He repeated similar statements [35]
and warned his readers that " it will be a shame for Russian
society if it should bring down [this ideal] from its height and
replace the universal task by little professional or class interests
under whatever great names." [36]   Typically enough, he would
mention that " the exterior form of a slave in which we found
our nation, the pitiful condition of Russia in economic and
other domains, far from being a contradiction of her vocation, rather confirms it." [37]   Not only the glorious task of the
country was expressed in terms of Christianity but, as we see,
" the form of a slave only confirmed " such vocation. This
" kenotic " national self-definition was made even more precise when I. Aksakov explained that " the call of the highest
free activities of the human spirit—thought, science, art and
so-called civilization—is to *serve* the gradual incarnation of the
Christian ideal in human society." [38]   That is why all the
Slavophils were anxious that Russia should not fail her call
and that she should live a *worthy* existence.[39]

What characteristics of their nation justified, in the mind of
the Slavophils, the claims of holy and universal Russia? What
manner of life did they themselves propose to her as necessary
for the realization of her task?

Great champions of freedom, the Slavophils spoke nevertheless in terms of obedience, the way and the result of a
Christian life. Within the state, the long-standing tendency
" to turn citizens into things " will be reversed, for, owing to
Christianity, such slavery of one man to another will change
" into voluntary, free obedience." [40]   True life, temporal and
eternal, depends " upon one general condition, namely, upon
the moral act of the self-denial of individuals and nations . . .

[34] V. Soloviev, t. I, p. 238, *Three Powers*. His poem, "Ex Oriente
Lux," 1890, proposes to Russia to choose between becoming the East of
worldly might or that of Christ.
[35] *Ibid., Letters*, ed. by E. L. Radlov (SPB. 1908, 1911), t. I, p. 189, to
Bishop Strossmayer in 1866 ; also p. 198 to E. Tavernier in 1896.
[36] *Ibid.*, speech on Dostoevsky, t. III, p. 204.
[37] *Ibid., Three Powers*, t. I, p. 238.
[38] I. Aksakov, *Civilization and the Christian ideals* (1883), t. II, p. 721.
[39] M. d'Herbigny, *V. Soloviev, un Newman russe* (Paris, 1934), p. 170.
[40] I. Aksakov, *Life of Tyutchev* (M. 1886), p. 177.

the fruit of such an act is *faith* and *obedience*." [41]   In the
country as represented by the Slavophils there will be no compulsion.   Freedom of conscience will be guaranteed; the only
arm employed will be " the word, this spiritual sword of sacred
truth which suffers the use of no other and material one." [42]
There will be no slavery and, above all, no penalty of death
which for all the Slavophils, no less than for Tolstoy, is
" legalized murder " [43] contrary to the spirit and mind of the
teaching of Christ.[44]   Dostoevsky, with his experience of being
sentenced to death, pleaded against capital punishment in
fiction.[45]

" Loving humility," [46] love forgetful of self, foolish in the
eyes of the world, should be the basis of life, personal, national
and universal.   The Christian spirit could not be replaced " by
any gentleness of manners," [46] nor can it be reconciled with
any sort of gain.[47]   There can be no compromise, no mingling
of the extreme demand of God with human ideals.

Poverty should be kept in greatest respect.   Simplicity of
life was posited as an ideal.   Luxury or even comfort which
one accepted were still felt to be " an unlawfulness not only
from the religious point of view but also from the moral and
social. . . . A Russian respects the rags of a fool for Christ's
sake more than the golden brocade of a courtier." [48]   A beggar
was regarded as the possible divine visitor " in the form of a
servant."   Hence, the Slavophil's distrust of organized charity.
The possibility of giving help personally was felt to be a
privilege.   Not through festivities with charitable aims but in

[41] V. Soloviev, *The great controversy*, etc., t. IV, p. 53.
[42] I. Aksakov, *Social questions in ecclesiastical affairs*, t. IV, p. 607.
[43] N. L. Brodsky, *The early Slavophils* (M. 1909), p. 117.
[44] I. Aksakov, *Despotism of theory over life* (1868), t. II, pp. 395, 400.
[45] Sentenced in 1849 and *The Idiot* written in 1868.   " Murder by
legal sentence is immeasurably more terrible than murder by brigands.
Who can tell whether human nature is able to bear it without madness?
Perhaps there is some man who has been sentenced to death, been exposed to this torture and has then been told, ' you can go, you are
pardoned.'   Perhaps such a man could tell us.   It was of this torture and
of this agony that Christ spoke too." tr. C. Garnett (1913), p. 19.
[46] C. N. Leontiev, t. VII, p. 385.
[47] I. Aksakov, *Letters* (M. 1888–92); to his parents, 1848.
[48] I. Kireevsky, t. II, p. 214, on the Character of European Civilization,
1852.

prayerful love should alms be given. "The beggar makes the sign of the cross, and everybody round repeats it giving thanks that the Lord had made them worthy to give something to a beggar. . . . They do not ask for money only, but that we should give a sign from the soul." [49] There was also a suspicion that gold hardly ever derives from a completely pure source. On the other hand, anxiety to take part in a holy act of charity often took the form of self-denial, of actual "self-beggary"—"the innate quality, as it were" of the nation.[50] No learning or civilization were thought necessary to create such a true spirit of charity, obedience and self-sacrifice. "Christianity does not teach but illuminates." [51] Therefore, once more, the peasant, even in his state of serfdom, can become almost a leader of life.

We can sum up the religious and national ideas of the Slavophils as those of self-limitation, humility, poverty and other virtues of "kenotic" character. It is easy to see that such ideas are liable to misinterpretation. In fact, they were often understood as expression of "obscurantism." T. G. Masaryk states disapprovingly that with the Slavophils "passive Christian virtues were esteemed; even suffering was a good thing; conciliatory, patient, pious humility and lowliness was posited as the chief Christian virtue of Orthodox Russia." [52]

In the heat of the controversy, the Slavophils and the Westernisers sometimes used harsh words against each other. In fact, the early Westernisers shared with their opponents " a passionate feeling [for Russia which] the Slavophils took for remembrance and we—for prophecy." [53] In order that Russia should fulfil this prophecy and develop her best qualities she

[49] N. L. Brodsky, *The early Slavophils*, p. 85, from C. Aksakov's play "Prince Lupovitsky."
[50] V. Soloviev, *The spiritual foundations of life*, t. III, p. 385. This was perfectly true of Soloviev himself. Turgenev's *Cabbage Soup* gives a good example too.
[51] I. Aksakov, *Civilization and the Christian ideal* (1883), t. II, p. 711. This whole volume deals with Slavophilism and the Westernisers.
[52] T. G. Masaryk, *The spirit of Russia* (1919), 2 vols., t. I, p. 324.
[53] A. I. Herzen (or Gertsen), ed. Petersburg, 1919, 22 vols., t. IX, p. 11, on C. S. Aksakov, written in London, 1861.

should, according to the Westernisers, first of all learn from
" the elder brothers " of the West. In spite of their divergencies
"during the 'forties and the two following decades the
Westernisers were under Slavophil influence." [54]   As a background to both groups there grew up and has persisted a large
body of moderate Westernisers, liberal, progressive constitu-
tionalists.   The outstanding Westernisers often used a language
akin to that of the Slavophils, and it often involved more than
the mere use of similar vocabulary.

It seems significant that while the Slavophils are spoken of
chiefly as a group, the name of Westernisers evokes the picture
of individuals.   It may therefore be preferable to analyse the
movement as it was represented by its chief leaders.

The man who promoted the crystallization of the ideas of
both groups, P. Y. Chaadaev, criticized his country ruthlessly :
" We have given nothing to the world and received nothing
from it. . . . We exist only as a kind of object-lesson to remote
generations which will find the understanding of it." [55]

Many would expose with Chaadaev the absurdity of the
claims of Russia to defend peace in the West, to bring a solution of Western problems or to liberate the Slavonic peoples,
whilst within the empire the educated class had no freedom of
thought, and peasants were still serfs.   The criticism of
Chaadaev was the outcome of his philosophy of history.   For
him, too, history was the revelation or realization of the divine
kingdom on earth, so to say, divine energy incarnate.   God
was the aim of history, Christianity its centre.   Lacking a
personal devotion to Christ, Chaadaev saw in Christianity a
system having all the potentialities of development in a perfect
social and intellectual order, almost equal to the notion of
progress.   He even thought that " one cannot distinguish the
teaching of the Church from science." [56]   He found this
especially with regard to the Western Church, to which he
ascribed the social advantages of the Western world.   He
sought the centre of his system and declared it to be in the

[54] Masaryk, *ibid.*, t. I, p. 334.
[55] I. Gagarin, *S. J. Tendances catholiques dans la société Russe* (Paris,
1860), from Chaadaev's letter, p. 16.
[56] M. Gershenzon, *P. Y. Chaadaev* (SPB. 1908), p. 304.

person of the Pope. " Is it not rather in the idea of Christ? " Pushkin wrote to him. [57] The personal religious position of Chaadaev remained vague. He would conform to religious practices, because such " exercise of submission contains more than one imagines." [58]

After the publication of the *Letters,* the Government declared Chaadaev insane. Did he want to propitiate the authorities when he published his *Apology of a madman?* As some of his private letters reflected the same spirit, we think it possible to trust the author. There happened to Chaadaev what happened later on to many Westernisers: he redis-covered his land.[59] It now seemed to him that the social task of Western Christianity was already fulfilled and that the time had come " to yield place to a Christianity purely spiritual." [60] And suddenly he said that in Russia " Christianity remained pure from human passions and earthly interests, because here, like its divine Founder, it did nothing but pray and remain humble." [61] He expressed similar convictions in the *Apology:* " We are called to solve most of the problems of social order . . . to pronounce ourselves on the most important questions which are in the minds of mankind." [62]

Along with this new conception of the Russian place in history, Chaadaev adopted a new attitude towards the Ortho-dox Church " so humble and, at times, so heroic, which alone consoles us for the emptiness of our chronicles." [63] She was the educator of the nation and to her teaching Russia owes her best qualities.

---

[57] I. Gagarin, *ibid.,* p. 5, Letter from 6, 18/7/1830. Chaadaev never joined the Church of Rome, though many believed him to have done so. The destiny of V. S. Pecherin (1808—end of the 'eighties) was strange. He was not influenced by anybody nor had he any influence. Educated in the West, Professor of Greek at St. Petersburg University, he fled from Russia. After an adventurous life of poverty he was converted to Catholicism, joined the order of Redemptorists in Ireland (1840), then worked among the sick in Dublin.

[58] I. Gagarin, *op. cit.,* p. 8.

[59] V. V. Zen'kovsky, *Russian thinkers and Europe* (Paris).

[60] M. Gershenzon, *op. cit.,* p. 301.

[61] Ch. Quenet, *Tchaadaev et les lettres philosophiques* (Paris, 1931), p. 277, in a letter to Orloff.

[62] *Ibid.,* p. 267, from *The Apology of a madman.*

[63] M. Gershenzon, *op. cit.,* p. 294, from the *Apology.*

This change of front is noteworthy, since it brings us again face to face with the conception of the " humble " country.

Chaadaev was and remained a lonely figure. The first Westerniser with a widespread influence, a true writer and a professional political journalist was Alexander T. Herzen or Iskander, his revolutionary name (1812–70). The great majority of the intelligentsia followed him and Vissarion G. Belinsky (1810–48) rather than the Slavophils suspected of conservatism. One can hardly understand the Russian life of the nineteenth century without being acquainted with these two men. Therefore, though their contribution to our particular subject is small, it seems relevant to dwell on their life and thought.

The impressions of the Biblical reading of the young Herzen were summarized by him in a letter : as an answer to the longing of dissatisfied humanity, " was born the carpenter's son Christ " who brought to men the message of equality; " but men did not understand it." [64] Through all his further evolution Herzen will preserve this " democratic " and " socialistic " view of the Gospels. His personal faith did not survive the death of a cousin which made him " part with the romantic hope of a meeting beyond grave." [65] The study of science and of the history of political struggles persuaded him of the final triumph of death over the almost impersonal life-process. He said that, after all, science also led one " to humility before truth, to a self-forgetful acceptance of it."[66] Herzen was influenced by the French Socialists and together with them turned from Christianity to positivism.

The political attitude of Herzen was that of religious inspiration, and this remained all through his life. He expected a New City, an earthly reality for the preparation of which " the Gospels should penetrate life, preparing individuals capable of brotherhood." [67] Any Christian Socialist could say the same. But in the poem of Herzen's youth, which had no pretensions to historicity, there appears a note which strikingly reminds us

[64] Herzen, t. I, p. 126, Letter to Ogarev, 1838.
[65] Ibid., t. III, p. 49, Diary, 1838.
[66] Ibid., t. XIII, p. 357, " My Past and Thoughts."
[67] Ibid., t. III, p. 319, Diary, 1844.

of the " kenotic " mood of the Spiritual Songs. These Russian utterances were ascribed to George Fox.

> " The simple men are everywhere oppressed,
> Abandoned by all in poverty and sickness.
> Yet they alone are sons of Christ
> And have full right
> To beg in His almighty name." [68]

Fox is represented in opposition to the plans concerning America :

> " Humble thyself and beg
> Thy piece of daily bread.
> Endure refusal, bear offences,
> Hide both thy riches and thy name
> And as a beggar, bring the tidings to the beggars
> Of the New World." [69]

Christ's chief demand is expressed as follows :

> " He would have brotherhood, equality and freedom
> And that there should be no rich men at all." [70]

Oppression of the poor was hideous to Herzen and so was war, especially if accepted by those who called themselves Christians. He also noticed in his Diary his horror of capital punishment.

Herzen's conception of wealth was negative. Describing to his fiancée the poetry of the Russian Easter night, he thus explained the traditional kiss : " the Church is so good as to accept the *rich* man and forgetting his graspingness and lack of sympathy, she puts him on a level with her favourite son, the beggar." [71] Fifteen years later, as a political émigré, living in London he would notice with reproach that England despises a beggar.[72] In his youth, like the Slavophils, Herzen opposed Christianity not only to riches but also to the State. This last point was very soon radically changed.

The ideal Western Europe, when seen in the light of every-day reality, disappointed Herzen by the " weakly utilitarian-

[68] *Ibid.*, t. II, p. 282, William Penn, 1839.
[69] *Ibid.*, p. 325.
[70] *Ibid.*, p. 279.
[71] *Ibid.*, t. II, p. 150, Letter to his fiancée, 1838.
[72] *Ibid.*, t. XIII, p. 35, " My Past and Thoughts."

ism " [73] and the acute sense of property. He reacted as would a Slavophil : " It is not in vain that Christianity looks in such a hostile way upon property and belongings [where] man becomes possessed by things." [74] He had to acknowledge that the Western nations proved " lower than our picture " of them.[75] And he would soon declare himself to have become " alien to Western Europe." [76]

Like his opponents the Slavophils, Herzen now started " looking with hope towards our own East." [77] He read Koltsov's poetry and felt impressed by the world of the peasantry, "indescribably touching in its naïve naturalness and simplicity, in its humble poverty. Poor, forgotten peasant Russia ! " [78] This silent mass, not embittered in spite of so many hardships, had succeeded in preserving the brotherly, communal character of village life but, above all, it had some indefinable " intimate force unconscious of itself which has so marvellously preserved the Russian people." [79] And if even this Cinderella of the nations had in her " something foolish " it was neither " trivial nor petty-bourgeois." [80] Most probably it was so because " up to the present time one can speak to the people only through the Holy Scripture." [81]

The vision of peasant Russia provoked contradictory feelings of sympathy and indignation. The poor, always too submissive, seemed to share with the upper class a part of the responsibility for their condition. Nevertheless, sympathy prevailed. " The sad condition of the peasantry haunts us day and night as a reproach and an accusation," said Herzen.[82]

---

[73] In spite of the ideas he professed, the aristocratic and romantic Herzen had no less distaste for democracy than C. N. Leontiev.

[74] *Ibid.*, t. III, p. 347, Diary, May, 1844.

[75] *Ibid.*, t. XIII, p. 390, " My Past and Thoughts."

[76] *Ibid.*, t. XIV, p. 206, *op. cit.*

[77] *Ibid.*, in *The Bell* (1857), t. VIII, p. 492. One more variation on an old subject.

[78] *Ibid.*, t. IX, p. 98, on a novel from popular life in Russia. A. V. Koltsov (1808–42) was a poet of great talent of peasant origin. There is a religious element in his poetry but it is not connected with our thesis.

[79] *Ibid.*, t. V, p. 309, " La Russie," 1849.

[80] *Ibid.*, t. VI, p. 456, " Reply to Michelet," in Nice, 1851.

[81] *Ibid.*, t. III, p. 319, Diary, March, 1844.

[82] *Ibid.*, t. VI, p. 284, " Du développement des idées révolutionaires en Russie," Nice, 1851.

He wrote on serfdom in Russia for English readers in the following terms : " Let us thank those forgotten serfs for the wisdom which we have gained at the cost of the cruel hunger of some, the fierce sweat of many, the brutal degradation of all; let us who are the fine flower of this glorious civilization be grateful, we whose smiling gardens are watered with the blood and tears of the poor." [83] This attitude of compassion brought Herzen to some practical conclusions; he himself could not go back to Russia, but he suggested that in future the educated class should turn its attention not to Western problems and revolutions but " to the people." This suggestion became the watchword of the next generations; we shall examine it when speaking of the Populist movement.

Herzen's friend and fellow-exile Nicolas P. Ogarev (1813–77) should also be mentioned here. He was never as influential as Herzen, but his poetry was widely known and it also played its part in the revolutionary movement. There was a religious motive in his poetry, though it did not seem to affect his personal life. There was a desire of faith (" Discord," " Among the tombs "). God was spoken of as Eternal Soul. Christ, not necessarily divine, was " the Word of truth " (" Farewell "). Despised by the scribes, he could be understood by simple folk. He was an example of sacrifice : " Like Jesus, for the sake of men I long to suffer persecution " (" A Christian "). And Ogarev even expressed the hope that his own suffering and blood might save the persecutor by moving him to repentance. All these appeals to suffering and death were only poetry; but they were taken seriously by those young men and women within the country who read with awe the officially prohibited literature of the exiles. The Slavophils, convinced Christians and Churchmen, used much more reserved language in their religious poetry.

Already for some time Herzen had been meditating upon the contradictions of historical Christianity professing mastery over passions and contempt of earthly goods but acting quite differently. " Modern times," he thought, " positing the

[83] *Ibid., Russian serfdom,* t. VII, p. 346.

State as the most real substance (the Kingdom of God on earth according to the religious expression) abolish all deceit, for the State has its temporal as well as its eternal side. . . . Here is the true realization of what was dimly foreseen by Christianity." [84]   Logically, Herzen and with him many of the intelligentsia took the next step, leaving behind what was merely a foreboding : " Christianity was mighty by its universality ; this is even more true of Socialism." [85]

Herzen and Ogarev were romantics in their youth ; their religious language had something of that same exaggeration which made them " swear eternal friendship," etc.   Vissarion G. Belinsky's desire to find God sounds much more serious : " Do you know what the craving for God consuming a man means ? " [86]   An extreme character, Belinsky changed his ideas many times in his life ; one must always notice the exact epoch of his pronouncements.   His life is roughly divided into two periods—that of moderate political views and "mysticism" and that of " reality," i.e. Positivism and Socialism.

In the first period he would say that it was too early to give freedom to the peasants, they first needed education.   He passed through self-criticism and he expected to find in faith a philosophy—truth contemplated by intelligence.   He would not be contented with anything but the absolute.   Yet soon he grew tired of abstractions ; from 1837 onwards " reality " meant for him no less than " God."   In 1840 he spoke of the Gospels as the absolute truth of which individual immortality is the cornerstone.   But the death of a friend [87] was a shock which made him feel, in his turn, what Herzen had felt at his cousin's death.   His personal religion was at an end, though he continued to link Christianity with liberalism.   Finally, in 1841, Socialism became for him the central devotion of his life, " The first and last word of faith and knowledge." [88]   And this is the Belinsky who, for the ideas such as he had himself

[84] A. Herzen, t. III, p. 44, Diary, 1842.
[85] *Ibid.*, t. VI, p. 127.
[86] A. N. Puypin, *V. Belinsky, his life and correspondence* (SPB. 1876), 2 vols., t. II, p. 163 ; also in *Turgenev's Literary memoirs* (ed. SPB. 1898), t. XII.
[87] Nicolas V. Stankevich (1813–40), a Westerniser.
[88] A. N. Puypin, *op. cit.*, t. II, p. 122, Letter to Botkin, 1841.

professed a few years earlier, styled Gogol " an apostle of ignorance." [89]

For Belinsky, seeking for truth meant readiness for self-accusation, self-denial, self-sacrifice. The contemplation of the Absolute could not be achieved without suffering and self-abandonment. He related this seeking for truth more directly to the Person of Christ and felt that where the Crucified was held in view there could be no more self-deceit and happy self-satisfaction. He wanted even books for children to teach the mystery of free and voluntary suffering. Eternal life could not be reached save by way " of death and humiliation." In this period (1834) he thus speaks of Derzhavin (1743—1816): " God in his poetry is severe. The poet has not yet understood the love of Him who called to Him all who labour." [90]

Belinsky as an ardent Westerniser had to face the problem of Russia. He did it by choosing Peter I as his true hero, who breathed life and spirit into Russia. And suddenly Belinsky would interpret his thought in a language already so familiar to us, though so far not applied to Peter I : " Peter expressed the great idea of denial. . . . Only big men and great nations possess this quality of self-denial, and just by this the Russian race elevated itself above the other Slavonic races, and in this quality consists the source of her present might and her future

[89] There is no room on these pages to study in detail the instructive evolution of Belinsky. Known and very influential as literary critic and political thinker, he as far as we know was never approached on religious ground. A. M. Bukharev, then still the Archimandrite Theodor, attentive as he was to secular life and thought, wrote in his *Three Letters to Gogol* in 1848 : " Belinsky had the genius to realize and the burning force of conviction to say that the Supreme Truth must be contemplated from now onwards not only by oneself but in application to all fields of real earthly life. . . . One should help such a man with brotherly self-sacrifice. . . . But those among us who understand Christ as the Supreme Truth not only did not want or could not recognize fully in B. the champion of the same truth not *known* as yet to himself in all its significance but they called even Gogol after the publication of his Correspondence a *shallow person* " (published only in 1861, SPB.), p. 257.

[90] V. Belinsky, *Complete works* (M. 1892), 12 vols., t. I, p. 44, in Literary dreams, 1834 *Rumour* (Molva). All these thoughts were expressed in articles pretending to be purely literary criticism. The big periodicals in which Belinsky took a leading part were educators of the reader, and for Belinsky himself criticism, " these dynamic æsthetics " could be of use if only lofty and instructive, it should be " the true tutor of society." *Ibid.*, t. II, p. 75, on criticism and literary opinions, 1836.

greatness." [91]   But when the Slavophils spoke of the same features as national qualities, Belinsky would angrily reply that there is no historical evidence of such a fact.   In any case, we notice that with regard to Russia all the writers we have examined were inclined to use similar language.

After the years of crisis, Belinsky with his usual violence, cursed his past dream and declared " fanaticism and mysticism to be the enemies of science." [92] Even his attitude towards art was now changed ; the sad reality of life had to be redeemed through Socialism.   With Belinsky, Socialism was not a technical and economical ideal but righteous organization of society.

> " What does it matter to me to understand an idea if I cannot share it with all ? . . . Away from me, bliss, if given to me alone out of thousands !   Distress, deep affliction overwhelm me at the sight of boys playing bare-footed in the street, of a beggar in rags, a drunken coachman. . . . Tossing a copeck to a beggar woman, I fly from her as if I had done evil. . . . Has a man, after all this, any right to forget himself in art, in knowledge ? " [93]

Sensitive as he was to artistic values, he now denied any meaning to a work of art unless it expressed some call to action.   The now dominant attitude was defined by the poet N. A. Nekrasov (1821–77): " You are not forced to be a poet —a citizen you must be " (" A poet and a citizen "). This utilitarian tendency prevailed until the end of the century, only reinforced by the critics who succeeded Belinsky, and was responsible for many misleading and even barbaric estimates of literary works.

In 1847, ill, fearing the approach of death, and moved by the desire to leave some useful work, Gogol published his *Selected pages from correspondence with friends.*   But what seemed " useful " and even " only necessary " to him provoked the furious indignation of Belinsky.   He wrote :

[91] V. Belinsky, t. VII, p. 106, on Derzhavin, 1843. In 1888, V. Soloviev, t. V, " On the national problem in Russia," a few words in defence of Peter I expressed similar ideas.

[92] *Ibid.,* t. IX, p. 431, Russian literature in 1844 (Otechestvennija Zapisky).

[93] F. Nelidov, *The Westernisers of the 'Forties* (M. 1909), p. 169.

" Have you not noticed that Russia does not see her
salvation in mysticism or pietism but in the achievements
of civilization, of enlightenment, of humanitarianism? . . .
The Orthodox Church has always been the supporter of
despotism and the whip; but why did you bring Christ
into all this? What have you found in common between
Him and any other thing and particularly the Orthodox
Church? He was the first to proclaim to men the teaching of freedom, equality and brotherhood, and in His
martyrdom He sealed the truth of His doctrine." [94]

This letter was circulated in manuscript and for nearly half a
century it obscured for Russian readers the true sense of
Gogol's poignant book.

We have allowed ourselves to bring in this letter not only
because it was famous but because, to our mind, it sum-
marizes the whole Slavophil-Westernising controversy, though
without direct reference to it. It makes perfectly clear what
Christ meant finally to a Westerniser. It also brings in the
sore point of the Russian Church. In the beginning of their
career the Westernisers were prepared to take Christ not as a
revolutionary but as their Master, perhaps even as their Lord.
As for the Church, it personified in their eyes the Government;
the reactionary attitude of both repelled them. Indeed, in the
great work of emancipation the Church took hardly any part.
With some of the best men it was an attitude of asceticism and
other-worldliness which prevented them from feeling the vital
need for reform. The liberally-minded sons of the clergy
therefore deserted their class and went to swell the ranks of the
revolutionaries. This indifference of the Church to the
suffering around her was greatly responsible for the growing
alienation of the intelligentsia. The actual leader of thought
became literature.

How did it happen that the Slavophils kept faithful to the
Church? Did they not see its failings? They certainly did.
Loyal orthodox and religious thinkers, they suffered in a more
direct way than the Westernisers. Their own works could not
pass the ecclesiastical censorship. Yet they insisted on work-

[94] *Ibid.,* p. 181.

ing together with the Church. I. Kireevsky's letters to the monks of Optina, with whom he was translating ancient Greek Fathers, were strikingly humble. The harsh criticism of I. Aksakov's essays was such because the destiny of the Church was dear to him. We find the explanation of the desertion of the Church by the Westernisers and the fidelity of the Slavophils in the fact that the Westernisers did not identify that Christ, whom they often loved, with the Church. The Church was only an institution and a very imperfect one. The Slavophils, with their organic conception of the Church, could not look upon her as only an institution, neither could they separate her from Christ. It was not a question of criticizing something outside; they themselves were " in it," they were living members of this body and whatever they did was done, already, in the nature of things, for and within the Church. Incorporated into it through the sacraments and consciously obedient to it, individuals, according to Samarin, became in the Church a new creation. However they might have suffered within and from the Church, the conception held by the Slavophils excluded for them all possibility of abandoning it.

CHAPTER II

THE IDEAL OF HOLINESS IN RUSSIAN FICTION

WORKS of fiction were rightly considered the chief form of self-expression in nineteenth century Russia. "The national character, the merits and defects of the Russian mind and heart and the meaning of the movements within our life, are much more clearly expressed in the works of Pushkin, Gogol, Tolstoy than in all the ratiocinations of our historians and publicists."[1] The works of fiction were so widely known and so typical that often the name of the author and that of his hero were treated as interchangeable—sometimes to the confusion of the unwarned Western reader. Some protagonists became the symbol of a certain type and epoch. Literature was less restricted by the censorship than journalism or philosophy. In the nineteenth century "literature acquired an importance which it had long lost in the other countries of Europe."[2] The writers of this period belonged to the upper class, which gave them some degree of moral and material independence, even though they also were under the strict observation of the authorities. In the domain of religion these men could bring their contribution of "free religious thought and experience"—aspects "lacking in school theology."[3] Some authors, like Gogol, had more to say than their imaginary heroes; or, like Turgenev, they reproduced the religious life of others. We allow ourselves to dwell on the life of a writer when we consider him in his personal experience a significant illustration of the theme of humiliation.[4]

Being directly connected or at least well acquainted with the

---

[1] N. N. Strakhov, *Critical essays on Turgenev and Tolstoy* (SPB. 3 ed. 1895), p. 434.
[2] A. Herzen, *Du développement des idées russes,* t. VI, p. 245.
[3] M. M. Tareev, *Foundations of Christianity,* t. II, p. 10, Preface to the volume on the Gospels.
[4] We assume the biographies of the great writers of the nineteenth century to be generally known. We shall have to give more information of a biographical character dealing with the theologians.

East-and-West controversy, the writers of fiction thought of the character of their land as a whole, though the theoretical considerations of what Russia is and what is her place in history and among other nations did not interest all of them. In a way, their production was an answer to the other, deeper problem raised by the Slavophils: what does the definition of Russia as " holy " mean? The type of life and character aimed at by the writers or represented by their heroes did not differ widely from that extolled in the early oral or written literature, and had much in common with the ideal conceived by the Slavophils (paradoxically, even in Turgenev). Studying them all in relation to the " kenotic " idea we mention only in passing the prose works of Pushkin and Lermontov. Pushkin's *Station Master* (1830), people from the *Captain's Daughter* (1831–6), or the *Maxim Maximovich* of Lermontov (1840) are the first in the picture-gallery of lower or middle-class characters, courageous, modest and meek. But there is no explicit religious tendency in them.

Gogol's *The Cloak* is the recognized source of the inspiration of all subsequent fiction. The stupid clerk, teased by everybody in the office, used to say sometimes in his defence, " Why do you always disturb me at work? " But he had another plea: " Am I not your brother? "[5] These words seem to have reached the writers, who responded by their production. *The Cloak* was projected in 1834 but achieved only in 1840. In between appeared humorous stories, *Arabesques, Mirgorod* and the play the *Inspector General.* The Slavophils recognized Gogol as their own, though he gave them no particular reason for so doing and, on the whole, remained indifferent to their problems. He lacked the sense of historical reality and did not realize the importance of the controversy.

Gogol is one of the most disputed figures of the Russian nineteenth century. He continuously disconcerted his contemporaries. When one section expected amusing stories of Ukrainian life, he wrote his realistic and fantastic *Nevsky*

---

[5] Gogol, *The Cloak,* tr. C. Field (1916), p. 24.

Prospect (1835) or the ridiculous idyll of the *Oldworld Land-owners* (1835) with a sudden frightening note in it, the sudden summons of death. When the public protested or laughed at the characters in the *Inspector General*, Gogol himself declared that he wept. A political satire was expected, yet the author claimed to have reproduced his own inner world. He refused to " make an epoch in the literary sphere " according to his friends' plans because he considered his true work to be " simpler "—" my work is the *soul* and the solid *fact of life.*" [6]

Gogol himself reveals his creative method and it is of some importance. *Dead Souls* (1842) in itself lies outside our field. But we know that it was the author's way of self-examination. Merciless judgment of himself and repentance produced those monsters of triviality and petty unromantic vices which the author claimed to be one collective portrait of himself. The ideal treatment of impressions from outside would be, as with the artist of *The Portrait* (1842), first to enclose all within his soul " and only therefrom, from the very source of his soul, to direct it out in an harmonious, triumphant song." [7] The second part of *Dead Souls,* unfinished and partly burnt by the author, was meant to become the expression of such an harmony. Gogol preached the purification of an artist's soul and body, and himself lived a life of increasing asceticism in order to produce a great and instructive work. He was too interested in man's inner world to pay much attention to his political surroundings, and merely advised complete obedience to God and loyalty to the existing order as established by God; and he believed that the personal perfection of individuals would build a righteous society better than any systems, however good, applied from without. At the same time he constantly asked friends and unknown readers to provide him with facts of Russian life. There was more in this request than the desire for information of an author living for long periods outside his country; there was a sincere readiness to be taught.

[6] Gogol, in ed. Lodizhnikov (Berlin, 1922), pp. 375–6. Four letters to different persons about *Dead Souls.*
[7] *Ibid.,* the same edition, p. 91, *The Portrait.*

All the efforts of Gogol, his vigilant (according to some of his friends morbid) self-examination and his asceticism were due to his desire to serve, and his conviction that to serve one must first become worthy of being used by God. Service was his device. He had sought it from childhood, and the difficulty for him was to decide which field would best answer his intentions. Hence his hesitations between the Civil Service, lecturing at the University, literature and, later, concentration on the " soul and the fact of life." This desire to be of service runs all through his life and writings.[8] " Even in my boyhood . . . it always seemed to me that there would be in my life some great self-sacrifice and that in order to serve my country I should have to be educated somewhere far outside it." [9] It so happened that Gogol, who disliked travelling, had in fact to leave Russia because he wrote better abroad, seeing his country, as it were, in truer perspective. But this " education " referred even more to the upbringing of his soul and his relation to God.

The contemporaries of Gogol and many generations after them were too much fascinated by the writer to perceive the man. It was agreed that, after the publication of *Dead Souls*, he fell into a sort of religious mania chiefly due to his fear of death and his fear of God as severe Judge. His decision to renounce the craft of fiction provoked indignation even among his religiously-minded friends.[10] He protested that there was no " change " in him and illustrated it from his early writings of no artistic value; but nobody paid any attention. Yet in 1832, in his vague theories about the teaching of history, Gogol had already pointed out that in the midst of the tumults

[8] Gogol, ed. by N. Tihkonravov (M. 1889), 5 vols., t. II, p. 351, in the dénouement of the *Inspector General*, the words put in the mouth of the chief comic actor (1846). More strongly in *Confession*, t. IV, p. 273.

[9] *Ibid.*, t. II, p. 260.

[10] Aksakov, *Correspondence and Poems* (M. 1888–92), p. 41, in letters to his mother mentioned that Gogol was sending *The Imitation of Christ* to people and expressed some apprehension lest " his art should suffer from excess of religion " (1844). A penetrating portrait of Gogol and analysis of his vision of the powers of evil is given by G. V. Florovsky, *The ways of Russian Theology*, pp. 360–70. C. V. Mochulsky, *The spiritual way of Gogol* (Paris, 1934) shows understanding and sympathy with Gogol's seeking of true life.

of the ancient world an event had happened unnoticed. "Within the Old covenant the New is born! Unrecognized, the divine Saviour of the world is incarnate, and the eternal Word, not understood by the rulers, resounds in prisons and deserts, awaiting mysteriously new nations yet to come." [11] The same thought was expressed in picturesque form in the poem in prose " Life," (1834). From the West, Gogol constantly wrote to his friends asking them to send him religious literature.[12] In Paris in 1845 he attended the liturgy daily and for two years worked on his *Meditations on the divine liturgy,* which he also revised shortly before his death. But this work remained unknown to the public.[13]

This work reveals in Gogol several features besides his universally recognized attitude of fear of God. There is a reference to the Virgin Mary " glorified " in order that all may learn how " humility is the highest virtue and how God becomes incarnate in the heart of the humble." [14] The divinity of Christ is never doubted. The meditations certainly preserve the tone of awe and reverential amazement. But the author calls attention to the fact that " there appeared among us one like unto us . . . though not in the form which unhallowed imagination had pictured. Not in proud splendour and greatness; not as the chastiser of crime; not as a judge come to condemn some and reward others." [15] Among the aspects of condescension—incarnation, birth in a manger—there is one more moment felt by Gogol: the Eucharist. Before the consecration, at the great entrance he was struck " at the sight of the King of all, carried in under the humble guise of the Lamb lying on the paten . . . surrounded by the instruments of His earthly passion." [16] And these few remarks bring the author closer to " kenotic " thought. Gogol never concealed that he first approached Christ as a writer dealing with the

---

[11] Gogol, t. V, p. 147, " On teaching of universal history," 1834, first published in the *Journal of Ministry for Education,* February 1834.
[12] Among Russian works he read Bishop Tykhon of Voronezh.
[13] First posthumous edition by Kulish (SPB. 1857).
[14] Gogol, *Meditations on the divine liturgy* (1913), p. 74.
[15] *Ibid.,* p. 2.
[16] *Ibid.,* p. 54.

inner world of men. Christ's unique knowledge of the human soul convinced him—it gave him a kind of rational verification of what he dimly believed.

Even more than his writings, the life of Gogol attracts our attention. In this man who is generally accused of pride we detect features of humility, almost of foolishness for Christ's sake.

After the publication of the first part of *Dead Souls* all Gogol's circle pressed him to hasten with the printing of the second part. But he refused to hurry. He was terrified of the monsters which had sprung up under his pen. He became too aware of the wide echoes which his work had produced throughout the country. And he felt that he must be duly prepared and purified before giving out any new work. After having exposed darkness, he desired to create an harmonious, positive Christian type. By a strange paradox, Gogol starving himself to death, body and soul, was not granted the success which befell the tragic and disorderly Dostoevsky. In the end he felt that he ought not to write fiction. This decision provoked a storm no less than that roused by Tolstoy's corresponding action later. Hardly anybody, even among later generations, appreciated Gogol's distress. "Surely, it was much harder for me than for anyone to renounce writing, since it was the unique object of all my meditations, for which I had given up all the rest, all the strongest attractions of life and, like a monk, had broken the link with all that on earth is dear to a man, in order to think of nothing else except my work." [17] At this period Gogol was the only living writer of his stature. Pushkin was killed in a duel in 1836 and Lermontov in 1841. One can understand those who felt it a personal loss that this one hope of the new-born Russian literature should retire into silence. But there was a deeper problem still involved: that of the relation between art and holiness.[18] Gogol, for the sake of holiness, destroyed almost

[17] Gogol, t. IV, p. 269, Confession.
[18] We do not think it relevant to dwell on the greatly discussed question whether or not Gogol was wrongly influenced by his spiritual adviser and acted in obedience to him.

the whole second part of *Dead Souls*. Here is his own witness: " It was not easy to burn a work of five years, created with such painful tension, where each line was wrung from me by force, where there were many of the best meditations which had occupied my soul. Yet all was burnt, and this in a moment when, seeing death before me, I was determined to leave behind me some better memorial. I thank God for having given me the strength to do it." He was afraid that his immature work might do harm to human souls which mattered for him more than the " delight of any lovers of art." And he added: " Unless it dieth. . . . One must first die in order to rise again." [19]

Haunted by the thought of death, though bearing his long and painful illness as a divine gift, Gogol collected his letters sent at different periods to his friends. [20] He knew that some of them had been helpful to those to whom they were first addressed. And he decided to print them, hoping that, by God's mercy, " they might serve others also, taking thus off my soul at least a part of the burden of responsibility for the uselessness of all I have written hitherto." [21] Never was his desire to serve so great as when he collected these letters. Meanwhile, he reduced his own belongings and needs to extreme simplicity, sent money in secret to the students, and possessed nothing but one suit-case and what could be put into it. The scandal produced by the *Select pages from correspondence with the friends* (1847) was beyond imagination. The book was completely misunderstood and misinterpreted by all, whether the friendly Aksakov family or Belinsky. In fact, it contained some naïve statements but also much sound spiritual advice often precise and widely applicable. None of his critics was ready to learn from him, even though Gogol explained that he spoke without any pretention to be taken for a master, but rather as a schoolboy helping his fellows in the school of life. This book which was the " outpouring of the

---

[19] Gogol, ed. Berlin, 1922, p. 374, four letters about the *Dead Souls*.
[20] Some of them written on purpose in form of articles. This is rightly noticed by V. Hippius, *Gogol* (Leningrad, 1924).
[21] *Ibid.*, p. 259, *Testament*.

soul and heart " of the author seemed to him of some value if
only because of its sincerity. But all felt justified in treating
him as—at best—an abnormal.

> " They practised upon the body of a man still alive a
> terrifying dissection which would put into a cold sweat
> even those of a strong constitution. But however stun-
> ning and offensive to a generous and honest man
> were many of these deductions and conclusions—taking
> courage as far as my small forces would allow, I decided
> to endure it all and, using the case as an indication from
> above, to examine myself with more severity." [22]

In one of the letters of this ill-fated book, Gogol said to a
friend : " I say to God . . . that someone should so disgrace
you in the sight of others that you would not know where to
hide yourself from shame. . . . That man would be your true
brother and deliverer. Oh! how we need at times a slap in
the face in public, given in front of all ! " [23] This was not the
hyperbolic style of his early writings. The general tone of the
Correspondence was indeed restrained. Nor was it empty
words. After the whole country had done its worst in the way
of " dissecting " his soul, Gogol wrote : " As for the fact that
my person did suffer. . . . Why, one must sacrifice something.
I myself also need a slap in public and, perhaps, more than
anybody else." [24]

Nothing would have been easier for Gogol with his unani-
mously recognized genius than to end his life in wealth, glory
and general respect and admiration. Instead of all this he
turned his eyes towards his Lord and accepted the reputation
of obscurantism and insanity. He was ready to ascribe even
this general blindness to his own fault. And, though knowing
himself a sinful man, he yet felt an imperative call to pray not
so much for himself as for his country. This also was mocked
as an unheard-of pretension. It seems only just that the
humiliation and agony of this man to whom Russian literature
owes so much should be remembered in a survey of Russian
spiritual destinies.

[22] Gogol, ed. Berlin, p. 569, " An author's confession."
[23] *Ibid.,* " Correspondence," p. 452, to a short-sighted friend.
[24] *Ibid.,* p. 560, " To A. O. Rosseti."

With Turgenev, unlike Gogol, it is his writings only, not his personality which can throw any light upon our investigation. He emphatically claimed to be a Westerniser and scorned the spectacle of a " cultivated man standing before a peasant, doing homage to him : Heal me, dear master-peasant, I am perishing of moral corruption! and the peasant in his turn doing homage to the cultivated man : Teach me, dear master-gentleman, I am perishing from ignorance! . . . We ought to . . . feel really humble for a little . . . and to borrow from our elder brothers [of the West] what they have already discovered before us." [25]

He was an unbeliever though theoretically he understood, not without a certain irony, the supernatural character and power of prayer. "Whatever a man pray, he prays for a miracle. . . . Only such prayer is a real prayer from person to person. To pray to the God [of the philosophers] is impossible and unthinkable." [26] In another place he said of a monk : " I understood him and perhaps envied him ; but let him too understand me and not condemn me ; me, for whom his joys are inaccessible. He has attained to annihilating himself, his hateful ego ; but I too ; it is not for egoism I pray not." [27] Like many of his time, he tried to find an aim in either art, beauty or nature. But he felt no response. " Are there no great conceptions, no great words of consolation : patriotism, right, freedom, humanity, art? [but] at the end nature is inexorable. . . . Unconsciously and inflexibly obedient to her laws, she knows not art, as she knows no freedom, as she knows no good. . . . She suffers nothing immortal, nothing unchanging ; and [man] hurries feverishly to an unknown, uncomprehended goal." [28] We can roughly reduce his philosophy to this pessimistic determinism. It sometimes seems that his gift of acute observation and his keen feeling for natural beauty gain in

---

[25] Ivan S. Turgenev, *Smoke* (1867), tr. C. Garnett (1896), p. 49. We shall constantly refer to this edition of Turgenev's works, giving the date of the original and mentioning the translator only in reference to some other edition. In the passage above we have departed from Mrs. Garnett.

[26] *Dream*, etc. (1881), *Poems in prose*, p. 323, " Prayer."

[27] *Ibid.* (The monk) (1879), p. 321.

[28] *Ibid.* (Enough), pp. 315–21. In the volume *The Jew*, etc.

intensity because he looks upon all as it were for the last time. Death is there, close behind, stimulating, adding to all his human and artistic enjoyment a bitter and exciting tang.

How to explain that Turgenev's work gives us such rich material? How could he have noticed all these types of meekness and devotion? He himself declared that, returning to his estate after his studies in Germany and seeing the lamentable state of the lower classes, he pledged himself to fight the landlords' despotism. Hence, he would claim, his peasant portraits.[29] Turgenev liked to be counted among liberal minds. But his artistic intuition was richer than his conscious programme. He painted the Russian masses as he saw them, though he himself was perhaps frightened or at least puzzled by them. Contemplating a sphinx he would suddenly feel: " I know those features. In them there is nothing Egyptian . . . but it is thou, peasant, my countryman, flesh and blood, Russian! Art thou, too, among the sphinxes? . . . Wouldst thou, too, say somewhat? " [30]

Going round with his gun, instead of pitiful slaves, Turgenev met men and women endowed with greatness of character and, often, knowing more about the aim of their lives than he himself did. To his question—What is your occupation?— Kassian answered : " I live as the Lord commands. . . . I have no occupation. . . . We all are in God's hands, and a man should be righteous—that is all! Upright before God, that is it." [31] The same Kassian expressed his complete disapproval of hunting—it was a sin to kill God's birds. This peasant was known as one of the poorest, also as a healer by herbs and prayer—a fact which he sought to conceal, adding that " he who has faith shall be saved." [32]

In another case, Turgenev was shocked to hear a punished serf defend his master's reputation and maintain that he

---

[29] L. Crossman, *From Pushkin to Blok* (M. 1926), is convinced that country-life and villagers formed for Turgenev no more than an original subject. It is true he examines all the authors from a merely literary-formal point of view. Both statements seem somewhat partial.

[30] Turgenev, " The sphinx," in volume *Dream*, p. 297.

[31] *Ibid.*, " Kassian of fair springs," in volume *A sportsman's sketches*, p. 185.

[32] *Ibid.*, p. 185.

himself had surely merited a correction. Likewise, Kalinich,[33] idealist and dreamer, a romantic and enthusiastic spirit, revered his master, who actually was responsible for his extreme poverty as he always wanted Kalinich to accompany him in his hunting tours, leaving him thus no time to work. Kalinich could charm away hæmorrhages; his bees always did well. It is as if the essential quality of meekness and complete disinterestedness is joined with a certain power over nature.

Turgenev often referred to a childlike, half-artist and half-saint type of peasant, knowing the language of birds and animals. He drew an original picture of a " revolutionary," who could write but was not readily employed by the land-owners because he did not allow the corporal punishment of his fellow-men and carried with him a poor friend. He did it " as an act of justice, as it is the duty of one poor man to help another poor man. . . . For a rich man, if I may venture to say so, it is an entertainment." [34] Another kind of disinterested love was shown by Matrona, a girl whose lady did not allow her to get married. The girl ran away but, after a short period of happiness with the man she loved, afraid of bringing him into trouble and in spite of his energetic protests, " she went and gave herself up. What b came of Matrona? I asked. Karataev waved his hand." [35]

This facing of danger and suffering was not only courageous—it was without reproach. In many cases the man would even accuse himself of whatever happened and would take his suffering as an expiation. Such was Akim of *The Inn* (1852), ruined by the lover of his wife. His lady pretended not to understand, sold his house to his rival and allowed the true owner to be cast off. The inn was bought, moreover, with the money Akim's wife had stolen in her own home. After a stormy reaction, Akim forgave all, became a pilgrim and went away to expiate his sin—the sin of having married a girl much

[33] The first story of the sketches, *Khor and Kalinich,* published in 1847. The first volume finished in 1851.
[34] Turgenev, *Punin and Baburin* (1874), p. 81.
[35] *Ibid.,* " Piotr Petrovich Karataev," in volume *Sportsman's sketches,* p. 86.

younger than himself.   Even more unresisting was the laun-
dress Tatiana, perfectly ready to marry a drunkard proposed
by her lady, though at the same time almost sure that another
man, a deaf giant, would kill her if this marriage should take
place (*Mummu.* 1852).   A similar character was Malanya
whom her master Lavretzky married chiefly in order to annoy
his parents.   " All her life she had never been able to oppose
anything."   And, when she died, " her features expressed, as of
old, bewildered resignation and constant, uncomplaining
meekness." [36]   This meekness and silence were not the result
of complete loss of personality or of lack of intelligence.   The
same resignation was shown by Agafya, the nurse of Lisa.   In
her youth she was a favourite with the landlord.   After his
death she was degraded, but

> " to the astonishment of everyone, she accepted with
> humble resignation the blow that had fallen upon her.
> . . . The time had come for her to reflect. . . . She spent
> fifteen years quietly, peacefully and soberly, never quar-
> relling with anyone and giving way to everyone.   If any
> one scolded her, she only bowed to them and thanked
> them for the admonition.   Her mistress had long ago
> forgiven her . . . but she was herself unwilling [to be
> raised] and always wore a dark dress.   After her mistress'
> death she became still more quiet and humble. . . ."

She taught Lisa religion, she told her the lives of saints, speaking " gravely and meekly, as though she felt herself to be
unworthy to utter such high and holy words." [37]

Agafya's attitude may be that of repentance and expiation.
But what of the soldier whom a woman wrongly accused of
having stolen her chicken and whom a general, passing by,
condemned to be hanged?   The woman was distressed—she
had never expected such a result of her complaint.   The
soldier received the last sacraments and said : " Please, sir, tell
her not to take it so much to heart. . . . I have forgiven her." [38]
The acceptance of death, the confident serenity of peasants at

---

[36] Turgenev, *A House of Gentlefolk* (1858), p. 60.
[37] *Ibid.*, pp. 216, 218.
[38] *Ibid., Poems in prose* (1879), tr. S. J. McMullan, " Hang him,"
p. 130.

their passing, was emphasized not only by Turgenev but by almost all Russian novelists.

This executed soldier and Lukeria, *The Living Relic,* are the fullest illustrations of our theme. Lukeria, the village beauty and its best singer, fell by accident from a staircase. Withered, paralysed, left alone in a remote hut, hardly ever visited by anyone, she is all love and praise of God. She does not pray much : " Why should I worry the Lord God ? What can I ask of Him ? He knows better than I do what I need. He has sent me a cross which signifies that He loves me. We are commanded to understand it so."[39] This last remark is not that of protest, but of wholehearted acceptance. In the undisturbed silence of her hut, she felt especially thankful for having preserved and even developed her fine hearing. It sometimes seemed to her as if she alone were living, and as though something were blessing her. In dreams she sometimes had seen Christ. Once, though she was not asleep, she saw her dead parents, thanking her for her suffering, which had removed a great burden from them. The priest to whom she confessed explained to her " that it was not a vision because only persons of the ecclesiastical profession have visions." When asked by the narrator whether he could do anything to help her she replied : " I want nothing, I am content with everything, thank God. . . . But you ought to persuade your mother to reduce the quit rent of the peasants here." These same peasants spoke of her as " the quietest of the quiet. [She] has been smitten by God for her sins it must be. . . . But . . . we do not condemn her."[40] When the author mentioned her patience, Lukeria enthusiastically spoke of martyrs ; her own deformity was nothing in comparison with them. Some time later Turgenev enquired for Lukeria. She was dead. The peasants reported that " the day of her death she had heard uninterruptedly the chiming of bells—although there was no church near, and it was a week-day." Moreover,

[39] Turgenev, " The Living Relic," from *Memoirs of a sportsman,* tr. I. Hapgood, p. 292.

[40] This remark is valuable : it shows the background of indifference and " common sense," realism which allows one to believe in Lukeria's real existence.

Lukeria said it proceeded from up above. Probably she had not dared to say from heaven.[41]

Is it so surprising that once when the author found himself " in a humble village church " he had a vision of Christ—and Christ looked like a peasant, had " a face like that of all others " ? [42]

Turgenev's conception of poverty and beggary remains wholly traditional. Even the nobleman Lezhniov, who criticized Rudin, finally acknowledged : " I have learnt to value you. You will not make yourself a position. And I love you for that." [43] There is that peasant—richer than Rothschild— for whom to take an orphan in his house means to be reduced to unsalted soup. (Cabbage Soup.) There is the ruined rich man who used to help others and now feels it hard to beg. But when, in the end, he held out his hand, and many passed by without taking any notice, when one gave him a penny— a calm joy returned to his heart. (Poems in prose, 1878, " The alms.") Turgenev speaks of how he himself, once ashamed of having no money on him, seized a beggar's hand and asked him to excuse him. " The beggar murmured : ' I thank you all the same . . . that too is alms, brother ! ' I felt that I also received alms of my brother." [44] And in the delightful " Old portraits " (1881) there is a country gentleman who used to say : " Give to a beggar once, and give him twice, and three times. . . . The fourth time, ask whether he would not rather have a job. But, uncle, somebody once asked : ' Suppose . . . the beggar came again the fifth time ? ' Oh, well, give again the fifth time." [45]

The upper class heroes of Turgenev are also of interest, though less religious. They are very typical reflections of Russian life and its " ten years " rhythm. His weak, dreamy, undecided men are often contrasted with active or sacrificial women. All alike are restlessly looking for something. And this is especially true of his women. Sometimes their other-

[41] Turgenev, " The Living Relic," p. 293.
[42] Ibid., Poems in prose, tr. McMullan, " Christ," p. 114.
[43] Ibid., Rudin (1855), p. 245.
[44] Ibid., Poems in prose, p. 21, " The Beggar."
[45] Ibid., " Old portraits " in volume Punin and Baburin, p. 191.

wise inexplicable fantastic behaviour may be understood as a
result of this unsettled spirit. The princess R., " the sphinx "
beloved by Paul Kirsanov, shortly before her death " sent him
word that the solution of the enigma was the cross." [46] The
vicious and beautiful Eulampia ended the leader of a sect (*A
Lear of the steppes,* 1870). Assia said she would like " to go
far away on a pilgrimage, on some great exploit. . . . As it is,
the days pass by, life passes by, and what have we done? " [47]
Elena, of *On the Eve* (1860), used to collect all the crippled
animals she could find. She prayed also—occasionally, under
the influence of some emotion. But what could these girls of
the nobility do, whose destiny consisted in love and marriage,
happy or unhappy? Naturally, their heroism was chiefly
expressed in the domain of sentiment. Turgenev, like many
of his time, admired George Sand. In his own creation he
liked to lay stress on the consciously " revolutionary " character
of the women. Elena married secretly and followed her
Bulgarian husband to his suffering land. Marianna of the
Virgin Soil (1876) ran away with a young man with whom she
intended not to teach the peasants but to serve them. Even
Lisa, a practising believer, took the veil chiefly because of her
unfortunate love for an unhappily married man. Yet she,
taught by Agafya, had a real love of God, and a deep sense
of duty, of sin and of that forgiveness which belongs to God
alone. One man is worth some attention—Misha Poletaev,
A desperate character (1881). All his life long he vacillates
between the calm gentleness of a child, the folly of a drunkard
risking his life for nothing—and a deep repentance, taking
upon himself vows of almost monastic severity. When, after
many incredible adventures, including beggary, he is collected
by his uncle and brought home, he first feels happy and
redeemed, but after a few days cries in a fury : " I can't live
in your respectable thrice accursed house ! It makes me sick
and ashamed to live so quietly." [48] Death finds him in a
country town, married to a working girl, having given up

[46] Turgenev, *Fathers and children*, p. 51.
[47] *Ibid.*, " Assia " (1857), p. 276 in the volume *A Lear of the
steppes.*
[48] *Ibid.*, *A desperate character*, p. 34.

drink, trying but unable to work.   And his uncle wonders
what this dissatisfaction, this thirst for self-destruction, can
mean.

Last among Turgenev's characters we should notice Sophie
of " A strange story," an aristocratic girl of seventeen, very
quiet, almost *distraite,* whom the author had met at her
father's house.   Meeting her again at a ball and not knowing
how to awaken her attention, Turgenev spoke to her about a
strange peasant thereabouts who could make people see any
dead person they chose to think about.   The girl took it all
seriously and proved disposed to believe in miracles.   She also
added :   " The beginning of faith is self-abasement, humiliation."   " Even humiliation ? " I asked.   " Yes.   The pride of
man, haughtiness, presumption—that is what must be utterly
rooted up.   You spoke of the will—that is what must be
broken.   [And, when her astonished partner asked whether she
got such ideas from her priest, Sophie replied :] ' My ghostly
father tells me what I ought to do; but what I want is a
leader who would show me himself in action how to sacrifice
one's self.' " [49]   She then recalled some grand person of whom
she had read, who wanted to be buried " under a church
porch so that all who came in should tread him under foot and
trample on him.   That is what one ought to do in life." [50]
Sophie finally found the leader in whom she could believe and,
dressed as a working woman, ran away to follow and wait
upon a holy tramp. They went round together, people speaking
of Sophie as one probably " seeking salvation, atoning for her
sin."   Turgenev met the strange pair in a village inn; she was
winding the strips of rag wrapped round the vagrant's legs.
On the sole of his foot there was a wound.   He could be heard
teaching the innkeeper :   " Give all thou hast, give thy head,
give thy shirt.   If they ask not of thee, yet give! " [51]   The
author even suspected the possibility of a romantic relation,
but realized that there was nothing of the kind here.   Sophie
was found by her family and brought back.   " But at home

[49] Turgenev, " A strange story," p. 62, in the volume *A desperate
character.*
[50] *Ibid.,* p. 63.
[51] *Ibid.,* p. 63.

she did not live long and died like a Sister of silence without having spoken a word to anyone." [52]

Turgenev traced thus portraits of lovers of obedience, forbearance and humility, even though such lives were for the artist himself no more than a " strange story."

Leo Tolstoy's critics or admirers usually fall into one of two groups : those who praise his mastery of the craft of letters and neglect his writings of religious tendency and those who, following the master himself, consider only his last works important. Yet both aspects of his work express one and the same Tolstoy. Nicolenka of *Boyhood,* with his craving for perfection and his failures, at last gains victory over himself when the celebrated writer, Count Tolstoy, leaves wealth, fame and home, and hurries through a winter night towards a purified new life. As with many of his heroes, this beginning of a new life coincided with his earthly end.

Tolstoy seemed to have given to the form of the novel its full development, almost exhausting the possibility of further achievements, though we may ask in passing whether the hasty and apparently disorderly style of Dostoevsky, his disregard of classical construction, his monologue (one, his own, all through his conflicting heroes), were not a response to Tolstoy and a new artistic opening. Tolstoy, the man of means, the *grand seigneur* with his acknowledged masterpieces and his religious influence—erroneous in the eyes of Dostoevsky—was perhaps opposed by him through the very style of his novels. There was as it were an indirect, unacknowledged yet none the less passionate controversy between them.

The inner tragedy of Gogol was worked out without affecting his readers. The religious contribution of the Slavophils was overshadowed for many by their national theories. Hardly anybody knew Bukharev. Dostoevsky's ideas reached the public only towards the end of the century. It was Tolstoy who brought home the immediate task of self-perfection and pointed to the model of perfection in the person of Jesus

[52] *Ibid.,* p. 75.

Christ. We cannot overemphasize his moral influence and his role in the religious revival of Russia. The Orthodox apologists had to face problems raised by him in all their vital importance. He is thus spoken of by M. M. Tareev: "Tolstoy has not become and will not become our prophet. But will he not awaken us by his destiny? Have we not to think out what is lacking in his writings, so lofty and of such perfection of form? Have we not to find out, what we must answer to his questions? And is not his way, after all, a way of foolishness for Christ's sake?"[53] A great many of Tolstoy's opponents from the Orthodox side were far from the moderate tone of Tareev; it is true, Tolstoy was no less violent in his utterances against not only the temporal failures of the historical Church to which he belonged but against all the main Christian dogmas. Attracted by the moral teaching of Christ, Tolstoy did not realize the meaning of the Person of the teacher. In the light of his rationalism, which increased with age, Tolstoy condemned all the mysteries of faith; but with them he logically rejected life also, and love in its human forms, and art.

Though Tolstoy judged his own earlier writings as vain and "immoral," it is impossible not to see that from the very beginning of his literary activity he possessed that earnestness and striving for perfection which gave such weight and meaning to all his works. As his late production reflected more of his religious views, we shall not study separately his great novels but rather dwell on the stories of his last period.

1852 saw the publication of *The Cossacks,* of *Boyhood* and of *The Squire's Morning.* The strong and almost animal types of the Cossacks showed Tolstoy's almost unique gift of rendering the life of people, nature and things, as well as his intuition of the body, its movements, its unreasoning joy of living. Tolstoy painted people who just live without any problems and are not less attractive and even good for that. This attraction to the pagan type, the vigorous natural man, remained proper to Tolstoy all his life long, though in the light of his religion this type tended to become a peasant—the

[53] M. Tareev, *Foundations of Christianity,* t. III, p. 177.

synonym of godly life. Not by chance the later works of Tolstoy mark the reappearance of the name of Nekhludov. All his life long the author was trying to answer the questions he had raised in his first stories. Nicolenka Irtenev grew into the moralizing Tolstoy. The squire Nekhludov became the begetter of Levin (in *Anna Karenina*, 1873–6) and of his namesake in *Resurrection* (1899). The early Nekhludov asked how to live righteously; the later replied: by considering oneself not as a master but a servant.

Reconciliation with life was often the result of contact with simple folk living " true " life, that is, for God and their soul. But among the peasantry painted by Tolstoy many convince in fact not so much by religious beauty of character as by their undisturbed force of life and their integrity. This is obvious of the old Cossack or of the girl Marianka. In spite of the author's intention, we hesitate to range among Christian types even his famous Karataev. (*War and peace*, 1864–9.) He seems more harmonious than Christian; his wisdom is probably unconscious, and so is his pity for all living creatures; he lives and dies, perfect in his kind as a leaf on a tree. But one wonders whether there is any righteousness in him just as one is not quite sure there is any personality. In a way, he is a collective figure, the expression of this sane life of the poor which so appealed to Tolstoy. The simple and poor are better, purer and wiser than the learned and refined. The problem of chastity is often presented by Tolstoy as a class-problem. The leisured, the well fed and well dressed are slaves of selfishness and lust. This runs through all his novels, and in a letter he would advise a person seeking chastity to take as means against temptation such shabby clothes as to be prevented by them from attracting anyone. The privileges of the rich are in fact their ruin.

Poverty is the true way back to peace with one's self and with others. The *Stories for Peasant Readers* illustrate this point. In 1860 in his *Talks to children on moral problems* Tolstoy contended that riches are obtained not by labour but by sin and therefore become a burden rather than a source of enjoyment. In 1876 he wrote stories in which he spoke of the joys of poverty, especially if willingly accepted (" How much land does a man need ? " " Two old men," " The two brothers and the gold," " What men live by.") [54] Very important are the *Memoirs of a lunatic* written in 1884. The man, taken one night by a sudden uneasiness and fear of death, recurs instinctively to a superstitious prayer, which finally turns into a sincere cry : " If Thou art, ' reveal Thine existence to me.' " [55] It is a short and powerful story of conversion which results practically in the refusal to buy an estate at great advantage, in attendance at the liturgy which now appears to have a meaning, in the distribution of all the money which the hero had in his pockets. " At that moment the full light of the truth was kindled " in him, he felt no fear, he felt that death was no more.

The first step of a man who is ready to give up his possessions, even if he would in any case use them only for good purposes, is inevitably leading him towards true perfection. So it happens to the peasant who never achieved his pilgrimage to the Holy Land since he stopped half-way at the sight of other people's misery. Not only did he give them all he had, but he remained in their house to work until things went better with them. He himself felt very ashamed of his failure, as proving his lack of zeal (" Two old men," 1885). Yet, of course, his sacrifice and service are shown to be acceptable to God no less than that of the cobbler sharing his meal with an old soldier, warming a frozen woman with her baby, reconciling an apple-woman with the boy who has stolen one of her apples (" Where love is there God is," 1885). This activity of love proves to be effective contact with God. And is it not this same assurance of His reality in love which sanctifies " The old men " (1886), three hermits unable even to remember the Lord's Prayer and repeating their own : " Three are you, three are we—have mercy upon us " ? In a letter, Tolstoy mentioned a paralysed monk who suffered during thirty years and was so radiant with joy, love and gratitude that thousands

---

[54] *In Twenty-three Tales,* tr. Aylmer Maude.
[55] Tolstoy, " Memoirs of a lunatic." In the volume *Hadji Murad,* ed. by C. H. Wright (1912), pp. 296, 302.

of visitors came to him, and this man, deprived of the possibility of any activity, was actually a source of help and
encouragement to others.

The other aspect of the blessed life is the spirit of obedience,
forgiveness, meekness and non-resistance.   Among the popular
stories we notice in illustration of these themes " The God-
father," " The story of Ivan the fool " (1885), who became a
king, and built a happy realm only because he never opposed
evil otherwise than by gentleness; " The Candle " (1885),
and above all, " God sees the Truth but waits."   A merchant,
falsely accused of murder, meets after long years in prison the
actual murderer who, at first, only laughs at him but finally
repents; the merchant had suffered too much to forgive
easily, yet after a struggle he says : " God forgive you ; maybe
I am a hundred times worse than you."   This final victory
brought to the merchant an indescribable peace and the
sensation of his heart growing wondrously light.   The tru
criminal having declared the truth, the merchant's releas .vas
ordered, but before he could leave prison he died.[56]

D. Merejkowsky justly remarks that the thought of death
is central in Tolstoy's works.   The horrified cry of Nicolenka
confronted by his mother's coffin is echoed by Ivan Ilitch.   Is
it mere fright at the unknown, or too strong an attachment to
earthly things, or the pain of parting with people whom one
loves?   With his extreme honesty Tolstoy admits that a dying
man seldom thinks of anybody but himself.   Is it then that he
is afraid of disappearing for ever?   *Three deaths,* written in
1859, shows a restless, unhappy young woman of the upper
class, a serene peasant, and a tree.   The lady alone complains.
The peasant here is like those scattered in other volumes.   The
soldiers of *Sebastopol* (1854) and those of *War and Peace*
would probably dislike a sudden death; they prepare themselves on the eve of battle, wash, and put on a clean shirt.
The young married man Avdeev, who had just been com-
plaining of his own generosity which had made him accept

[56] Tolstoy, " God sees the Truth but waits."   *Tales,* tr. N. Bain (1901),
p. 243.   This tale is also recounted to Bezukhov by Karataev in *War and
Peace.*

the hardships of military service instead of his brother who had children, when gravely wounded asked to send a message to his people : " say : Your son . . . envied his brother—and now he is himself glad. Don't worry him. Let him live . . . [and, after enquiring whether a pipe which a fellow-soldier had lost was found, he added :] Now, bring a candle. I am going to die." [57]

Why are these simple men so calm about it ? Tolstoy, in his later period, explained that " the fear of death is only the consciousness of the unsolved contradiction of life." [58] Would it be one more proof of the essential truth of simple lives ? All tend to take it this way. Yet this would be too poor an explanation. The fact of death insistently attracts Tolstoy's attention, and together with his heroes he undergoes the striking experience which Leo Shestov has well defined as " the revelations of death." [59] We can dispense with quotations of passages already well known. Who does not remember Prince Andrew on the battlefield revaluing his whole life, with hardly a thought for his hero Napoleon bending over him ? All his past efforts seem senseless, and even his craving for glory fades. There is only silence, and the sky, and the abiding worth of love. Later, recognizing his rival wounded, Andrew suddenly realizes : " love of one's enemies . . . that is why I was sorry to part with life, that is what would remain to me if I were to live." [60] But this intuition would never have come to his mind before the experience of the battle-field. This again is explained by Tolstoy himself : " the manifestation of the feeling of love is impossible to men who do not understand the meaning of their life." [61] One thinks immediately of another powerful scene—the reconciliation of Karenin and Vronsky at the bedside of Anna. *The death of Ivan Ilyitch* (1885) is the most realistic of all. Step by step

---

[57] Tolstoy, *Hadji Murad,* ed. by C. H. Wright (1912), p. 80.
[58] *Ibid., On life,* the Free Age Press, Christchurch (1902), p. 126.
[59] L. Shestov, *Les Révélations de la mort, Dostoievsky-Tolstoi,* ed. Plon (Paris, 1923).
[60] Tolstoy, *War and peace,* ed. Birukov, t. VII, p. 210, 24 vols. (M. 1913).
[61] *Ibid., On life,* p. 108.

the reader follows his fight with death, hour by hour he watches the pain working its mysterious destructive way within him. Ivan Ilyitch felt at first offended at the usual life of his family and friends going on as if nothing had happened. He enjoyed making them feel uneasy. But little by little he re-examined his life, his whole scale of values. And then he began to pity his wife and his little son, of whom he felt that his life would be wasted too. This unselfish glance was a beginning. He accepted death. Then suddenly all changed : " ' How right and how simple ! ' he thought. ' And the pain? Where's it gone? . . . Yes, here it is. . . . And death. Where is it?' In the place of death there was light. ' So this is it ! ' he suddenly exclaimed aloud. What joy ! . . . ' He is gone,' someone said. . . . He caught those words and repeated them in his soul. ' Death is gone,' he said to himself. ' It is no more.' " [62] Whilst Tolstoy the thinker doubted personal survival, the artist in him had the strongest intuition of eternal and perhaps also personal life. Death is presented as light, and it throws its beams back upon life and makes clear what there is of true value. To accept death is already to pass into the world of light and love.

Even more striking than the feelings expressed by the refined Prince Andrew or by the educated Ivan Ilyitch is what happens to the merchant Vassily Brekhunov overtaken by a snow-storm together with his servant Nikita. When, after long efforts to find the way, the latter comes to tell him that there is no hope left, the merchant is unwilling to take it in. Nikita sits quietly, prepared to die. Brekhunov makes new efforts, all in vain. After a time, Nikita comes to say that he is dying. And suddenly it seemed to Brekhunov of absolute importance that Nikita should live—this same ragged Nikita whom he had exploited and cheated for years. Warming him and protecting him with his own body, " Nikita is alive, and that is the same as my being alive he said to himself triumphantly. . . . And he thought of his money and his shop, and of his buying and selling . . . and it was hard for him to understand why

[62] Tolstoy, *The death of Ivan Ilyitch,* tr. C. Garnett (amended) (1915), p. 69.

that man whom they called Vassily Brekhunov had occupied himself with all those things. . . . 'He did not know what I know now . . . and he heard the voice of Him who was calling him. And his whole being cried out joyfully and comprehendingly ' I am coming ! " [63]

If death often reveals the true, sacrificial love, life as it is lived in the world is constantly driving men into false relationships. The finest and more tempting substitute for love is, for the heroes of Tolstoy, not sensuality or selfish affection for a man's flesh and blood but the admiration of other men—human glory. His heroes are ambitious and never at rest because never satisfied. The only remedy is that true love of which the dying Prince Andrew caught a glimpse, together with profound and sincere humility. There is real greatness in the peasant who saved the life of an aristocratic girl crushed by the crowd watching the coronation. He learnt who the girl was and then disappeared refusing a reward and without giving his name (*Khodinka,* 1910). Pierre Bezukhov imprisoned in burning Moscow and saving a child experiences something of the kind. The most prominent illustration is to be found in *Father Sergius* (1898). The brilliant young man, rushing into a monastery when he realized the true character of the relation between his fiancée and the Emperor, is of course moved by grief and pride and not by religious feelings. But slowly and not without resistance he is gained by God. Yet vain-glory is still alive in him and he is tempted by his reputation as a saint. Peace and light come only in the end, when he flies from his hermitage, is taken for a tramp without a passport and sent to Siberia. The real saint he meets is a poor old woman working hard to keep her daughter with her many children and her drunkard of a husband. Too busy to pray, the woman is convinced of her own wickedness. Another striking figure is *Feodor Kuzmich* (1905), an actual hermit, believed to be the Emperor Alexander I. The conqueror of Napoleon is represented in this fragment as assailed by poignant remorse when unexpectedly he witnesses the

---

[63] Tolstoy, "Master and man," in *Tales,* tr. R. N. Bain (1901–2), pp. 75–6 (written in 1895).

punishment of a soldier. The desire of his youth comes back to him : to abdicate, " to go away from all, but without vanity, regardless of the glory of men, only for himself, for the sake of God." [64] And he flies from his earthly glory to end his life in a peasant's hut in a remote corner of Siberia. It would be difficult to represent a more clearly " kenotic " way than that chosen by the Prince Stepan, later Father Sergius, or by the supposed Alexander I.

It is evident that in his fiction Tolstoy, especially in the last period of his work, was attracted by the types which were pointed to by previous Russian writers. With him it was not mere description, as in the case of Tugenev, but an ideal to which he called other men. He ascribed this ideal to his conversion. But it would be a complete mistake to think that Tolstoy's religious thought had any connection whatever with the doctrine of kenosis. All the writers whom we examine in this chapter (except Turgenev) wrote or thought of religion. Tolstoy alone attempted to give a systematic account of his belief. His doctrinal position is that of deism. He refused to believe in the dogma of the Trinity because he could not verify it by reason. For him reason alone was not an illusion and could not be denied. He explained that the sin against the Holy Ghost is that of those " who are against reason." [65] He angrily rejected the idea of original sin. The incarnation, redemption and resurrection seemed to him also ideas " unacceptable to common sense "—which they certainly are —and also " senseless and immoral." [66]

Tolstoy's Christology is regardless of the Gospel records and quite inadequate. Christ is for him simply the best man known to us. There could be neither kenosis nor return to the glory of the Father. The divinity of Christ is explained away, and so is His redemptive work : " Everyone who reads the Gospels knows that in them Christ says nothing, or speaks very vaguely about that. . . . The chief content of Christ's message is the teaching of life : how men should live with one another." [67]

[64] L. Tolstoy, in Birukov's ed. t. XX, p. 108.
[65] *Ibid., Letters* from 1901, t. XXIII, p. 35.
[66] *Ibid., What is religion?* tr. by V. Tchertkoff and A. C. Fifield (Christchurch, 1902).
[67] *Ibid., What is religion?* p. 169.

E

According to Tolstoy, Christ "never spoke at all" of His resurrection, though he found in the Gospels an appeal to some better sort of life with eternal elements in it—"the life of the whole of humanity, the life of the Son of Man." [68] In spite of his disbelief not only in the resurrection but even in personal immortality, Tolstoy experienced after the death of his brother something which convinced him of some sort of survival of souls. He was ready to ascribe such survival to Christ and to those men who, while on earth, entered "the life of the spirit." The life of love and reason is such true life and it is also true fellowship with God. It excludes any need of personal or corporate prayer, since God knows all without our words; all ritual or sacramental expressions of faith are but heathenism. (We prefer not to quote mockeries which are far from honouring Tolstoy.) Tolstoy was devoid of metaphysical and mystical sense. But he acknowledged Christ to be Messiah because He gave commandments of peace and had thus shown the "Kingdom of God on earth"; and because, by "having shown the path of perfection, Christ" has proved to be "the Saviour of the world." [69] None, it seems, had less feeling for the cross than Tolstoy. His "reasonable" religion only allowed him to notice that Jesus died a victim to human hatred.

Not even in his moral teaching could Tolstoy embrace the fullness of the Gospel narrative. All the mystery of the life of prayer was beyond his grasp. He was able to ascribe to Christ such utterances as that "love among men is not an aim towards which people should strive but . . . their natural condition, in which children are born." [70] The teaching of Christ

[68] Tolstoy, *Christ's Christianity*, ed. Kegan Paul (1885), p. 271.

[69] *Ibid., What is religion?* pp. 225, 277. These few lines make clear why the Church had to protest against T.'s teaching by his excommunication in 1901. Some Protestant bodies mistook T. for their ally; yet he definitely declared that he could not belong to any of these fellowships quarrelling with one another and asserting their own truth. All the churches should realize their responsibility for having scandalized by their disunion this human soul. The other cause of scandal was the attitude of the churches with regard to violence and war. T. appreciated the Society of Friends and the Russian Dukhobor for their pacifism.

[70] *Ibid., What I believe*, tr. by Aylmer Maude (Oxford, 1921), p. 371.

in the Sermon on the Mount, so central for the whole
system of Tolstoy, was reduced to five commandments : (1)
live at peace—no anger, no enmity ; (2) no adultery—man
must remain with the one with whom he first had sexual relations (later in life Tolstoy expressed total disapproval of the
life of the flesh, including marriage); (3) never take an oath ;
(4) resist not evil ; (5) love your enemies—no national or racial
distinctions, no war, no armaments, no personal hatred.

Though Tolstoy gave 1878 as the date of his " complete
rebirth," much of his later thought was foreshadowed in his
early writings.   The optimistic view of the " natural condition " of man was apparent when he wrote *The Cossacks*. And
though he now criticized the " false conception of man's right
to a blissful life," [71] he yet believed that the way to it was
shown to mankind.   For him this true happiness consisted in
life with nature, in work, family, free amicable intercourse
with all the different peoples in the world, and in " healthy "
and painless death.   So far, there was no need of conversion :
all the squires of his previous fiction had already felt similar
appeals for " simplification " of their lives.   They also noticed
how much more quietly a peasant accepts death.   But, in a
way, a tree is even more perfect, because more calmly
" natural."   These ideas have a dangerous nihilistic flavour
and it was precisely this exterior " simplification " of life which
appealed to many of Tolstoy's disciples.

Much more radical were Tolstoy's conclusions after he came
to understand the words "resist not evil" in an absolute sense.
" Everything became intelligible.   Christ never represents His
disciples . . . otherwise than as turning the cheek to the smiter,
giving up the cloak, persecuted, beaten and destitute." [72]
Tolstoy did not refer here to Phil. ii. 5, but his interpretation
of what a disciple true to the mind of his Master should be
became suddenly nearer to the spirit of the Gospels, than when
he attempted to summarize his own creed.   There is no need
to repeat the universally known appeal against violence in all
its forms, preached by Tolstoy with such prophetic flame and

[71] Tolstoy, *op. cit.*, p. 235.
[72] *Op. cit.*, p. 118.

sincerity. Even resistance to violence was declared to be the supreme sin and to involve separation from Christ. He exposed the fact that " the worldly heathen governments are supported by the Churches with arms, which is a perversion of true Christianity." [73] War being usually justified as defence of one's own land, state or civilization, all these should be rejected as occasions of sin. Each organized nation being necessarily—at the best—on the defensive, its citizens are subjected to unchristian standards and duties, which should be rejected. Only love, which Tolstoy calls " the unity of the Son of man," should hold men together. Tolstoy protested against any form of co-operation with worldly authorities; even so peaceful an activity as, for instance, the training of children seemed wrong to him because based on false, if not criminal, principles. Nevertheless, there was one occasion when Tolstoy was not only ready to become a loyal citizen, but promised the Emperor Alexander III to become his " slave, his dog." It was in 1881, after the assassination of Alexander II. Tolstoy besought the new Tsar to forgive the murderers of his father. The whole country knew of his letter to the Tsar and awaited its result. He was not alone in hoping for an act of Christian forgiveness, and had this forgiveness been granted, it might have changed much in Russian history.

Tolstoy understood Christ's commandment to those who desired to become His disciples as a call to " be beggars, to be ready without resisting evil to accept persecution, suffering and death."[74] The homeless and the wandering follower of Christ should denounce " the hypocrisy of modern times, where both clergy and nominal Christians and the unbelievers, Socialists or men of science, say: ' We do not want all to be as poor as the poor; we want all to be as rich as the rich.' " [75] Poverty was precious to him as one of the characteristics of Christlike life. At the same time—and here was the greatness of Tolstoy—while he wanted to take upon himself evangelical poverty, he realized the sufferings of those pushed into it by

[73] Tolstoy, *What is religion?* p. 73.
[74] *Ibid., What I believe,* p. 300.
[75] *Ibid., The Kingdom of God is within us,* tr. C. Garnett (1894), p. 236.

cruel and unjust relationships within society. He felt indignant with the Encyclical on Socialism, " this teaching of selfishness which prescribes that you should give to your neighbours only what you do not want yourself." [76] Tolstoy went round the poorer quarters of Moscow, and in contact with the real misery of his fellow-men he forgot all his theories, gave way to his heart and allowed his conscience to speak for him :

> " I beheld the misery, cold, hunger and humiliation of thousands of my fellow-men. . . . I might have given away not only the drink and the small sum of money I had with me but also the coat from my shoulders, and all that I possessed at home. Yet I have not done so, and therefore felt and feel and can never cease to feel myself a partaker in a crime which is continually being committed, so long as I have superfluous food whilst others have none, so long as I have two coats whilst there exists one man without any." [77]

These passionate words are proof of a sound moral approach : there is here not so much indignation against the existing order of things as a feeling of personal responsibility and a personal self-condemnation. With his alarming frankness Tolstoy relates how once when walking in the street with a peasant he met a beggar. The peasant wanted to give him a copeck but had only a three-copeck piece; the beggar had no small change ; so the peasant crossed himself and gave him his three copecks. Tolstoy gave twenty, but he reckoned that to equal this peasant, whose income he knew, he would need to have given three thousand roubles—three hundred thousand copecks.

This contact with the inhabitants of the slums, the example of the poor helping the poor, made Tolstoy ashamed not only of his wealth but also of his origin, his education, of all the privileges which set him apart from his suffering fellow-men. He confessed himself guilty in accepting these privileges. Were

[76] Tolstoy, *The first step,* tr. A. Maude (1891), p. 19. The teaching of the Encyclical is misinterpreted by Tolstoy.
[77] *Ibid., What is to be done?* ed. Walter Scott (not dated), p. 10, written in 1885.

he alone concerned he would gladly have changed his whole manner of life. But he had a family. The play *The light shines in darkness* (1900–2) gave a poignant picture of a man who, out of pity for his wife, consciously and willingly bore the humiliation of the taunts of those who accused him of being a preacher not practising his doctrine.[78] The play showed also the disastrous results of this Sarintsov's theories and preaching: the priest to whom he taught religion " within the bounds of pure reason " recanted; a young man who had refused military service was to be tried. And the author or Sarintsov asked the agonized question : " Can it be that I have been mistaken? Mistaken in believing in Thee? No. Father. Help me! " [79]

Here Tolstoy, who started from a doctrinal position quite other than Gogol's, began to approach the desire for humiliation. His letters constantly refer to it :

> " Take my yoke . . . learn of me. . . . I cannot express in words the feelings which these words always did and do provoke within me and how they answer everything. Not for me, this proud, nasty me to become perfect, but accepting my own position, my own body, health, character, my past, even my sins, to seek in my heart at every moment, with meekness and humility, some opportunity of doing some job He wants done. Can I not be of use to stop up some hole? To wipe something with? Can I not be used as an example of meanness, of vice and of sin; or at least cannot my body be used as manure? All is easy and assured when I feel like this." [80]

Trying to sum up his life before and after conversion, Tolstoy wrote :

> " Now I remember that he alone is superior to others who humbles himself and is the servant of all. I now understand why that which is exalted by men is an abomination before God, and why woe befalls the rich and famous while the poor and humble are blessed. . . .

---

[78] Tolstoy was not spared. Thus Merezhkovsky's *Tolstoy as man and artist* (SPB. 1900), otherwise interesting and acute, illustrates it well enough.

[79] *Ibid., The light shines in darkness,* tr. L. A. Maude (1914), p. 411.

[80] *Ibid., Letter to V. V. Rakhmanov,* in ed. Birukov, t. XXII, p. 61.

This belief has changed my whole appreciation of what
is good and lofty. . . .   I can no longer yield to that
temptation which, setting me above my fellows, deprived
me of my true welfare, the union of love. . . . I can recognize . . . no title, rank, or distinction. . . . I cannot seek
fame and applause; I cannot seek even such knowledge
as would divide me from others.   I cannot but seek to set
myself free from my wealth."

But, deeper than this desire for union with men in simplicity
and on their level, however low, was his conclusion :

" The very thing which formerly militated against the
truth and practicability of Christ's teaching and drove
me away from it : the possibility of privation, suffering
and death inflicted by those who do not know this teaching—that very thing now confirms for me the truth of the
teaching and attracts me to it." [81]

Nothing could put more clearly why Tolstoy became hostile
not only towards riches but towards science, art and intellectual riches as well.   His personal drama involved all he had,
all he was, and divided his family into two camps, while the
whole country looked on.   But on his way of renunciation and
humiliation Tolstoy still clung to the one form of wealth : he
could not or would not give up his reasoning powers and so he
never could recognize the divine Christ whom he so sought to
love and to follow.   But his artistic perception, if not his dis-
cursive mind, showed him the true way of perfection—in the
complete renunciation of a Father Sergius, in the unceasing
praise and naïve prayer of the three old men and in the sacrificial death of the merchant Brekhunov.

However different the theoretical conceptions of the Russian
writers, all of them seem to be of one accord when they seek
to express the type of true holiness.

Nothing in Feodor M. Dostoevsky as man and writer repeats
Tolstoy.   The difference between them is more than the mere
surface contrast of their lives, surroundings and achievement.
Tolstoy and Gogol were tormented by the question whether
they should write.   Dostoevsky, usually so alive to difficulties,

[81] Tolstoy, *What I believe*, pp. 372, 385.

was never troubled by this one. He never repudiated his work, though he too had his experience of conversion. After his period of Socialism, after the trial and the last-moment reprieve from capital punishment, after years of prison and soldiering in Siberia, he returned " renewed " and reconciled with God. Whilst Tolstoy wanted to get rid of his possessions and was unable to, Dostoevsky incurred endless debts, struggled for money and begged from all his friends. His real difficulties and heavy family responsibility were aggravated by his gambling. All this, however harassing, was nothing compared with the conjunction of creative tension with the constant fear that illness (his epilepsy) or death might prevent him from finishing his work. He had no time to discuss " what is art?" For him, art was the only way of self-expression, or rather of expressing what he had to say about God. The novels of Dostoevsky are his testimony, his confession of faith.

It was a hard-won faith. The difficulties of life did not frighten him; in prison he lived by the hope of liberation and of the new life which he could start once set free. But readjustment to normal conditions of existence brought with it, in a way, greater difficulties. All the conflicts and contradictions of life and thought pressed upon him. Nobody could write the pages he wrote out of pure imagination. In his heroes, blinded by hatred, passion or religious doubts, Dostoevsky was winning in fair fight his right to believe. He learned rebellion, pride and self-assertion in their bitterest form : not in relation to people or society but in relation to God. His " hosanna went through fire of doubts." " The rascals teased me with my ' uncivilized ' and reactionary faith in God. Those idiots never dreamt of such a power of denial of God as there is in the Inquisitor and in the preceding chapter, the answer to which lies in *all the novel*." [82] In its actual form, it is an incomplete answer : death interrupted *The Brothers Karamazov*.

In spite of their suggestive titles and deeply humanitarian character there is no need for us to dwell on such early works

---

[82] O. Miller, *Biography,* letters and notes by Th. M. Dostoevsky (SPB. 1883), p. 368, from his note-book in 1880.

of Dostoevsky as *Poor Folk* (1846) and *Netochka Nezvanova* (1849), nor even upon his first publications after his banishment : the *Insulted and Injured* and *The House of the Dead* (both in 1861). Many among these " poor folk " are the victims of social conditions and of the appetites of the privileged classes.

The important feature of *The House of the Dead* is that it illustrates the period of " return to the soil." The liberal, international tendencies of Dostoevsky faded. In his works from 1860 onwards the theme of Russia expanded side by side with Christian motives. He attributed his return to the faith to contact with the peasantry. There was that unforgettable incident when, dressed as a convict, he was given a penny —alms from a soldier's widow, brought to him " in the name of Christ " by her little daughter.[83] The remembrance of a gentle peasant, whom he had met as a boy, helped him to bear the repulsive scenes he witnessed in prison.[84] But of all the Russian writers of his time, Dostoevsky was the least partial in his representation of the peasants. He did not sentimentalize. On the whole, he was never concerned with class problems in the manner of Tolstoy. His Christlike characters are drawn from among all classes of society, indeed predominantly from the upper class. But what impressed him in the peasantry, and even among criminals, was their essentially sound moral conviction of what was right and wrong. Through them he realized clearly the error of the " advanced " thinkers to whose circle he had once belonged— people who were ready to take upon themselves the decision as to who among their fellow-men had or had not the right of existence. That is why the convicts disliked Raskolnikov, guessing him to be an unbeliever. That is why Shatov, the mouthpiece of the author, exhorted Stavrogin : " You've lost the distinction between good and evil because you've lost touch with your own people. . . . Attain to God by work, by peasant's work. Go, give up all your wealth." [85] This utter-

---

[83] Dostoevsky, *Complete works* (ed. SPB. 1905–6), 12 vols., t. IV, p. 21, *The House of the Dead.*
[84] Peasant Marej, in *The Journal of a Writer.*
[85] *The Possessed,* tr. C. Garnett (1913), p. 238 (1871).

ance brings in a note we have heard already. In opposition to those who would reduce the good life to a matter of external " simplification," there are the words of the humble Prince Myshkin : why should the upper class disappear? " We might remain in advance and be leaders. . . . Let us be servants in order to be leaders." [86]   Dostoevsky himself would always remember that it was from and through " the people " that he " regained in his soul the Christ " whom he had lost whilst he was " a European liberal." [87]

To accept Christ meant also to accept life, and not only good or moral life but the life of suffering and death. Just because he had received Christ back into his heart, he could face the problem of suffering. The conversation—almost a duel—between the novice Aliosha and his brother Ivan made this clear. Ivan was ready to accept not only the existence of God or even His wisdom and His purpose. He went so far as to be ready to believe " in the Word to which the universe is striving, and which itself was ' with God ' and which itself is God and so on, and so on to infinity." [88]   Almost, it seems that Ivan is a believer. But the subtle denial began after all these declarations. Ivan rejected the world with the suffering of the innocent in it and " most respectfully " he wanted to give back " the entrance ticket " to it. Tolstoy could never feel that " the Word was God," and he denied life. Ivan could think of the Word as divine but he also denied life. The answer to both, from their different points of departure, would be the acceptance of the incarnation. S. N. Bulgakov had pointed out that " what really matters is that the Word became flesh." [89]   In the materials and first drafts of the *Possessed*, there is a striking dialogue between Stavrogin and Shatov. The former thinks the problem of Christ the fundamental problem of existence. Their understanding of Orthodoxy comes to them through " the people." But the question is whether an educated man can believe, or whether the Christian belief is only a product of the ignorance and

[86] *The Idiot* (1868), tr. C. Garnett (1913), p. 556.
[87] In O. Miller, *Note-book*, p. 440.
[88] Dostoevsky, *The brothers Karamazov* (1881), (1912), p. 258.
[89] S. N. Bulgakov, Preface to ed. SPB. 1906, p. ix.

backwardness of the nation.   If so, the sooner the nation grows
out of it, the better.   In fact, the question is even much more
important than this: "The whole question is: can one
believe unconditionally in the divinity of the Son of God,
Jesus Christ (because all belief consists only in this)."
Stavrogin says to Shatov: "We know that the Christ-man is
not the Saviour, as we know that science alone will never
fulfil the wholeness of the human ideal; peace for man,
source of life and salvation from despair of all men and the
condition *sine qua non* for the existence of the whole universe
is included in these three words: The *Word became Flesh,*
and in belief in these words." [90]   Shatov, who personifies
Dostoevsky, believed in these words.   This fullness of
orthodox belief helped Dostoevsky to perceive the mystery of
suffering and the final victory of Christ.   It saved him from
dualism; there was no need to deny the flesh, or the State,
or his own art.   Sinful men and nature were already
redeemed; they belonged to the cosmic process where all
were responsible for all.   Dostoevsky had the intuition that
both a good and a bad act affect the whole creation.   He felt
some particular bond with the earth—and this much more in
connection with the Incarnation than in the sense of any
"natural" bent towards it.   Stavrogin's crippled wife spoke
of mother-earth where lies "great joy for men; and every
earthly woe and every earthly tear is a joy for us; and when
you water the earth with your tears a foot deep, you will
rejoice." [91]   This half-conscious utterance was repeated more
definitely by Dimitry Karamazov and was ecstatically
experienced by his brother Aliosha in the crucial moment of his
life.   The monk Zossima insistently spoke of this link binding
men and nature in a process of transfiguration.

None knew better than Dostoevsky the evils of life, both in
the individual and in the whole human organization of life.
But instead of the political systems to which he trusted as a
young man, he now claimed "that *true* Christianity solves
social problems also, changing each one into a brother and a

[90] Dostoevsky, ed. 1906, t. VIII, pp. 597—626, esp. pp. 601 and 602.
[91] *The Possessed*, p. 238.

servant." [92]   The idea of civilization or of virtue apart from
Christ became abhorrent to him.   He realized that men
tended to seek their perfection in becoming super-men and
were therefore opposed to the humble God-Man.   For him,
the political world reflected the temptation of the wilderness :
" Bread alone."   To make material welfare the chief aim was
just as wrong for him on the social scale as it would be for
an individual.   He exposed also the readiness of mankind
to accept the servile state and to yield to coercion whether
social or ecclesiastical.   He condemned as the ethics of " the
ant-hill " the disposition to worship anything if only it could
be done in common with the swarm.   For him the only
safety from these three dangers and the only unity possible
was to be found in Christ and his freedom.

Like their creator, Dostoevsky's heroes tried to make their
choice and to find some philosophy of life.   He portrayed
hardly any " neutral " type.   His heroes were classified not so
much by their origin, or by their personal destinies, as by
their attitude towards life and God.   They fall into two
groups : the lowly and the daring or, in other terms, the strong
and the weak.   Dostoevsky's classification does not deal with
customary human virtues and morals. The noble actions of the
lofty Katia in *The Brothers Karamazov* spring from pride.
The depraved Grushenka shows more humanity.   If Sonia,
of *Crime and Punishment,* is depicted as an innocent victim,
her father, whose drunkenness was the cause of her degradation, is nevertheless presented as a victim also and, like his
daughter, a believer, he was sure that Christ " who understood all men and all things will pity " all of them " because
none of them has believed himself to be worthy of it." [93]
The same was emphatically felt by Dimitry Karamazov :
" Let me be wild and base, only let me kiss the hem of the veil
in which my God is shrouded.   Though I may be following
the devil, I am Thy son, O Lord, and I feel the joy without
which the world cannot stand." [94]   Nastassya Filippovna, more

[92] Dostoevsky, *Journal of a Writer,* t. XII, pp. 452, 463 (against
Granovsky).
[93] *Crime and Punishment* (1865), (1914), pp. 20, 21.
[94] *Brothers Karamazov,* p. 109.

complicated, proud and tormented than any of these fallen people, found some bitter satisfaction in her degradation, yet Prince Myshkin understood her deep conviction that she alone was to blame. And she also used to think of Christ.

There was hope for all the immoral people because there was in them conviction of their unworthiness. The way of repentance was opened to them. All Dostoevsky's characters knew this school of repentance and the test of tears.[95] The fragment, *Stavrogin's confession,* recorded the visit of the sinner to the hermit. The confession was written and the man almost ready to publish his "ridiculous manuscript" and to bear the results. The hermit, aware of the fact that man can sometimes speak of his sin without being ashamed of it, but is ashamed of repentance, answered that "even this form will conquer if only you accept sincerely the blows and the spitting. It always ended in the most ignominious cross becoming a great glory and a great strength, if the humility of the deed was sincere. Perhaps even in your lifetime you will be comforted." [96]

It is of interest to notice that the hermit who calls the sinner to the way of humiliation was given the name Tykhon. He is not a figure of fiction. Dostoevsky was deeply impressed by the person of the Bishop of Voronezh and wanted to revive his memory. He was truly anxious to create this figure before his death. [97] Once more, literature and actual sainthood proved to be deeply connected with each other. This fragment was not included in *The Possessed* as was first intended. But the idea remained, and Zossima from the Karamazovs was inspired by St. Tykhon. [98]

Stavrogin, who wanted to repent and could not, was one of the "strong and daring." All these proud, self-assertive men

---

[95] Especially the story of the cruel merchant in *The Raw Youth* (1875), pp. 394ff.

[96] *Stavrogin's Confession* and the plan of a Life of a great sinner, tr. by S. Koteliansky and V. Woolf (1922), p. 78.

[97] Already in 1870 he mentions his desire in a letter to A. N. Maikov, in *Miller*, p. 233, also in letters to Katkov.

[98] In his materials and first drafts D. retains for him the name of Tykhon, see Dostoevsky, *Materials,* ed. by N. S. Dolinin, Academy of U.S.S.R. (Leningrad, 1935).

were setting themselves up as judges of the others or of the existing order, whether the political order of their time or the universal order of things.[99]   They were never caricatured by Dostoevsky; he represented them at their best: clever, often strong, sincere and at times ascetic.   But this is the asceticism of negation.   It is a reversed form of a possible way to God, just as the immobility of Stavrogin, who was struck on the face, was a form of pride.   All these men are animated by the craving for power.   With some it takes the form of trivial immorality; but more often it is connected with the right they assume to pronounce sentence of death on other men. All his life long, Dostoevsky protested against this "right to eliminate" living people if even in the name of future harmony and "until the New Jerusalem." [100]   Like his Aliosha, he would not have a happy world built on injustice or suffering.   The logic of murder and suicide was powerfully proved to be the outcome of disbelief.   With Kirilov, suicide becomes an act of rebellion against the fear of death; his own voluntary end seems to him to assert the power of his own ego and to destroy God.   The rebellious fall into a perverted passion for martyrdom.   Beyond good and evil they pass into a realm of mystical terror.   These men, energetic, active and passionate, seem as yet to belong to a metaphysical world.   There is something unreal in them.   They develop some ghostly properties, they seem to vanish through the wall, their faces are mask-like.   The devil of Ivan Karamazov, "his caricature," feels all this and expresses the desire to be incarnate in some fat merchant's wife.

These God-fighting and God-tormented men are contrasted with the firm and silent mass of peasantry, "the God-bearing people."   If they seem to say: "I deny, therefore I live," there are others, meek and sacrificial, who seem to answer: "I love, therefore I live."   The super-men are shown unable to stand by their denial or crime in spite of their strength and

[99] The super-men of D. were prior to the works of Nietzsche: *Memoirs of the Underworld* in 1864, *Crime and Punishment* in 1865, *Possessed* in 1871.

[100] *Crime and Punishment*, p. 238.

intelligence.[101]   Their victims, the weak, the submissive, survive and conquer.   They prove to be the only ones who really
exist.   They oppose self-assertion by self-denial and violence
by non-resistance.   Meekness is the true force of the mother
of the Raw Youth.   Prepared to serve, eager to sacrifice, they
could say, as Dasha: " You can never anyhow be my ruin.
. . . If I don't come to you, I shall be a sister of mercy, a nurse,
shall wait upon the sick or go selling the Gospels." [102]   Aliosha
Karamazov is of the meek also, though none thinks of it when
first approaching the smiling, healthy and strong-looking
youth.   All his ways seem gay and natural.   But if all end by
trusting him it is because all realize that Aliosha does not judge
them.   This is his form of humility.   One cannot say that
Aliosha chooses poverty as well : he simply does not notice
how he lives, and he accepts other people's help as simply as
he himself gives it.   The same features are typical of the
Prince Myshkin.   The destitute " idiot " becomes in a day a
recognized prince and a rich man.   This does not seem to
affect him in any way, just as poverty did not seem a burden.
In these two men it is difficult to choose examples of their
meekness or humility—the whole of their lives and characters
express it.   But with them it also becomes clear that true
humility, and humiliation accepted in the true spirit, become
a force.   They are true conquerors of life because they are not
afraid of any suffering or abasement of their persons.   The
broken marriage ceremony of the prince is an instance of such
silent triumph.   It is also interesting to notice the parallel
between Stavrogin, struck on the face and enduring it in
silence, and the behaviour of the prince in similar circum-
stance.   With him, one is in the world of non-resistance and
he would meet death with similar simplicity.

There is nothing depressed about the lowly people of
Dostoevsky.   They seem already to have approached the other
world, where " the body of humiliation " is changed into the

[101] In his article on " Crime and punishment," A. M. Bukharev proves
that Raskolnikov was not able to endure his crime because by nature he
was goodhearted ; he was a victim of the wrong conception of greatness.
(Published posthumously in t. I of the *Orth. Observer,* 1884.)
[102] *The Possessed,* p. 273.

body of glory. They are joyous because they give up everything. The old pilgrim Makar knew it and felt sorry for men
who give so little to the others. How different it is

> " from Christ's ' go and give all that thou hast to the poor
> and become the servant of all.' Then thou shalt be
> richer than ever before . . . by love multiplied immeasur-
> ably. . . . Then thou wilt attain wisdom, not from books
> alone, but wilt be face to face with God Himself, and the
> earth will shine more brightly than the sun, and there
> shall be no more sorrow nor sighing, nothing but one
> priceless paradise." [103]

Makar was said to be serene and consolatory; he used to tell
stories with a flash of something wonderfully accomplished and
touching in them. He used to say that he never met a complete unbeliever and assured people that a man of gay character cannot deny God. Himself an untaught man, he was glad
to see others educated, but he rather rejoiced in thinking that,
in spite of all learning, God and the world are still a mystery.
This " makes it only better; it fills the heart with awe and
wonder; and that awe maketh glad the heart; all is in Thee,
my Lord, and I, too, am in Thee; have me in Thy keeping.
. . . There is a limit to the memory of a man on earth . . .
but [once dead] I will pray to God for you, I will come to you
in your dreams; it is all the same—even in death there is
love." [104] Makar is touching here the mystery of the unique
everlasting life; but to enter it, one had first " to become the
servant of all "—a typical addition to the recommendation of
the Lord or rather an equivalent of the " Come, follow me "
of St. Luke xviii. 22. Makar says here in simpler and more
direct words what the dying heroes of Tolstoy tried to say.

Even the unreconciled Ippolit felt it. He spoke of an old
and very poor retired general visiting the prisoners who used to
remember him, though not necessarily with warmth. It is of
interest that the feeling of unity should be applied to almsgiving as well. Ippolit suggested something which throws new
light on an act of charity. For him, almsgiving with a loving

---

[103] Dostoevsky, *Raw Youth,* tr. C. Garnett (1916), p. 381.
[104] *Ibid.,* p. 355.

approach to man is already a self-emptying, though he does not use this term. "You are giving away, in one form or another, part of your personality and taking into yourself part of another; you are in mutual communion with one another; a little more effort and you will be rewarded with the knowledge of the most unexpected discoveries." [105]

The monk Zossima, "the Russian monk," should be considered at length, which is impossible in this work. In creating him, Dostoevsky tried to present a positive type of Russian sainthood. He did not intend to make a portrait of the historical saint, but he said definitely that he wanted " to show the *real* Tykhon whom long ago and with enthusiasm [he] took into [his] heart." [106] He wondered whether this man were not the positive type sought so eagerly by Russian writers. There is, as a matter of fact, a likeness in the atmosphere of Zossima's talks to the ideas of St. Tykhon of Voronezh. His words about the love of God had, even in style, some kinship to the writings of the bishop. There is no outspoken teaching of humility in Zossima. The only act of self-abasement from the human point of view was that day in his life when he refused to fight in a duel. (His life story is imaginary and has no traits in common with the life of Bishop Tykhon.) But this disregard of conventional honour was easily forgiven when people round him realized that he wanted to become a monk. One has the impression that towards the end of his life Zossima would not specially mention the way of humiliation because this was too evident for him. He himself already approached the realm of radiance. From this victorious assurance of divine love, Zossima understands human sorrow. A young woman weeping after the death of her child asks for consolation. He knows that conventional words would not comfort her. And he gives her leave, so to

---

[105] Dostoevsky, *The Idiot,* p. 406.
[106] Letter to Maikov, in *O. Miller,* p. 233 ; quoted also by Rozanov in *The Great Inquisitor* (SPB. 1894), note on p. 6. In spite of the letter, many persisted in thinking that D. painted one of the monks of Optina, Father Amvrossy, whom he met during his visits there, in 1879 (according to D. P. Bogdanov, in 1877). Bogdanov holds up this idea, see *Historical Messenger,* t. CXXII, 1910. "Optina and pilgrimages there of the Russian writers."

say, to carry on her " lot " of tears. He knows that this sorrow, accepted by her, will be her way of godly life.   In spite of the caricatured presentations of the Russian mind disseminated in the West there is no artificial seeking of suffering, except by definitely unsound souls of the type of Nastassya Filippovna. Not suffering in itself, not mortification of the body, but the obedient attitude, appeals to the Russian mind.   This is not a passive obedience.   The force of rebellion proves what these souls are capable of.   Dostoevsky gives striking instances of both.   Even the young brother of Zossima, who so impressed him, passed through a period of rebellion. In brief, this youth, converted shortly before his untimely death, illustrated what was later on the line of Zossima.

Rediscovering God, the young man felt first of all his own sin and his own share of responsibility for all the wrongs of the life round him.   " One is really responsible to all men for all men and for everything." [107]   He felt ashamed to be waited upon and wanted to become the servant of his servants.   He asked forgiveness not only of people but of birds. His mother objected that he was too young and too good to have committed all the sins he was ready to take upon himself.   He then answered : " I like to humble myself before them, for I don't know how to love them enough."   Certainly, this is a reflection of the condescending love of the Incarnate.   On the other hand, with relation to his fellow-men, the youth explained : " If I have sinned against everyone, yet all forgive me, and that's heaven." [108]   Through this way of repentance and self-abasement he enters into joy because now he realizes the unity of " all creation and all creatures where every leaf is striving to the Word, singing glory to God, weeping to Christ, unconsciously accomplishing this by the mystery of their sinless life." [109]   In spite of the difference in their education and surroundings this youth, dying of consumption, has much in common with the " Living relic," Lukeria.   This allows one to repeat with S. N. Bulgakov that there exists " a purely Russian

[107] Dostoevsky, *The brothers Karamazov*, p. 304.
[108] *Ibid.*, p. 305.
[109] *Ibid.*, p. 311.

manner of the artistic interpretation of Christ's image which brings together writers so unlike and so remote from each other in spirit as Turgenev and Dostoevsky." [110]

Death interrupted the Karamazovs. Aliosha, who was intended to become the chief personage, hardly begins to act. But we know whose pupil he was and though, according to his spiritual father, he had to go out in the world and to marry, and according to the notes of Dostoevsky he had to pass through the period of rebellion and participation in the revolutionary movement, he would still come back to the purified vision of Christ. Dostoevsky, with his merciless criticism of the revolutionary ideal as an ideal " of virtue without Christ," realized also the religious significance of the movement. Already his Shatov was earnestly ready to believe in God and expected Christ's actual second coming : Aliosha, eager for love and justice, would probably endeavour to hasten this Kingdom on earth. We shall try to detect the Christian features of the revolutionary leaders, especially as they also seem to be in the line of the humiliation of Christ. One more writer must be examined now. He belongs to the generation of the 'sixties, but he is still wholly in the Christian tradition and he is a believer.

Nicolas S. Leskov (1831–95) was for a long time disregarded by literary critics because of his political conservatism. He is of great interest to us. His " political " novels *No Way Out* (1864) or *At Daggers Drawn* (1870–1) are not characteristic of his art and give us hardly any material. But his stories are a real contribution to the collection of " kenotic " figures or thoughts, expressed moreover in an extremely rich and picturesque language which we do not attempt to render in translation.

Grandson of a priest who married a girl of merchant family, son of a civil servant and gently-born mother, he had an exceptional field of observation among different classes of society. In addition to this, he was employed as a travelling agent or steward of a rich estate and came thus into touch

[110] S. N. Bulgakov, *From Marxism to Idealism* (SPB. 1903), p. 100.

with the peasantry and with small country folk.   He met
Sectarians, he knew well the Old Believers on whom he wrote
articles (" With People of Old Belief " and " Monk Paul and
his books," 1863–5, in *Biblioteka dlia Chtenija*) and many
stories as, for example, his famous *Sealed Angel* (1873). Leskov
did not think of becoming a professional writer.   He started by
occasional correspondences from Kiev to a St. Petersburg
newspaper (*Peterbyrgskija Vedomosti*).   His first paper was a
protest against the exorbitant prices charged for the Gospel in
a Russian translation (1860).   Religious problems preoccupied
Leskov all his life long.   He met Protestants—hence his novel
The Islanders (1866) and the story *The Quakeresses* (1892).
In his last years he became a follower of Tolstoy.[111] As one who
knew from within the life of the clergy and who abundantly
wrote on the subject, he serves as a true link with those whom
we shall examine in the theological world.   Some of his stories
preserved even the actual names (*Details of Episcopal Life,*
1878, at first prohibited by the censor, and also historical
portraits given in *The Just Men,* 1880).

There is no idealization of either class in Leskov's works.
There is no moralization either, except in the stories of the last
"Tolstoyian" period. With the earnestness of a Russian writer,
further increased through the influence of Tolstoy, Leskov
studies all whom he meets and, depicting people, he tries to
remain faithful to his model.   This was especially important
for him, as he had an acute sense of the language, and each of
his picturesque personages speaks in a kind of vernacular,
peculiar to him alone.   Many did not recognize his gift and
ascribed to his work only a descriptive, documental value.[112]
Leskov has a fine sense of humour, his descriptions are naturalistic and full of local colour.   His heroes are living people,
except the pale figures of his " political " novels and the

---

[111] Leskov, *Letters to Tolstoy,* ed. Gosizdat, M. Leningrad, 1928 ; also
Vera Mikulich, *The meetings with the writers,* ed. Gosizdat, 1929.

[112] Ossip Lourié, *La Psychologie des romanciers russes du XIX siécle*
(Bruxelles, 1905), holds this opinion.   The artistic contribution of Leskov
is defended by R. I. Sementkovsky in his preface to the *Works of Leskov*
(SPB. 1902–3), from which edition we quote. Fuller exposition of L.'s life
and work in P. Kovalevsky, *Leskov peintre méconnu de la vie nationale
russe* (Paris, 1925).

imaginary holy men of the *Legends* (1880).   Aza and Daniel
are pale expressions of virtues.   But none could doubt the
existence of old Kiriak or of Ivan in *The Enchanted Wanderer*
(1874), however incredible may seem his adventures.   No class
or confessional prejudice hinders Leskov's observation.   He is
full of sympathy for the *Unbaptized Priest* (1877), Savva, an
Orthodox by origin, but brought up by the sectarians, who
always kept " the law of love."   Leskov shares with the Old
Believers their love and knowledge of old iconography.   And
he paints, in the old lady Plodomasova, a serf-owner, the
picture of a defender of truth, full of generosity and understanding in spite of her authoritative ways and her fancies—
those of a rich woman of her epoch.

Leskov has drawn various types of religious people.   The
three figures of his *Cathedral Folk* (Soboryane, 1872) are quite
unlike each other.   The giant deacon Akhila, a Cossack of
great physical strength and of childish stubbornness, is often a
scandal to the town.   He is not intelligent, but he is alone able
to understand the old, perfectly silent and " most humble "
priest Zakharia, as well as the central figure of this chronicle,
the Archpriest Tuberozov.   This last is an indomitable wrestler
for truth.   He suffers from the separation between religion
and everyday life.   He shows the tendency to introduce into
his sermons episodes and examples from his surroundings—a
tendency disapproved of by the authorities.   He is ready to
suffer and one makes him suffer.   But he is not a submissive
character.   There is no false humility in him ; he denies the
charge that his zeal is arrogance.   In the midst of his struggle
with civil and ecclesiastical authorities, who " ruin God's living
work," he is comforted by an unexpected vision : a very poor
citizen who brought up two orphans is planting vegetables,
praying aloud : " Lord, multiply, grow enough of it for all
men hungry and poor, for all who bless and all the ungrateful
. . . this old man is planting for a thief and is praying for
him." [113]

Among the godly people of Leskov there are vigorous,
chaotic figures of men who could not explain why they are

[113] *The Cathedral Folk*, p. 101.

attracted by religion (*The enchanted Wanderer*). Some of them are "seekers of God" (*The Ovibos,* 1863). But, more than any of the writers already mentioned, Leskov had noticed the kenotic type. Some object to civilization, State, war : Ovtzebuyk, the officer Vigura (*Figura*), and the idealistic district police officer (*Laughter and woe*). Also *The teacher Chervev* (1871). A princess, who wished to appoint the teacher Chervev to instruct her children, did not dare to do so on account of his radical interpretation of the Christian life, which led him to renounce all property and to see in the State an instrument of evil. Great stress is laid upon poverty, and the men who, in the Russia of Nicolas I, occupied high position and never took any material advantage of it were almost heroic. In the series of *The Just men* one finds D. A. Bryanchaninov, future Bishop Ignaty of Caucasus, and his friend Chikhachev, engineers and musicians who renounced the world. There is the amusing and touching *Man of one thought,* man of low class, poorest of the poor, who read " all the Bible, up to Christ." [114] Having received a decoration, through the governor to whom he taught the true humble manner of entering the church, he never put it on because he did not possess the clothes which one is expected to wear with this distinction. The whole family of lovers of honest poverty is represented in many a generation of the Princes Protozanov (*A Decayed family,* 1874).

Even more outspoken in their direct reference to Christ are priests, whose names are not revealed by the author, but who are taken from life. An archimandrite who taught in the military school asked children once why Christ did not descend in His glory instead of being born in a manger. And he himself gave the answer :

> " When well fed (as my face shows) and dressed in silk I preach a sermon explaining that one should bear patiently hunger and frost, I read on the faces of my listeners : Easy to you, monk, to reason when you wear silk and are nourished. . . . And, I think, if our Lord came in glory we should say to Him something like this.

[114] Leskov, *Man of one thought,* t. III, p. 87.

We should say perhaps: 'Thou art happy in heaven, Thou camest here for a time to teach. No, wert Thou born among us, hadst Thou suffered from cradle to grave what we have to bear, then it would be different.' This is very important and well-reasoned and so He came barefooted and journeyed on earth without refuge." [115]

A man who hardly speaks at all, and yet is unforgettable, is the hermit Pamva—" authoritative little old man " and yet " the meekest of the meek " who is " all inspired by love." There are no books in his hut—which strikes an old believer who happened to seek shelter under his roof; the cross made out of two little sticks is all he has to worship. His young companion and servant treats him rudely. But the old man says of himself with tears: " I am not humble, I am arrogant, I want a place in the heavenly kingdom." [116] His silent power brings the dissident back into the Church. This conquering, humble love is the only missionary method of the old Kiriak also (*On the edge of the world*, 1876). He refuses to preach and to baptize because he is sure the Zirani cannot yet understand it. He makes necklaces for the little pagan girls, he begs for some food for the heathen magicians put in prison and visits them. When reproached by the bishop that he speaks of Christ in too familiar a way, he answers:

" Why, He does not mind simplicity. Who can tell His generation—yet He walked with the shepherds, He went with the sinners, He did not abhor the mangy sheep. Whenever He found one, He put it as it was, on His holy shoulders and carried it to His Father. Now, what could the Father do? He did not want to grieve His Son the sufferer—so, for His sake He let the untidy thing into His sheep-fold." [117]

The same man, perishing from cold on a tour in the North, implores the bishop's forgiveness for a Zirani man baptized but hardly conscious of his faith, who abandoned him and ate

---

[115] Leskov, *The cadet's monastery*, t. III, p. 151.

[116] *Ibid., The sealed angel*, t. III, p. 50. The description of Pamva— his bent body, his stick, the wood, remind one of St. Seraphim of Sarov as represented on icons of later origin. There is no direct indication whether L. wanted to represent him.

[117] *Ibid., On the edge of the world*, t. VII, p. 129.

the Eucharistic bread and wine carried by the monk. And, in his last prayer, he threatens God rather than implores : " Bless them all, otherwise I shan't leave Thee in peace." [118] After his death many of the tribe came and asked to be baptized " into Kiriak's God."

The story of this old monk is told by the bishop who, full of missionary zeal, wanted to visit the country and was unwillingly the cause of Kiriak's death; he began by scolding the old man for all his ways—but he himself speaks of Christ in very similar terms. " Whatever Messieurs the Greeks say and however they prove that we are obliged to them for having learnt of God through them—it is not they who revealed God to us. We did not find Him in their pompous Byzantinism and incense. He is our own, He goes everywhere with simplicity." [119] The same thought is expressed when, discussing Western religious art and its masterpieces, the bishop says :

" the typically Russian image is as simple as it could be. . . . It is true, Christ is even peasant-like, and yet worship is due to Him. . . . As He has revealed Himself in this or the other place, He goes on that way; to us, He came in the form of a servant, and that is how He walks having nowhere to lay His head, from Petersburg to Kamchatka. Probably He likes to receive, together with us, defamation from those who drink His blood and yet shed it. And in the measure in which, it seems to me, our popular art understood more simply and with greater success the exterior features of Christ, so also perhaps our popular spirit grasped His inner features more truly as well." [120]

These quotations do not need any comment : Leskov, whom Tolstoy described as " the first Christian idealist of the 'sixties," [121] seems even more precise in his portraits than his predecessors. The accusation of being merely an ethnographer make these portraits only more valuable to us. He completes our illustrations of the " holy Russia," and we turn now to the writers of revolutionary type who did not claim and in some cases denied any Christian inspiration in their lives and work.

[118] Leskov, *On the edge of the world*, t. VII, p. 168.
[119] *Ibid.*, p. 119.
[120] *Ibid.*, p. 109.
[121] A. I. Faressov, *Against the current* (SPB. 1904), p. 69.

CHAPTER III

No picture of religious tendencies in the Russian nineteenth century secular world would be complete without references to the left wing. It is more particularly so for anyone who wishes to follow the development of the idea of the humiliation of Christ. We do not want to present as purely religious and " kenotic " movements the events and ideas of the 'sixties and 'seventies. But we have to admit that " even for the writers of radical-populist tendency, Nekrasov, Saltykov, Gleb Uspensky, the seeking of justice had not only a social but also a religious significance." It also reminds one of the fact that " Russian religious problems of the nineteenth century were much more social in character than one usually thinks." [1] Many a feature of the movement known in literature under the name " *narodnichestvo* "—populism—and in the social and political world as " going down among the people " " *hozhdenije v narod* " seems to us a new aspect of the problem of humiliation. It is evident that here also " people " was still understood as peasantry, whilst the " going down " consisted in the actual sharing of the life of the lower classes, which were idealized and believed in no less than they were in their time by the Slavophils.

The whole movement could not be rightly understood if one omitted to mention the influence of the poet N. A. Nekrasov. Friend of Belinsky, he was regarded as a Westerniser, though he had no attraction to the West whatever. During his voyage in Italy he wrote his *Russian Women* (1871–2). On his return he was seized by emotion at the sight of villages. He expressed it in the poem " Silence " (1857).

---

[1] N. A. Berdyaeff, *The Russian religious thought of the nineteenth century,* p. 335. (M. E. Saltykov-Shchedrin, 1826–89, a satirical writer of great influence.)

" The living steppe—nothing but rye !
No castles, no mountains, no sea. . . .
I thank thee, my native land,
For thy healing spaciousness.
. . . However fair these foreign lands
It is not for them to heal our sorrow
And drive away a Russian grief.
. . . A temple of sighs, a temple of mourning,
This humble temple of my land
Go there !
And Christ will lay His hands upon you
And with His holy will remove
The soul's chains, the heart's pain
The plague of a conscience ill-at-ease.
. . . I listened ; and like a child was moved
And long I sobbed and beat my brow
Against the old flagstone, praying
That He might forgive and He might defend me,
And might bless me with the sign of the cross,
This God of the oppressed and mournful,
God of the generations standing
Before this altar, bare and poor."

These lines bring us to the very heart of Nekrasov's poetry.
The sorrow of his land, serfdom and oppression—this is what
made his conscience " ill-at-ease."   He thus expressed his call :

" I was called to sing thy sufferings,
O nation so incredibly patient
For the sake of one drop of your blood in me,
Forgive my sins, O my country."

(" To the unknown friend," 1867.)   His own sin, which tormented him and which was either made a reproach to him by
the intelligentsia or purposely covered by silence, was the fact
that he had made a fortune and lived the life of the rich.   His
conscience was certainly that of a Christian, and so was his
inspiration.   He himself said in the poem " Muse " (1857):

" No sweet-voiced, no soft-singing
Beautiful Muse can I ever remember.
Early was I burdened with the bonds
Of another Muse, unkind, unloved,
Sad companion of the sad and distressed,

> Born to labour, suffering, chains;
> A sorrowful, aching, accursed Muse,
> Preaching love in negation."

Known as the "singer of sorrow and revenge," Nekrasov sang sorrow much more than revenge. It is true that he said:

> "From the bread of slave-tilled fields
> I derive no benefit."

("In my country," 1855.) But when he addressed those who shared this shame he did not call them to rebellion. On the contrary he would advise:

> "Go to the humiliated,
> Go to the hurt
> Follow their steps."

("Who can be happy and Free in Russia?" 1873–6.) These words were religiously taken by the youth of his time. There was criticism in his poetry; for him, to live without sorrow and anger meant to lack love for his country. But the way out of it was not pictured by him as a triumphant march. He would remind us that

> ". . . there are times, there are ages
> When nothing is more desirable,
> Nothing more beautiful than the crown of thorns."

("Mother," 1868.) Of his own "unloved and unkind" Muse he would say:

> "But only the crown of thorns
> Suited thy sullen beauty."

("Poet and citizen," 1856.)
Following Belinsky in his utilitarian conception of art, Nekrasov refused to do purely artistic work. He wanted to be "a citizen":

> "The struggle hindered me from being a poet;
> The songs prevented me from becoming a fighter."

("To Z," 1876.) Many generations saw in him nothing but the "singer of the sorrow" of the nation. In fact, his rare poetic gifts saved him from himself and his surroundings, just as they saved him from his position as a Westerniser. And could not any one of the Slavophils sign the following lines:

> " Thou pitiable,
> Thou prosperous,
> Thou downtrodden,
> Thou almighty
> Mother Russia."

(" Who can be happy ? ")   Or would not any of them express
the same hopes when watching the hardships of unskilled
peasants building the first Russian railway :

> " Don't be afraid for your country !
> The Russians have borne much already,
> Even the building of this railway,
> They can stand whatever God sends them."

(" Railway," 1864.)

Whether Nekrasov spoke of the life of village or of town,
his eyes were attracted by the miseries round him.   He could
not pass unnoticed a horse beaten by a peasant, himself
unhappy and in distress.   He called one's attention to the
drunkard, to the woman in the streets, to the funeral of a poor
man, to the peasants waiting to be received by a magnate and
finally refused admission to his house.   The deeply humanitarian appeal of his poems, reinforced by their artistic value,
is unforgettable.   It was not in vain that his writings became
almost the Bible of the young.   All those who wanted to help
or to serve " the people " quoted him as their authority.
Especially influential were his poems describing the village.
" Peasant's children," 1861, " Who can be happy and Free in
Russia ? " " Orina, mother of a soldier," 1863, " Frost, The
red nosed," 1863, " Vlass," 1854 and many others became
classics.   The types of peasant recalled those of Turgenev.
Their attitude towards life and suffering was that of meek
forbearance, where people did not judge and where they died
with comforting words for those around them,

> " Extinguished like a candle,
> A waxen candle before an ikon." (" Orina.")

The peasants were presented as respectful of other people's
sorrow as well.   Symbolically, during the processions in a
village, the Innocent Ionushka followed often " the poorest
ikon in the poorest of all the huts."   The same bond of sym-

pathy united the peasants with the Decembrists and more so with their wives.[2] The " Russian women," princesses following their husbands in Siberia, became heroines of the revolutionary-minded youth. Typically, when speaking of her deported husband, the princess says :

> " He was more irreproachable than ever,
> And I loved him as Christ
> In his convict garments."

Here, for the revolutionary, meekness has the quality of greatness, and suffering has to be overcome by the way of patience. Such language recalls to the reader the tradition which united all the previous writers. The chief comfort of the young princesses in banishment was contact with the simple folk, whose tears " have fallen already," while they were preparing to weep for the first time.

> " Thou lovest the sufferer, o Russian folk ;
> The sufferings made us one."

The " Russian women," " The Night " (1858), " Grandfather " (1869) and many short poems were addressed to the left-wing reader and, though dealing with the historical past, they always brought in some note connected with the situation of the day. But, whichever was the content of the poems, two predominant motives remained : admiration of the humble forbearing and uncomplaining " people " and compassion mixed with repentance and shame for their own comfortable life on the side of the privileged class.

As elsewhere in Russian life, literature here took the leading part, criticizing the existing order and appealing to the reader's heart. Nekrasov was repeated, though with less talent, by the populists of the 'sixties. V. A. Sleptzov (1836–78), A. I. Levitov (1842–77), N. N. Zlatovratsky (1845—1911), and the gifted Gleb Uspensky (1840—1902) dealt chiefly with the " people," their true " mass-hero." It was no longer the peasantry alone ; it was also the new type which emerged after

[2] Which is not exact historically. In some places the crowd threw mud at them for having attempted the life of the Tzar. (Movement called by the date of the riot, 14th December, 1825, on the accession to the throne of Nicolas I.)

the emancipation: an artisan, a landless peasant, a worker
new to the factory and still rooted in village life, and the
raznochinetz, new intelligentsia of obscure origin, "the non-
tax-payers" with no property or definite income. The new
writers belonged themselves to this class and, without falling
into the exaggerations of criticism, detecting "class-interest"
in each work of art, one must acknowledge certain class-
resemblance in all of them. They are no more naturalistic
than the characters of Tolstoy. But certain crudenesses, and an
almost deliberate negligence of style, reflect as it were the
conditions of their life. The first impression is that Turgenev
and, for example, F. Reshetnikov (1841–71) speak of different
worlds. But one soon recognizes the features of meekness,
patience and non-resistance here as well.

The men of this group belonged nominally to the free-
thinkers. They called themselves "Nihilists" or "Thinking
Realists." In many cases sons of deacons or acolytes, they felt
embittered against the Church. Yet it would be inexact to call
them unbelievers. Christ was not alien to them. Perhaps the
most accurate way of defining their position would be to say
that they were ready to disbelieve in God but they still clung
to Christ. There was no room for any doctrine in their works;
but the religious element was present and such as it was it
could be related to the current of "humiliation" noticed in
the works of their predecessors.

The attitude of the writers themselves was typically a compassionate and condescending one. They seemed to bow down,
to associate themselves with the suffering of the poorer classes.
It was so with all the minor writers of the epoch.[3] A certain
sentimentality was typical of Levitov and of Zlatovratsky, of
whom the first felt just a "sufferer for the people" without
any political conclusions. With them, it was still the peasantry
who alone knew the Truth and lived righteously. The features
of this righteousness were manifest in compassion for a
prisoner, in repentance, in desire to expiate a fault humbly and

---

[3] So in Sleptzov's *Nursling,* a pathetic story of a defenceless peasant
woman working in town and unable to find traces of her little daughter
sent by the authorities to some village for upbringing.

voluntarily, all their life long. (So in Zlatovratsky's *Peasants'
jury*, 1874.) Refusal to judge and to condemn was noticed
by G. Uspensky also. A jury consisting of peasants " pitied "
and " forgave " a woman who, in incredible distress, caused
the death of her baby (*Lower than grass, stiller than water*).
Even if falsely accused, an evangelically disinterested deacon
would assure his accusers that he deserved reprobation
(Levitov, *Jacob Syroed*, 1863). In *Neighbours* (1863) a
silent, poor peasant took defence of the orphans. Another
meek old man used to give up anything he could, and even
other people's belongings; he was willing and glad to suffer
patiently in the name of the Lord (*Homeless*, 1870). All
these men belonged still to those who learnt by heart in their
school-days : " The cross is the keeper of the earth, the cross
is divine mercy and beauty." [4] This background influenced
men whether they were aware of it or not. In Levitov's
autobiographical *Lyrical memoirs of Ivan Sizov* (1863) the
young man, awakened by reading of the Russian poets and
writers, conceived a desire for learning; he could no longer
conform to his surroundings. Not being able to afford the
railway fare, he went walking to the capital. On his journey
he met a tramp, an ill-starred person, whom he pitied and to
whose story he gave himself the trouble of listening. And
suddenly he " saw almost palpably the bright face of the living
God who called to Him all that labour and are heavy laden
and who gives them peace." [5] It may be worth noticing that
this experience of charity reminds one of the beggars in the
Spiritual Songs as well as of the Idiot. The old general of
whom Ippolit spoke did not help by means of money either;
but this " giving up " of one's time or attention seemed pregnant with " unexpected discoveries "[6]; here in this " form
of a servant " the living God was revealed to the author.

The most influential man of this period was Gleb Uspensky.
With more clarity than any other he expressed the chief
inspiration of his group. Sickness of mind or heart or, more

[4] Levitov, *Village training*, 1870, Works ed. (M-Leningrad, 1932),
2 vols., t. II, p. 559.
[5] *Ibid., op. cit.*, t. I, p. 720.
[6] See our p. 67.

often, "sickness of conscience," that is how he defined the
general mood. It was the awakening of conscience, the shame
for one's selfish life. But one must not confuse this "shining"
of conscience, suddenly bringing to light the miseries of life
round the author, with personal repentance after some failure.
In a great many cases it affected the imagination only and
tormented people literally to death without affecting their
will. In life and in fiction, the victims of such an awakened
conscience often fled from reality and sought escape in something stupefying, most frequently in drink.[7] That is what
happened to a rough and suspicious village deacon when he
was finally convinced that the young woman teaching in the
village had voluntarily given up her wealth and home in order
to serve in this place where she met nothing but opposition
and general distrust (*On the old hearth; An evening in
a lonely place*). A clerk in a tea-business, unable to bear the
pain for others which had simply overwhelmed him, committed suicide. The author added that it is an almost universal
phenomenon in Russia to find hearts tortured by a vision of
truth and justice, which they see to be unrealized in human
lives.[8] According to him, one could hardly expect anything
more than a mere awakening of conscience because the life of
all had been too hard for too long a time. "How dimly these
men felt the needs of their souls; what inadequate means of
expressing their wishes they had; how they lost the habit of
having these essential needs of the soul." [9]

Contradicting this statement he went on giving examples of
conscientious people, most of them, it is true, still divided in
their minds. The peasant Egor, eager to live a godly life, was
married against his will. He refused his wife, who finally
loved another man. The conflict within the ascetic husband's
conscience brought him finally to drunkenness and allowed
the author to discover this "drama lying in a gutter."

---

[7] So it was with Uspensky himself; he ended in religious mania.
Levitov, Reshetnikov, Sleptzov, Pomialovsky (1835–63), died early ruined
by alcohol. The young and over-sensitive Garshin committed suicide.
[8] Uspensky, *New times, new worries; Works,* ed. with biography by
N. K. Mikhaylovsky (SPB. 1908), third ed., 6 vols., t. II, p. 57.
[9] *Ibid.,* t. I, p. 595. *Lower than grass, stiller than water.*

(*Sketches. He wanted to act according to his conscience.*)
A different form " of a particular cross laid on her by God,
which she should carry to the end "[10] was that of a widow
letting out corners in a slum. Herself destitute, she made all
sorts of sacrifices in order to provide her lodgers (who did not
pay her) with all that a proper landlady would give to well-
paying boarders.

In these two instances the desire for sacrifice was visible and
direct. In many other cases the " conscience " and compassion were vague and concerned not so much with particular
people as with " masses." Uspensky realized himself the
danger of such feelings, impersonal and not supported by will.
As for these " masses " they seemed to him, he confessed,
" terrifying when without Christ."[11] He spoke of the need of
the country : that somebody should go to share completely
and sacrificially the life of low classes, contented without
salaries and living just on what the peasants could offer. He
added, by the way, that priests, even if not of the best type,
are understood by the peasants, who know their lives, needs
and income. What Uspensky preached was more than the
action of a " *kultur-träger.*" " What a truly tremendous and
necessary act it would be to go into this crowd, to take upon
oneself the sorrow for its darkness . . . to enlighten the mind
and conscience. Had it not been for Christ and His loving
heart, these unenlightened people, silly as they are, could kill
an innocent man."[12] Certainly, he recognized the sacrificial
spirit of teachers, doctors, nurses working in villages. But he
wondered how much their work helped in " building up the
personality and spiritual life of a peasant."[13] Unexpectedly
for many, Uspensky contrasted with them the unlettered
Rodion with his vision of the Blessed Virgin and his call to
repentance. He mentioned also the saints appearing, in spite
of the conventional presentation of pious stories, as men of

[10] Uspensky, *The poor of the capital; Old cloth man,* t. I, p. 246.
[11] *Ibid., Willy-nilly,* t. IV, p. 658. U. accused all the Russian history
for the lack of respect to a personality. Cf. also *Three Letters,* t. II,
p. 285.
[12] *Ibid., From village diary,* t. IV, p. 91.
[13] *Ibid., Rodion the paintaker,* t. IV, p. 701.

G

active love who " gave up and carried to all who needed
them, to the crowd, to the masses, all the treasures of their
souls, all their knowledge." [14]　One of those whom he distinguished was St. Tykhon.

Uspensky gave an example of such sacrificial abasement :
the " Foreigner " sacrificed his position on behalf of a dis-
agreeable, disunited family and ended as a joiner (*Three
letters*).　Self-abasement was also the way of expiation.　The
tramp who appeared once at the author's door quoting
Tyutchev's " Christ went round Russia blessing her " and
adding :　" Certainly, no one will refuse me a bowl of
soup ? " [15] was, in fact, an official.　A member of the police
force, he ruled mercilessly over the political prisoners in Siberia
until the sufferings of one of his victims brought him to
repentance.　Another case was a country gentleman, a tyrant
and a drunkard. Returning once after an orgy, he was refused
entrance to the house by his wife.　He disappeared and
came back again calm and lowly.　He did not go to the manor
house but " without haughtiness " he went to his former serf
saying, " Provide me with food, I'll help you as long as I can ;
just command me."　He declined the help of his family :　" I
have been greedy for too long a time."　The peasants showed
sympathy and understanding, for " it is a hard job, repentance." [16]　There was already living an " Odd Gentleman "
who dwelt in the village, having distributed all his goods, yet
misunderstood by the peasants.　Another one felt an imperative, total demand to go down into the village life and would
not even continue his activity as an arbitrator.　He gave up
everything, including his useful occupation and, dissatisfied
and tormented by his conscience, he went on living in the
country " just so " (" A sheep outside the flock ").　These last
two types were social rather than religious, but the motive
force of their queer behaviour was their uneasy conscience.
They prefigured those who, in actual life, were preparing to
" go down among the people."

[14] Uspensky, *Good Russian type,* t. V, p. 507 ; without any knowledge
of Dostoevsky's letters, he uses a similar definition.
[15] *Ibid., Free Cossacks,* t. III, p. 752.
[16] *Ibid., New times, new worries,* t. II, pp. 67ff.

Vsevolod M. Garshin (1855–88) should be mentioned separately. He lived and died as one whose chief concern was the sufferings of others. A workman, a woman led into a life of vice, a soldier, all those whom he met or pictured excited in him a burning, unbearable compassion. In 1877, himself a convinced pacifist, he took part in the war in order to share the lot of the others. He refused to enjoy better conditions which he was offered as an officer's son. His *Four days* (1877) was a powerful and artistic plea against war. For some time he lived also the life of a peasant. One of his friends being arrested in connection with the revolutionary movement, Garshin tried to intervene in his favour. Refusal produced on him a disastrous effect : it was the beginning of the mental disease which was never completely cured and brought him finally to suicide.

With this group of writers, literature and life were closely interwoven. Very often it was almost photography, or at best a sketch-literature. It revealed a perplexed world, men who lost their land, who on the one hand were themselves struggling to make a position in society (if only a literary society) and on the other hand felt ashamed of abandoning their minor brethren, the peasants or artisans, and calling everyone " back " to the land and " down " among the people. Detached from the Church and from dogma, they still loved Christ, but this sentimental admiration, unsupported by either thought or will, was not enough to guide them through life. The 'sixties, this " epoch of great reforms," proved at the same time to be a transitional epoch which produced these brokenhearted and unsettled men. Calling the attention of their readers to the dark mass of the Russian lower classes, they themselves did not possess either religion, or the high social standing and education which would justify a move " down towards the people." This call, vague as it was, reached many hearts. The young men, chiefly those of the upper classes, offered their lives in the hope " of serving the people."

The definition " political " is inexact when applied to the origin of the movement of the 'seventies. It was essentially a

youth-movement inspired by the desire " to satisfy the deep
need of personal moral justification." [17]   Membership did not
imply the acceptance of any programme.   The whole started
as study-groups; the new applicant's character was earnestly
discussed by those already in a group; " the slightest sign of
insincerity or of self-complacency, and the person was
rejected." [18]   Rigorism and the puritan spirit were typical of
this youth.   Brought up on " realism," the " scientific conception of the world " and the " nihilism " of the previous generations, nourished by Western socialistic doctrines, the young
felt that none of these satisfied the profound need either of
their own soul or of the life round them.   " It is important to
state that it was precisely a seeking of religion." [19]   This
explains a basic difference between what was going on in the
West and what happened in Russia.   Whilst the working class
leaders fought for the defence of *interests,* Russian Socialism
was coming into life as " a current of ideas among the intelligentsia, as moral conviction . . . as a demand for a right
personal life and just social order." [20]   As G. V. Florovsky
defines it, it was the same problem as in the case of Gogol:
how to live righteously.   This is why for all these young men
and women " the ideal of personal perfection became the
nearest way to the [achievement] of final social benefit." [21]
This mood found its best expression in the writings of N. K.
Mikhaylovsky (1842—1904), theoretical expounder of the new
conception of progress and, even more, in the *Historical
letters* (1873) of P. L. Lavrov (1823—1900).   Natural science,
the science of the 'sixties, was assigned a secondary place.   The
author came back to the problems of history raised by the
East-and-West controversy, though without referring to it.   It
was of real benefit that the Russians, with their tendency to
neglect both personality and history, should be reminded of

[17] V. Y. Bogucharsky, *The active populism of the 'Seventies,* p. 179.
[18] P. A. Kropotkin, *Memoirs of a revolutionary* (SPB. 1905), edition
Znanije, p. 277.
[19] G. Florovsky, *The ways of Russian Theology,* p. 294.
[20] *Materials for the history of the Russian social-revolutionary movement,* ed. of the *Old Members of Land and Freedom* (Geneva, 1893,
etc.), in N. 5, vii 1895, p. 21.
[21] *Ibid.,* p. 35.

the necessity of developing a personality, of its role and responsibility in the process of history, as well as of the need to realize
truth and justice in social life.   Moreover, the author called on
those who have profited by education to understand the price
of it : progress being made through the destruction of the
weak, the educated had now to pay back their debt to the
poor.

It is paradoxical that the new " lay-religion " of the 'seventies was inspired by Lavrov, a professed atheist.[22]   One
should remember also among the ancestors of the movement Chaadaev, with his social interests and his statement that the Russians who came late into history should do
something new and better than other nations.   The Slavophils,
though despised by this generation as conservatives, had certainly their say in the movement : it would be enough to
mention their conviction of the uniqueness of Russian destinies
and their admiration of the village community.   Like them,
those of the 'seventies were ready not so much to teach " the
people" as to be taught by him.   That is why they tried to translate into terms of the peasantry what was meant by Western
thought in connection with the proletariat.[23]   This particular
emphasis on the peasantry is especially reminiscent of the Slavophils and was noticed in their own time.[24]   It even produced
some similar religious experiences.   A Jewish medical student
Aptekman came in touch with Christianity through a nurse of
peasant origin whom he tried to " enlighten " with his propaganda ; he started reading the Gospels and was convinced
and baptized.   For him, there was not only the joy of a conversion but also of the fact that he was ever afterwards in full

[22] L. G. Deich, himself not religiously minded, denies Lavrov's influence
and considers M. Bakunin as chief inspirer of the youth, but there is the
witness of Vera Figner, M. Frolenko, O. V. Aptekman.

[23] It finally brought a split within the group.   From 1875 onwards
some turned from peaceful propaganda to a revolutionary agitation.   In
the trial of the Fifty, 21/11/1877 one used still the name of " populists " ; during the trial of the Hundred and ninety-three, on 25/5/1878
there was already mentioned the Russian revolutionary party of " social-
revolutionaries " or the group of Land and Freedom.

[24] I. Aksakov wrote in *Russia*, 1883, n. 6, that populism is an incon-
sistent Slavophilism.   He reproached their weakness, result of detachment
from true foundations (quoted by Bogucharsky, note 2 on p. 16).

" communion with the people." [25]   In a way I. Kireevsky and
Dostoevsky underwent a similar process.   On the whole, all
the revolutionaries, from Herzen onwards, had to take into
account religious belief among the peasantry. [26]   " We became
persuaded that it is impossible to avoid discussions on religion,
especially with those among the peasants who are outstanding
by reason of their gifts and their habit of thinking. . . .
Socialism is an integral world-conception; here . . . it faced
another world conception, a theological one."   They started
to " destroy the faith " whilst some among the more naïve
and less logical still mixed these two philosophies. [27]

Many did not think definitely of religion when they
followed so many voices calling them " back " or " down "
into the masses.   Their mood was admirably illustrated by the
poetry of Nekrasov and, in particular, by the desire to
approach those

> " Who bear all in the name of the Christ,
>   Whose austere eyes do not cry,
>   Whose silent lips do not murmur,
>   Whose rough hands labour
>   Having respectfully left it to us
>   To plunge into science and arts,
>   To give ourselves to dreams and passions " (*Night*).

Herzen and Ogarev, we remember, emphasized in the
Christian message equality and brotherhood.   One could
easily imagine a revolutionary inspired either by this idea or
else by the image of Christ purging the temple.   It was not
so in the case of active populists.   They sought first of all to
resemble those " who bear all in the name of Christ " by
denying their privileges and by humbling themselves.   If one
could object that it was an imitation of peasant, rather than
an imitation of Christ, the answer would be that a revolutionary movement is not bound to imitate Christ, but that as
far as peasants were taken as an example, they were chosen

[25] O. V. Aptekman, *From the history of revolutionary populism* (Rostov-
on-Don, 1907), (written in 1879), p. 65 ; on p. 212 he acknowledges the
link with the Slavophils.

[26] A. I. Herzen, *Works*, t. III, p. 319, *Diary*, 1844.   Our p. 20.

[27] P. L. Lavrov, *Populists of 1873–98 in Materials for the history*, etc.
(Génève, 1893), nn. 6, 7, p. 202.

in their " kenotic " aspect.   One of the members of the movement thus explained their mood :

> " Youth brought up on the ideas of the 'sixties was
> imbued by the idea of serving the people and sacrificing
> personal career or goods.   Many had, in their childhood,
> sincere belief.   The teaching of Christ : to lay down
> one's soul, to give away one's possessions, to suffer for
> one's faith and ideal, to leave father and mother for their
> sake, to give oneself wholly for the service of others, was a
> testament of God.   It was not difficult with such a back-
> ground to take in the teaching of the 'sixties about one's
> debt to people and the necessity to pay back for all the
> privileges received in their childhood." [28]

Vera Zassulich, influenced in her early youth by the poetry
of Lermontov, Ryleev, Nekrasov, felt that her attraction
towards the lower classes was almost of the same character
as the one she felt towards Christ when first reading the
Gospels.   " I have not betrayed Him ; He is the best ; but
they also are good enough to gain a crown of thorn ; I will
find them, I shall try to be of some use in the fight. . . . And
I considered, not as a privilege but as a pain, the fact that I
lived meanwhile as a rich woman." [29]   Similar witness, and
in almost equal terms, was given by many.   Unprepared even
for simple house work, they went into villages and factories
ready to face all hardships.   " One considered it almost
treason to occupy any privileged position, however modest,
which would free us from the compulsion of ' sharing the
sufferings of people.'   The girls used to seigneurial surroundings . . . had to work literally fifteen hours and have revolt-
ing food. . . . They slept on desks in dormitories, using straw
mattresses and pillows without any linen ; moreover, there was
vermin." [30]   This desire for self-abasement was so great that

---

[28] M. Th. Frolenko, *Memoirs of a man of the 'Seventies* (M. 1927),
p. 87.
[29] L. G. Deich, Preface to V. Zassulich *Revolutionaries from upper
classes* (SPB. 1921), p. 6.   K. F. Ryleev (1795—1826), revolutionary
poet.
[30] P. L. Lavrov, *Populists-propagators of 1873–78*, pp. 234–5. Turgenev,
The Virgin Soil (1876), gives a somewhat ironical but illuminating picture
of this movement.   In practice, it often resulted in complete misunderstanding between the disguised youth and the peasants.

it was extended even to the field of education. The members of the upper classes were sure that they had no right to study " on peasants' money whilst these last starve and sink into ignorance. . . . If we wait and finish our studies, we may become bourgeois-minded and no longer wish to go down among the people." [31] They would say that diplomas " demoralize men by opening better positions to them." [32] They consequently deserted the universities. These utterances were echoed by those who themselves were born among the lower classes, and whose upbringing and advancement was often the only hope of their families. These were afraid of becoming exploiters of the peasants.[33] For this same reason O. V. Aptekman abandoned a successful university career and went to work under a carpenter, who finally advised him to use his knowledge rather than his hands. Let us remember that all these experiments were carried on in a country desperately short of doctors, teachers, technical workers.[34] It is true a few tried to apply their education in a more adequate way. But these also shared the conditions of the people round them. They " did not use white bread, did not see meat for weeks; each superfluous slice of bread stuck in their throat in the midst of the general poverty." [35] Just as Nekrasov said, though bread came now from the fields which were no longer " slave-tilled."

That the character of the movement is in the line of humiliation is evident. It is more difficult to define the exact religious position of the populists. All use an extremely confusing and inaccurate language. The word " mysticism " was too often used by the writers when they spoke of any sort of

[31] P. L. Lavrov, *Populists-propagandists*, p. 171.

[32] *Ibid.*, p. 46.

[33] So I. F. Fesenko, see L. G. Deich, *Russian revolutionary emigration of the 'Seventies* (Petersburg, 1920), p. 5.

[34] Gogol who never denied the need of education was accused of " obscurantism "—the revolutionary youth with no education preached " enlightenment." It is time to protest that, except for Tolstoy, the Russian writers advocated learning, even if some of them thought religion as an experience of higher intelligence to be of more importance.

[35] Vera Figner, *The sealed work,* t. I, p. 128, Complete Works and Letters, 7 vols. (M. 1932).

religion or devotion.[36] In spite of such vagueness, Vera Figner's *Memoires* are very valuable. She noticed the religious character of a great many of her comrades; they spent years together in prison and used to have long talks. She affirmed that " an abstract God in the sense of truth or goodness or the soul of the universe did not satisfy them." [37] She spoke of personal devotion to Christ in many and in herself, though in her case it was more related to her past :

" Though there is no more faith in the heart,
There is a trace of the feelings of my childhood." [38]

This feeling, as expressed in her adolescent diary, was the desire " to die like Jesus." [39] There was in all of them a tragical paradox proper to all who emphasize part only of the Gospels. They admired obedience unto death, non-resistance, self-sacrifice and yet they were able at some moment of their lives to pass from peaceful propaganda to acts of terrorism.[40] Convinced of the justice of their ideas, they wanted to force their truth. This was one of the temptations so strongly felt and opposed by Dostoevsky in his Inquisitor. Still, Figner expressed herself in terms of Christianity.

" Whosoever has been once charmed by Jesus who, for the sake of His ideal endured sufferings, rejection and death; whosoever in his childhood and youth regarded Him as an ideal and His life as the supreme example of sacrificial love, such a one would understand the mind of a revolutionary thrown into a sort of tomb for the work of liberation of the people. . . . The time of proof has come; the force of His love is tried . . . no physical or even wordy warfare is possible. Jesus did not resist when one slandered or struck Him. Every thought of it would be a profanation of His pure person and His meek greatness.[41]

[36] The expression is used by M. Gershenzon speaking about Kireevsky; also by A. I. Faressov speaking of the men of the 'seventies. The same was already noticed by Ch. Quenet in his book on Chaadaev.
[37] V. Figner, *The prisoners of Schlüsselburg*, t. IV, p. 169.
[38] *Ibid., Poems*, t. IV, p. 268.
[39] *Ibid., Memoires*, t. V, pp. 94–5.
[40] The nucleus of the group stood against terrorism. It divided the party, autumn 1879. " Those of the villages " (the early populists) opposed the group of Land and Freedom. The non-terrorist body took the name of the Black Re-allotment.
[41] *Ibid., The prisoners of Schlüsselburg*, t. IV, p. 34.

The idea of non-resistance was strongly felt by A. K. Malikov (1894). He was the true predecessor of Tolstoy, whom he used to call " a nihilist born too late." [42] Son of a peasant, Malikov studied in Moscow University and worked as an examining magistrate. He joined the social movement but in 1874 he underwent a sudden conversion. Instead of a political programme, he preached to his fellow members: " Renounce the idea of destroying evil by evil. . . . Our salvation is neither in science nor in political organization but in the union of men in the name of Christ. . . . We are to become peacemakers, all of us. A beggar, a capitalist, a judge and an accused, all are Godmen." [43] Malikov reflected also the " soborny " organic conception of Christianity. He affirmed that for a Christian " a bad man is to be considered as some defect in his own body." [44] He succeeded in converting some other revolutionaries. He was arrested at the trial of the Hundred and Ninety-Three (1878), proclaimed his new programme and was set free as " mentally deficient." He went over to America and organized, together with the idealist-positivist N.C. Heyns (or William Frey, 1839–88) an agricultural community. The " theoretical " approach and tyrannical puritanism of Frey proved unbearable. [45] The colony disappeared.

More striking was the return of Malikov into the Orthodox Church. If in his first experience he forestalled Tolstoy, in the second phase he illustrated some thoughts of Dostoevsky. He was converted by that very prayer of St. Ephraim the Syrian which, according to Dostoevsky, " contained all the essence of Christianity " and formed the basis of the popular belief. [46] It happened in 1881 when Tolstoy was already well known.

[42] A. I. Faressov, *Men of the 'Seventies* (SPB. 1905), p. 317.

[43] *Ibid.*, p. 297. Cf. Dostoevsky, *The Possessed*. Kirilov and Shatov have been over to America as the group of Malikov. Kirilov reflects the nihilistic asceticism and the idea of mengodhood bringing him to suicide; Shatov's religion is " the people bearer of God."

[44] *Ibid.*, p. 300.

[45] *Ibid.*, *Men of the 'Seventies*, p. 323, mentions a violent reaction of the children of atheistic parents. The daughter of Herzen fainted when first entering a Roman Catholic church during a service. Frey's daughter became a fanatical Roman Catholic.

[46] Dostoevsky, *An Author's Journal*, ed. 1906, t. XII, p. 438, our p. 8.

Malikov objected to his free " reconstruction " of the Gospels. Moreover, the appeal to " simplification " did not touch him : it was his own past. Through this prayer Malikov realized that he had been " a dreamer, a vain talker, despondent and yet craving for life . . . and that the victory over oneself consisted in chastity with regard to women, in love, patience and humility before every mortal. . . . We have made ourselves Perfection, we worshipped man and prayed to him but he was and remained just a worm." [47]

The movement of the 'seventies in its original form was of short duration. There is no need to insist upon the political and practical *naïveté* of its early members. Their inconsistency with regard to violence is also obvious. Tolstoy explained their failures by the mixing of political and eternal elements. He even hoped they could succeed on condition that " the evangelical teaching will become necessary to them in itself and not for their social purposes. These last may never come to realization, whilst the Christian teaching must remain for ever." [48] Faithful to himself, Tolstoy spoke of the " teaching." Men of the 'seventies spoke of the " mood " or " mind " or else of the Person of Christ. The religious current among the revolutionary youth had to be taken into account by their leaders. Lavrov summarized the movement towards the 'eighties in terms which, for him, sounded pessimistic :

" Together with Chernyshevsky and Saltykov . . . Russian literature buried also the forgotten words of these, almost the last representatives of the fight for the ideal. Lonely and depressed were those who remained on the literary stage. The literary " youth " of the 'eighties openly renounced the traditions of Belinsky and Dobrolubov. The leading writers began to recognize as their fellow workers the adherents of vague and idealistic metaphysics and the defenders of more or less heretical Christian theology. The preaching of non-resistance gained numerous followers." [49]

---

[47] Faressov, *op. cit.*, p. 324.
[48] *Ibid.*, *op. cit.*, p. 331.
[49] P. L. Lavrov, Preface to the second edition of *Historical Letters* (Génève, 1891), p. vi. N. G. Chernyshevsky (1828–89), novelist and radical leader. N. A. Dobrolubov (1836–61), literary critic of the Left.

These words allude to Tolstoy and also to Vl. Soloviev whose Lectures on Godmanhood (1877–81), to the great surprise and indignation of many on the left wing, were crowded with young people. Dostoevsky was not understood; he was regarded as a political conservative and his works, especially the *Possessed* (1871), as a slander against the revolutionary groups.

This movement ends our inevitably incomplete and scanty survey of the Russian secular world of the nineteenth century. We did not pretend to attribute definite theological ideas to anyone who did not specially write on theology. But our attention was attracted again and again by the fact that all the writers or political leaders whom we met were seeking more than human happiness or social justice. However different in their upbringing, interests and way of self-expression, they seemed all to seek righteousness or even holiness, whether personal or national and social. Some of them were professed Christians and orthodox; others rejected the Church but recognized Christ as their teacher; some, again, spoke of the Christian idea or ideal. Studying their pronouncements on the Orthodox country, on the Christian character or ideal, we become convinced that they pointed all to the one and the same image, that of the humiliated Christ.

CHAPTER IV

DEVOTIONAL AND MORAL APPLICATION OF THE
HUMILIATION

WHAT place was assigned in the life and thought of the
Russian Church of the nineteenth century to the humiliation
of Christ? We have seen that the secular world tended to
emphasize the importance of this image of the Saviour. But
we know also that many of the secular world did not recognize
the Church as their spiritual home. Could it happen that just
in this particular point the Church did not coincide with the
ideal and devotion of the nation? What sort of link did there
exist between the Church and the country in this particular
point? Or was it that the Church, whether recognized or
not by those from the world, supported and nourished the
inspiration of the cult of the humiliated Christ? And how
could one reconcile this type of devotion with the exterior
beauty and riches of the churches?

It is justice to say that magnificent buildings were seen in
the capitals, but that ordinary parishes in the country and
villages were simple and poor; the poverty of clergy throughout the country was an acknowledged fact. Paradoxically,
monasteries, owing to donations in money, jewellery and land,
became wealthy. This goes back to the controversies of the
early sixteenth century and to the defeat of the " non-
possessors " represented by St. Nil of Sorsk (1433–1508) [1]
But there existed a deep and to a certain extent justified conviction that the Russians, taking upon themselves lowliness
and poverty, would bring as rich an offering as they could
" to God." The temple is for them a part of heaven; they
seek there " all different from everyday life. . . . Nothing to
remind them of worldly luxury . . . only special ' sacred '
materials, ' sacred ' drawing and colours, ' sacred ' scents,
' sacred ' tunes and voices "; moreover, a Russian, artistic by
nature, " thinks in images, in plastic forms." [2] In the nine-

[1] N. Zernov, *Moscow the Third Rome* (S.P.C.K. 1937), pp. 39—46.
[2] A. V. Kartashov, *The Russian Christianity, Putj* (the Way), (Paris,
n. 51, 1936), pp. 19—31.

95

teenth century this view was advocated by the Bishop Ignaty (1807–67): " The people are pressed like ants in their poor huts, but they would build a high and beautiful temple of God . . . they walk almost in rags, but they long to see the church shining with gold and silver . . . " because their own houses are for them but a night lodging of a pilgrim, whilst the church is the reflection of eternal life and bliss : " Do not prevent the living people of holy Russia from hoping and loving in a splendid church." [3] Generally speaking, we could object that the small chapels (*chasovni*) did attract popular devotion no less than big and magnificent churches. We could repeat with N. Leskov : " A Russian likes to look at splendour but what he respects is simplicity." [4] But for our present purpose it is enough to notice that ornamentation of places of worship was not regarded as contradictory to the spirit of humility or poverty.

More important is to realize what were the services attended in these churches, whether rich or poor. We consider that the liturgy, apart from its sacramental character, was a constant reminder of the evangelical tradition and of the humiliation and glorification of the Son of God. The liturgy displays symbolically the history of redemption. The earthly life of the Lord is represented in the movements of the priest. The moment could not pass unnoticed when the priest takes from the altar the book of the Gospels and, preceded by a light, comes by the side door signifying Jesus Christ coming to preach the good tidings. It is accompanied by the singing of the Beatitudes, and more than anything it explains why the Sermon on the Mount is so deeply engraved in all Russian conscience.[5] The reading of the Gospels in the middle of the

[3] Ignaty (Bryanchaninov), Speech in defence of the monasteries, quoted by L. Sokolov, *Bishop Ignaty* (Kiev, 1915), 2 vols., t. I, pp. 151–2.

[4] N. Leskov, *Details of Episcopal Life* (SPB. 1902), third ed., p. 76.

[5] Such a critic of the Orthodox Church as A. Harnack confirms also that the Orthodox Church had maintained in the people the knowledge of the Gospels. " Ich kann aber auch mancher eigenen Anschaung und Erfahrung bestaten, wie sich selbst beim Russischen Bauern oder niederen Priester trotz Bilder und Heiligen Dienst doch auch eine Kraft des schlichten Gottvertrauens, eine Zartheit der sittlichen Ursprung und eine thatkräftige Brüderliebe findet, die ihren Ursprung aus dem Evangelium nicht verleugnet." *Das Wesen des Christentums* (Leipzig), p. 151.

nave was more than edification : it was, as it were, the new
coming of Jesus in the midst of men.   The crowd used to draw
nearer, almost to press the priest, the sick knelt round the
lectern or touched the vestments of the priest, representative
of the preaching and healing Christ.   As for the priest himself,
he repeated secretly (sometimes in a voice heard by those
outside the altar) the prayers before the consecration.   This
of the liturgy of St. Basil runs as follows : " Thou didst speak
unto us by Thy Son Himself . . . who being the brightness
of Thy glory and the express image of Thy Person, and
upholding all things by the word of His power, thought it not
robbery to be equal to Thee, the God and Father.   But albeit
He was God before all ages, yet He appeared upon earth and
dwelt among men ; and was incarnate of the Holy Virgin and
did lay aside His godhead, taking on the form of a servant,
and becoming conformed to the fashion of our lowliness, that
He might make us conformable to the image of His glory." [6]
It seems to us that the repetition of the Beatitudes, the lessons
from the New Testament and such a prayer would help one
to remember in what consisted " the mind of Christ."   We
must also remember that for any member of the Orthodox
Church, whatever his upbringing, the liturgy was always the
expression of the fullness of Orthodox belief.   In the country,
with great numbers of illiterate people, it was often the only
way of catechization.   The popular masses were educated
through these services of the liturgy which, as Dostoevsky said,
" are better than sermons."

One more factor of the Church life seems to us important
for the preservation and development of the kenotic devotion :
it is the veneration of Saints.   What the secular world
cherished in the folk-lore or in the works of art of the nineteenth century, which we have already examined, was even
more expressive within the Church.   The undying memory
of the " passion-bearers," Boris and Gleb, of St. Nil, of many
an Innocent, reminded continually the church people of those
who had chosen to follow the humiliation of Christ.   The
saints, especially if Russians by origin, did belong to different

[6] *Service book of the Orthodox Church,* tr. I. Hapgood (Boston and
New York, 1906), p. 103.

classes of society, some were married and had children; all
had their place in the history of the country, often in folk-
lore and in family traditions and formed thus not only the
link between the past and the present of the church but also
between the Church and the whole country.

The monasteries were of particular importance in the
spiritual life of the country.   A Russian of any class was able
to wander from one holy place to another in search of religious
help and inspiration.[7]   The monasteries were places of retreat,
govenije :   preparation for confession and communion.   But
they were also places of great ethnographical interest with
their picturesque crowds of pilgrims.   Nowhere could one
collect more of the true and legendary lives of saints than near
some monastery, where a " kalika " would sit on the grass
chanting the Spiritual Songs.

The Optina, already mentioned in these pages, was
especially important for the revival of contemplative
monasticism.   The educated monks " Gentlefolk and of good
life "[8] connected strict asceticism with the works of writing
and translation and they produced many a revered and
influential spiritual director (*starets*).   The scattered information which one could gather concerning the character of this
community makes it impossible to link them directly to our
subject.[9]   The Church of Russia and the secular clergy had
never completely recovered since the reforms of Peter I.   But
the spiritual life went on in the silence of monasteries and
hermitages.[10]   The eighteenth century produced a Tykhon

---

[7] *The way of a pilgrim,* tr. R. M. French (1931), is the story told by an
anonymous peasant in search of a teacher of incessant prayer.   The life
of Motovilov, biographer of St. Seraphim of Sarov, was to a great extent
such continuous pilgrimage.

[8] L. Sokolov, *Bishop Ignaty,* t. II, p. 176, from a letter in 1856.

[9] As we remember, the men of Optina translated the *Philokalia,* which
was done also by the Bishop Theophan.   The Slavophils, especially
I. Kireevsky, were spiritual sons and fellow-workers of the monks in this
work.   Among the writers who went on pilgrimages to Optina we should
remember Gogol, Leontiev, Dostoevsky, Tolstoy, V. Soloviev.

[10] It is " Wahrhaft ergreifend, wie tief die Kirche mit ihren Predigt
vom Ewigen, von der Selbstaufopferung, dem Mitleiden und der Brüder-
lichkeit in die Volksseele eingedrungen ist. Die niedrige Stufe, auf welcher
der Klerus steht, und die Missachtung, mit der ihm vielfach begegnet
wird, dürfen darüber nicht täuschen, das er als Repräsentant der Kirche
eine unvergleichlich hohe Stellung einnimmt, und das Ideal des Mönch-

Zadonsky and the nineteenth century gave a Seraphim of Sarov (Prokhor Moshnin, 1759–1833, canonized in 1903).[11]

The influence of which we spoke just now could be qualified as indirect and unconscious. But there was, on the part of the Church, a much more outspoken influence and instruction dealing with the humiliation of Christ. We shall try to show it through some of the outstanding men of the epoch. The first figure whom we shall consider is Tykhon of Voronezh. He belongs to the eighteenth century but, popular as he may have been in his lifetime, his influence actually begins and increases after his death. This man is particularly interesting for us as he formed a true link with the artistic, secular thought of the nineteenth century.

St. Tykhon, Bishop of Voronezh (Timofey S. Sokolov, 1724–83, canonized in 1861), was, as we know, the " positive type" of Russian sainthood which Dostoevsky tried to reproduce in his novels. Gogol read his works before the canonization. Uspensky mentioned him with admiration. The Princess Sophie S. Meschersky published fragments of his works.[12] The ecclesiastical world recognized his writings as useful for the reading of the students of St. Petersburg Alexander Seminary as early as 1788–99. They were included by St. Petersburg Theological Seminary in the programme of 1809–84. Since 1884 his works were introduced into all ecclesiastical schools together with early Fathers and the Imitation. The lectures on moral theology were indebted to the system of St. Tykhon.[13] G. V. Florovsky in his masterly characterization of the Saint rightly says :

" St. Tykhon was a great writer. His books fascinate

tums haltet tief in der Seele der ostlichen Völker." And Harnack applied this remark most particularly to Russia and illustrates it from the peasant stories of Tolstoy (*Das Wesen des Christentums*), p. 137.

[11] St. Seraphim, ascetic, contemplative and pneumatophore. He had a special devotion for our Lady and considered that the chief aim of a Christian is to " acquire " the Holy Ghost. On him, in English, A. F. Dobbie-Bateman (S.P.C.K. 1936).

[12] She also translated and published for popular reading pamphlets of the Religious Tract Society and some Russian sermons of her time ; see G. Florovsky, *The Ways*, p. 149.

[13] Information from A. Bronzov, *Moral theology in Russia ;* in *Christian Reading* (1901), tt. CCXI, CCXII, part I, II.

by light yet plastic images. His *True Christianity* (1770–2) in particular had a historical significance. It is not a dogmatical system; it is rather mystical ethics or ascetics. But it was a first experiment of living theology and of experimental theology in distinction and counterbalance of school erudition devoid of authentic experience." [14]

The life of St. Tykhon is near enough to be historically known, though unfortunately the documents are not very numerous. Two of his cell-attendants wrote about him and related many a trait of his childhood or of his inner life as told by himself. These and other documents and service records were taken in consideration by his first biographer who had also met him personally—the scholarly Metropolitan Evgeny Bolokhvitinov, in 1796. Moreover, St. Tykhon left his writings.

The childhood of Timofey was that of extreme poverty. Orphan of a village acolyte, he used to work in fields literally for bread. When, with great difficulty, his mother sent him to the Novgorod Seminary he had to sell half of his portion of food in order to buy a candle for studies at nights.[15] He

[14] G. Florovsky, p. 125; on St. Tykhon, pp. 122–5. The author finds in the book on *True Christianity* the influence of John Arndt read by the Bishop. (Existed also in Russian translation in 1735, was prohibited in 1743 but read nevertheless.)

[15] The difficulties of learning were increased by the fact that the official language of the ecclesiastical school was Latin. Already in the seventeenth century there was the controversy as to the language in theological schools. Kiev tradition was for the Latin. The Greeks residing in Moscow advocated their own language as that of the Orthodox Church. The Slavo-Græco-Latin School, founded in 1687 under the Likhudi and in the Greek tradition, soon returned to the Latin. The eighteenth century clergy read even the Greek Fathers in Latin translations. The Catechism of the Moscow Metropolitan Platon (Levshin, 1737—1811), printed in 1765, was a first venture of theological exposition in Russian. The struggle went on so far as the nineteenth century. Filaret of Moscow, who had a rare and brilliant mastery of Russian and a refined and precise style, used to write letters to his father in Latin. "Thus 'school-theology' was without soil. It sprouted and grew on foreign ground," says G. V. Florovsky, p. 114, see also pp. 141–6, 174–6. From 1814 onwards the Russian became predominant, though so far as the 'forties there were teachers keeping to Latin. The practical and pastoral shortcomings due to such a system are too obvious. But at least it shows that, whilst the Church was artificially estranged in her scholarly methods from the people whom she addressed in Russian and with whom she prayed in Slavonic, the theological thought was inevitably much more acquainted and even influenced by the Christian West, both Catholic and Protestant, than the geographical and historical isolation of the country might suggest at first sight.

became himself teacher at the Seminary of (successively) rhetoric, philosophy and theology. Professed monk with the name Tykhon in 1758, in 1761 he was nominated bishop of Keksholm and Ladoga and in 1763 of Voronezh. In time of the pressure on monasteries and ecclesiastical schools under Catherine II he struggled to uphold the safety of the Church. He introduced the teaching of people by the theological students on Sundays in the cathedral.[16] His own writings met the needs and instruction of the clergy : 1763, *Duty of Priest* and *On Seven Sacraments;* 1764 addition *On Penitence,* etc. He was a partisan of the translation of the Holy Scriptures into Russian. After four years as a bishop he asked to retire and spend the rest of his life in monasteries (Tolmachevo 1767–9 and afterwards Zadonsk, by the name of which he was known after his canonization). He sold the silk, velvet and furs belonging to him as bishop and distributed all to the poor. There was no limit to his charity, secret to the utmost. He entered personally into the needs of everybody. Contented with almost peasant cloth, a straw-mattress and pillow and the simplest food, he felt distressed at meal-times thinking of all who starve : " Woe unto me." He never refused help even if he suspected some deceit. " It is a greater mercy to be in need with the needy than to help him simply without one's own sacrifice." [17] Not only was he convinced that " poverty is more blissful than riches " [18] but he urged that " no over-indulgence is without offence to God and insult to one's neighbour." [19] And if some were grieved by their hard circumstances, he comforted them by reminding them of " the

[16] The Moscow theological school, Troitzko-Sergievskaya Lavra, encouraged the preaching. In 1747 there were already some experiments. The young Levshin, later on Metropolitan of Moscow, was one of the preachers. There was a special function of a preacher who could be a layman of theological training. In 1769 the students were ordained preachers (" given a stikhar "—dalmatic). In 1806 the teacher, Vassily M. Drozdov, preached for the first time ; he became the famous Filaret of Moscow. See *The history of Troitzko-Lavrsk Seminary,* S. S. Smirnov (M. 1867), pp. 58–60, 400–1.

[17] St. Tykhon, *Works,* second ed. (M. 1860), 15 vols. in "flesh and spirit " ; on Almsgiving (1796), t. II, p. 85.

[18] t. VI, p. 259, on love of one's neighbour.

[19] t. V, p. 67, on sin.

voluntary poverty of Christ and of the holy apostles." [20]
Though advising extreme simplicity of life, he made a
reservation for those who, without vanity, had to conform in
their clothes and manner of life to certain social standards.
Like St. Nil, he was indifferent or even opposed to expense
on ornamentation of churches and reminded his readers that
a service could be celebrated anywhere, whilst man, " the
living temple of God, cannot exist without food, clothes and
rest." [21]   But he knew and loved good singing in the church.
He had a strong liturgical devotion.   He was grieved that
frequent communion had become almost a legend of past
times.   " Christ calls all to Himself and offers His Flesh and
Blood ; but nobody comes to the supper of such a benefactor," and he would add to the priest : " Suffer in your
heart from it." [22]

The charity and pastoral care of the bishop were well
known in his lifetime.   Solitude and silence, for which he
longed in order to read or write, and most especially because
he was a contemplative, were hardly possible to him even
after his retirement.   Men of all classes came for his advice.
He had to keep up a large correspondence.   An incident of
this period characterizes Tykhon's attitude towards an
offender.   During a discussion with him, short of argument,
a flighty landlord struck him on the face.   The bishop fell on
his knees, made a prostration and implored his pardon for
having induced him into temptation.[23]   The contact with men
was at times painful to him.   He knew periods of despondency,
of despair and darkness.   His correspondence contains much
helpful advice to those who went through similar tests.   But
he came to victory, he had visions of heavenly light and he
gained a particular gift of love and joy which he also com-
municated to others.   It was not in vain that children followed

---

[20] St. Tykhon, t. VIII, p. 243, consolation against spiritual temptations.
[21] t. VIII, p. 38, on churches.
[22] t. I, p. 27, instruction to clergy ; cf. t. VI, p. 303.
[23] The first biography containing this fact is altered by the respectfully
written life-stories of Tykhon of later origin.   The precious truth changes
into a vague " impoliteness " of the gentleman answered " meekly " by
the bishop.   One cannot help remembering Dostoevsky, who introduces
in *The Idiot* the incident of a slap.

him everywhere and daily visited his cell.[24] A few days before his death which he felt approaching, Tykhon forbade access to the cell to anybody and remained alone in prayer. Then he called everyone, took leave of them and died peacefully, ordering his last belongings to be distributed to the poor. There was hardly anything to distribute, and he had no episcopal vestments to be buried with. He asked to be buried under a stone prepared by him, on the way to the church, so that each one going to a service should step on it.[25] His testament is a true hymn of joy and praise.

The cross, the suffering of Christ, the crucified divine love were constantly present in the mind of St. Tykhon. His thought was nourished by the New Testament. His devotion to Christ is central for his life and thought. He had a vivid, almost palpable feeling of the crucifixion. But he also had a triumphant assurance of divine victory and of redemption already achieved. The humiliation of Christ had also a noticeable place in his writings. He underlined the moral application of the Epistle to the Philippians. Most particularly he recommended those who were misunderstood or falsely accused (which has been his own case many a time) to follow Christ, rejected by the world and even by his friends.[26] Such a following would be only the accomplishment of our baptismal vows. He often and most vividly spoke of the baptism and explained that grace received by us in this sacrament is bestowed according to the love of God as expressed in St. John iii. 13 and in Phil. ii. 6—8, " This condescension of the Son of God for our sake which He accepted by His own will and by the benevolence of His heavenly Father and

[24] The spiritual life of St. Tykhon is very well reflected in the naïve description of his cell-attendant V. I. Chebotarev; see *Orthodox Observer*, t. V, 1861, " Materials for the life of Tykhon of Voronezh," pp. 299—334, esp. pp. 311, 313, 318. See also life of the newly-revealed saint of God, Tykhon, Bishop of Voronezh, second ed. (M. 1862). On despondency in *Works*, t. VIII, p. 205, Consolation and in t. XIV, Correspondence, pp. 165, 172.

[25] Could it be the testimony of the anonymous " great man " mentioned by Sophie in Turgenev's *Strange Story?* The story was written in 1869; perhaps it reflects the conversations and facts brought forward by the canonization of the bishop in 1861? Cf. our p. 42.

[26] St. Tykhon, to clergy, t. I, p. 65, Admonition to a monk and p. 71, Consolation to a monk.

the co-operation of the Holy Ghost is the cause of all our spiritual bliss." [27]   He was assured that this image of the humiliation preserves one from sin and leads to beatitude.[28]

Christ, " the true image of humility," left to us the cross so that contemplating it we should learn of the " *voluntary obedience* of the Son of God for our sake, His deepest humility, greatest patience and meekness; willingly the Lord of Glory humbled Himself so that there can be no greater humility; voluntarily for our sake He deigned to be obedient unto death even the death of the cross; voluntarily " He suffered and prayed for His enemies.[29]   The manger, the subjection to His Mother and His foster father, temptation, poverty spoken of in 2 Cor. viii. 9—all this forms the " true image of humility." [30]   Christ was not ashamed of our poverty (sin); He became as one of us in order to enrich us.[31]   He is thus an eternal example to the Christian : " The Son of God humbled Himself for you—could you be proud?   The Son of God took the form of a servant—could you seek to rule?   He became poor—could you run after riches?   He accepted dis-honour—could you strive after honours?   He had nowhere to lay His head—could you enlarge magnificent buildings? He washed His disciples' feet—are you ashamed of serving your brethren?" [32]   This image should be particularly kept in mind by each priest preparing in true spirit for the celebra-tion of the divine office.[33]   And even if the attraction of the world is very great, the contemplation of the humiliation and cross of the Son of God will help one to remain faithful to Him.[34]   It is interesting that St. Tykhon recommended to those who exercised charity to compare always the insignifi-cance of all our gifts and efforts with the act of self-emptying

[27] St. Tykhon, t. VII, p. 64, on baptism.
[28] t. VIII, p. 149.
[29] t. IV, p. 131.   *True Christianity;* cf. p. 122 " of this wisdom of his we must learn "; cf. almost same words t. II, p. 129, *Flesh and spirit.*
[30] t. VII, pp. 280, 316, on veneration of the passion of Christ.
[31] t. 6, p. 215, on the love of our neighbour.
[32] t. II, p. 129, on almsgiving; cf. t. III, p. 142, on the Incarnation and t. IX, p. 96, on dignity of a Christian.
[33] t. I, p. 125, instructions to clergy.
[34] t. VI, pp. 96 and 107, on renunciation of the world; cf. t. XV, p. 191, correspondence.   " His temptation is our weapon," and p. 207— expansion of Phil. ii.—washing of feet, etc.

of the Son of God and His poverty for our enrichment. Let us notice also that, like many Russians, St. Tykhon felt the mystery of the Body : " Christ is begging through the poor." [35]

The voluntary self-emptying of the Son of God in the Incarnation, His earthly poverty and especially His voluntary obedience, suffering and death were for the bishop the way by which Christ merited to the believers the name of children of God.[36] Out of His humiliation Christ says to men : " remember who I am . . . but for your sake " He has taken the form of a servant so as to call them to repentance (Rom. ii. 4).[37] If the word *merit* may seem confusing, the following statement throws, it seems to us, sufficient light to make it clear how it was interpreted by St. Tykhon : the humiliation and humility of Christ is " the mode of love to God offended by sin and of pity of men." [38] We must also notice that sometimes the humiliation is spoken of in terms which differ from kenotic distinctness and remind one of the Tome of Leo : " Christ lived on earth among men but He was not separated from the Father's bosom (St. John i. 18); He walked in the form of a servant (Phil. ii. 7), but as the Lord He ordered the wind and sea." [39]

Such meditation upon Christ's self-abasement and cross is not morbid for a Russian ; St. Tykhon more particularly felt that " union in suffering leads to likeness in glory." [40] The resurrection, the spring of the soul and of nature were spoken of by him very frequently and with an unforgettable touch of joy and poetry. It is " not through our own but through Christ's obedience that we are delivered from eternal death, hell and torments and receive eternal life." [41] The " native country of a Christian is heaven " and it was given back to us through Christ's humble obedience unto the death of the cross.[42] But, together with the Redeemer, our

[35] t. VI, p. 245, on love of our neighbour.
[36] t. IV, pp. 164, 166, on true Christianity.
[37] t. IV, p. 167 ; cf. t. VI, pp. 4, 9.
[38] t. VI, p. 82, on humility ; also p. 91.
[39] t. VII, p. 288, on veneration of the passion of Christ.
[40] t. VIII, p. 194.
[41] t. VII, p. 104, on obedience, also p. 120.
[42] t. IX, p. 79, on the comforting fruit of the holy faith. Cf. t. IV, p. 176, on true Christianity.

"body of humility becomes the body of glory (Phil. iii. 21)." [43] This hope of reconciliation and this joy was the chief characteristic of St. Tykhon. Dostoevsky in his Zossima caught something of this radiance.

We entitled this chapter "the devotional and moral application of the humiliation." But we see at once that the writings of St. Tykhon touch dogmas as well. The same will be noticeable in the other ecclesiastical writers examined under this heading. It could not be otherwise with any Orthodox person for whom true Christianity includes not only a man's moral life but his mind as well. There can be people living good lives according to the "law written in their hearts." But a Christian cannot be moral in the profoundest sense unless he accepts some dogmas which, for an Orthodox, are a true philosophy of life and, more than that, the expression of some fundamental and objective facts of the divine world. Therefore we shall constantly meet doctrinal elements in the sermons which we propose to examine next in order to see to what extent the Church of the nineteenth century remembered in her teaching the humiliation of Christ.

It would be impossible to present here all the ecclesiastical writers of the epoch. Our great technical difficulty here is not so much in abundance as in absence of materials. Even before 1917 many of the writings of the churchmen were buried in periodicals, in diocesan papers, etc. The best illustration is the fact that the works of Filaret of Moscow, influential as he was, have never yet been collected. There is no up-to-date biography of any of the men of whom we shall speak (except V. Soloviev). The one work giving a general survey of Russian theological thought is G. V. Florovsky's *Ways of Russian Theology,* Paris 1937. It contains most valuable information and fifty pages of bibliography. We constantly refer to this book. But, precious as it is, it is often an appreciation rather than a presentation of an author and it presupposes the reader's acquaintance with those of whom it speaks. M. M. Tareev could not publish his prepared book on the subject after 1917. N. N. Glubokovsky's work perished after

[43] St. Tykhon, t. XV, p. 207, cellular letters.

1917. His pamphlet on "Russian theological science in its historical development and modern state," Warsaw 1928, is a pathetic reconstruction from memory and in form of a conspectus of some of the pages of his work which he had no more hope to publish. We regret to be reduced to scattered material available in the conditions of exile. But this difficulty makes us bold, as it shows the need of work in the domain of Russian theology.

The ecclesiastical world underwent during the nineteenth century an evolution which corresponded to the general development of Russia and which, owing to the close connection of the Church with the State, greatly reflected the government policy. The emotional, pietistic, mystically agitated epoch of Alexander I found its expression in the life of the church no less than the reactionary, suspicious and practical reign of Nicolas I or the period of reforms of Alexander II. One of the chief events of the century, the history of the translation of the Bible, seems to illustrate it in the most expressive way.[44] Like the secular world, the Church also had its awakening of the sense of history, both the history of Russia and the ecclesiastical one. Moreover, the translation of the Bible, with all the problems to which it gave rise, helped to develop "intuition of the sacred history and at the same time philosophical speculation : [it was the revival] of theology and philosophy."[45] Considering the unfavourable conditions the Church advanced in the way of thought and self-expression with great rapidity. Triumph of the Russian language in the ecclesiastical schools ; publication by the High Schools of Theology of the periodicals which often gave in their pages very valuable material of importance for theses

[44] I. A. Chistovich, *The history of the translation of the Bible,* second ed. (SPB. 1899) ; also his *St. Petersburg Theological Academy within the last thirty years* (1858–88), (SPB. 1889). In all materials on the Metropolitan Filaret. In Florovsky, pp. 147–50, 152–6, 171, 349–55. Russian Bible Society founded in 1812 ; 1816 decision to translate Bible in Russian ; Four Gospels came out in 1819, the whole New Testament in 1820. The Society cancelled in 1826. The translated Pentateuch was burnt in 1826. The disputes filled the 'forties and the 'sixties. Renewed from 1858, the translation of the Holy Synod of the whole Bible was finally accomplished in 1875.

[45] G. Florovsky, p. 232.

of doctorates; revival of contemplative monasticism and of translations of early Christian literature; reforms of the ecclesiastical schools, admission of the pupils of seminaries into the universities (from 1863); all this had as a result that about the 'sixties a Russian theologian was " entirely on the same historical level as his Western contemporary." [46] But there was not yet any school of thought as there was no public to encourage an ecclesiastical thinker and writer. Even at a much later period, theologians in Russia wrote still " chiefly according to their particular bent and printed at their own risk, not merely the material one." [47] This sad fact brings us back to our subject and allows us to notice that several among the ecclesiastical writers had " a particular inclination " to the problem of the humiliation of Christ.

We thought it necessary to inquire what place is given to kenosis, devotionally or in doctrine, in the works of the central ecclesiastical figure of the Russian nineteenth century, the Metropolitan of Moscow Filaret (Vassily Drozdov, 1782–1867), considered as an authority of the Orthodox world.

One of the best brains of his time, reserved, prudent and authoritative, he managed to remain at the head of the Church during three reigns extremely different in character. He was often accused of having no heart and of being chiefly a statesman.[48] It is certain that he would not be an example of " kenotic " type in his personal life. His position and the state of the Church required a man rather wise as a serpent than harmless as a dove. One must not forget important services rendered by Filaret as an energetic and convinced member of the Bible Society, as member of the Holy Synod, as professor, rector and almost creator of St. Petersburg Theological Academy. Overwhelmed with various occupations, Filaret had no time to write. His sermons remain " his chief theological heritage." [49] Read, copied, spoken of in his

[46] G. Florovsky, p. 232.
[47] N. Glubokovsky, *Russian theological science in its historical development and its present condition* (Warsaw, 1928), p. 3.
[48] View opposed by his spiritual son and biographer N. V. Sushkov. *Notes on the life and time of Moscow Metropolitan Filaret* (M. 1868).
[49] G. Florovsky, p. 176. On Filaret, pp. 166–84, the whole Chapter V, Fight for theology, and through the whole book.

lifetime, they still represent a true theological value and interest. He is more truly expressed in these *Words and sermons* than for instance in his *Catechism*.[50] His system is remarkably integral and harmonious; his orthodoxy lies chiefly in his faithfulness to the Scriptures and at the same time in his intelligent capacity of embracing the dogmas as a whole. He is a master of the Russian language and has the rare gift of putting into a few expressive words (unfortunately completely lost in translation) all the foundations of Orthodox belief. Addressed to ordinary Church people and later on preserved and studied by the clergy of following generations, these sermons show to us the devotional and at the same time doctrinal ideas which educated Russian Church people.

As all other ideas of the Christian revelation, the idea of the humilition of Christ is brought by Filaret within the whole problem of redemption. The cross was central for his thought and it was for him the expression of the crucifying, crucified and triumphant love of the Triune God. The divine love and the divine glory were for him the background of creation. Having created the world and man, God established a certain " circulation of glory " between Himself and His world. This glory belonging to Him alone was seized by man who conceived the desire to stop it and to keep it for himself. What happened then was what, on the physical plane, could happen to a person whose circulation suddenly stopped. In His mercy, God has since tried different ways of approaching man and of re-establishing him in the hope of glory (2 Cor. xiii. 5). " God approaches man and partakes of his humiliation. In order that sinful flesh should not fly again from the divine presence, the Son of God appears in the likeness of sinful flesh (Romans viii. 3). In order that the weakly creature should not vanish from the glory of the almighty Creator, He does no more clothe Himself with honour and majesty (Ps. civ. 1),

[50] The Catechism first published in 1823 aroused two main objections: for some, the fact that the Creed and the Lord's Prayer were given synoptically in Slavonic and in Russian seemed a blasphemous introduction of the vulgar language. The other objection pointed out that the Holy Scripture was indicated as the only source of religion. The later editions added the tradition. See *Christian Reading* (1881), t. II, pp. 763–91, and 1885, t. I, 732–40.

but with the weak and dumb babyhood, with the poor swaddling-clout." In this manner men test Christ's divinity before they realize what it is.[51]

The humiliation of Christ was thus put in the very centre of the redemptive process. On many an occasion the preacher reminded his listeners of this mystery. (So even on the occasion of the consecration of an altar in the Kazan Cathedral in St. Petersburg in 1811.)[52] Preaching on Christmas days, he would link the Incarnation with the Epistle to the Philippians. Sometimes he reminded his hearers of it in order that they should duly worship " the hidden divinity " of the Baby in a manger. "The manger (after the premundane life of the Lord was hidden) became the throne of the King of kings. The divine power and wisdom are hidden in the weaknesses of babyhood "—abasement into the " abyss of fallen nature " which is difficult for a human mind to grasp no less than His future ascension above the heaven.[53] Blessed is therefore anyone filled with awe at the sight of the manger as if " before the throne of majesty." [54] And the preacher would advise " never to practise any other way of ascension than that by which the Son of God descended according to Phil. ii. 5—7." [55] For Filaret, the very union of the eternal with the temporal, of the uncreated with the creature " formed already a cross," still more striking in the humble earthly conditions of the life of Jesus Christ—in the poverty of His childhood among the subjected Jewish nation.[56]

The growth of Jesus was also mentioned by Filaret, and together with it the fact that " the source of grace received grace " in order to increase in wisdom (St. Luke ii. 52).[57] The question of the human ignorance of Jesus was answered from Phil. ii.; verse 6 was interpreted as showing the divinity

---

[51] Filaret, *Works, Words and Sermons,* 5 vols. (M. 1873–7), t. II, p. 40. The sermon on the Christmas Day of 1821 and in remembrance of the liberation of the Russian world from the invasion of the French.

[52] *Ibid.,* t. I, p. 147.

[53] *Ibid.,* t. I, p. 18, on Christmas 1811.

[54] *Ibid.,* t. I, p. 188, on Christmas 1812; cf. t. II, p. 296, Christmas 1823.

[55] *Ibid.,* t. I, p. 186, Christmas 1812.

[56] *Ibid.,* t. I, p. 33, on Good Friday, 1813.

[57] *Ibid.,* t. I, p. 34, on Good Friday, 1813.

of the Lord; but His self-emptying made it possible that He could not answer some questions. " If Christ was tempted in all like man, it is not surprising that He deigned to be tempted by taking the likeness of ignorance in which He was hiding the light of divine wisdom and through which this light shone only when it was necessary for the illumination of men." [58] Let us notice that the version in the later edition (1820–1) gives more kenotic definitions : " As He abolished all divine greatness, hence in some way He emptied Himself of course of His divine omniscience as well."

The prayers of Jesus, His preparation for suffering, were presented as an example to the faithful who too often would refuse to follow not only the example of the praying Lord but even, say, of Elijah under the pretext that they were not of the stamp of such a great man. Therefore, the prayers of Jesus should be remembered in relation to the humble aspect of the Lord and the imitation of Him should be based on Phil. ii. 5.[59] There was a mighty appeal on one of the Good Fridays to fix one's eyes upon Him whom Pilate presented to the crowd : the *Man* : " Let us look at Him in order that this Man should be revealed in each of us, according to Phil. ii. 5." [60]

Obedience was spoken of as an active virtue. It was previous to the Incarnation on the side of the Son of God. It was prior to the Incarnation on the earthly plan because there was one who said : I am the handmaiden of the Lord. " The annunciation is uttered not only by the almighty will of God : it seeks the acquiescence of His servant." [61] The Russian word " obedience " (*poslushanije*) suggests the hearing and following and Filaret interprets it as in higher sense, a following of the divine will. Adam brought the sin of disobedience—a Christian is a child of obedience (1 Pet. i. 14). The overcoming of Adam's transgression was accomplished by the obedience of Christ as pictured in Phil. ii. 8, Rom. v. 19, Heb. v. 8, 9. " Lo, I come, says Christ (Ps. 40) coming down in His Incarnation." He starts His redemptive work by an act

---

[58] *Ibid.*, t. I, p. 74, 1814.
[59] t. I, p. 106, on Transfiguration, 1820.
[60] t. I, p. 231, on Good Friday, 1817.
[61] t. IV, p. 236, Annunciation Day, 1843.

of obedience and He fulfils it by submission : " not as I will "
(St. Matt. xxvi. 39) and so, according to St. Luke xxiii. 46,
" surrender to God is the beginning and the achievement of
eternal salvation." [62]

The whole dogmatic scheme of the humiliation and
redemption is summed up as follows : one has to distinguish
between the state of the Son of God before His Incarnation,
His state as God, and His state as man.   As God, He always
has an unlimited power over all that is created by Him and is
preserved and ruled by His providence.   In the second state,
entering the earthly life, He humbles Himself taking the form
of a servant.   The glory of His divinity is now hidden and He
is preparing to be glorified.   Offering Himself to God in His
humanity on behalf of guilty mankind " He obtained, in His
resurrection, the glorification of His humanity and together
with it the hope of glory for mankind. . . . To Him (with
His cross as with a key) is *given* to open the gates of hell
(Rev. iii. 7), to deliver those judged of old, to open heaven,
to bring there those who were forgiven.   Power, *given on
earth* to the risen Christ-Godman, is the same which worketh
on earth as the beginning of what is fulfilled in heaven.   On
earth, Christ introduces the believers from the realm of
fallen nature into the realm of grace and gives to the children
of Adam the share of becoming the children of God (St. John
i. 12); in heaven, from the kingdom of grace He brings them
into the Kingdom of glory." [63]   Thus the disturbed " circulation of glory " is restored through the humiliation of Christ.

The divine condescension has its expression in the life of the
Church.   The self-emptying, the coming down is perpetuated
in human lives and also in the fact of divine indwelling in the
churches where God, " so to say contracts His divine omnipresence reducing it to visible signs and passing phenomena." [64]
The utmost proof of this divine condescension and of the
humble approach of Jesus Christ is in the sacramental life

[62] Filaret, t. II, p. 270, Annunciation Day, 1822.
[63] t. V, p. 488, on Friday of the Easter Week, 1859, and the birthday
of the Emperor Alexander II.
[64] t. I, p. 146, on consecration in the Kazan Cathedral of the altar of
the Nativity of the Blessed Virgin, 1811.

and " is every day there on the altar." [65]   The Metropolitan
Filaret was, by the way, a supporter of frequent communion.[66]
He regarded relics also as an illustration of the humiliation
of Christ who through His earthly ways offers to men " and
even to flesh the way of incorruption and glorification " [67]
in the light of Phil. iii. 21.

The moral application of the kenosis was constantly
remembered by the preacher. He called his hearers to follow
the " mind of Christ Jesus " as it was expressed in Phil. ii.
5—9. Addressing the representatives of the upper class, he
reproached these members of the Body for desiring riches
and magnificence whilst " the Head is in poverty and
humiliation." [68] Spiritual poverty, as beatitude, was linked
with 2 Cor. viii. 9.[69] The suffering of the innocent was
presented as their participation in Christ's vicarious suffering
and accomplishment of the divine will; on this occasion the
Metropolitan remembered St. Alexis, so dear to popular
memory.[70] He would exhort clergy to work in the spirit of
Christ's message and ministry. He would recommend disinterestedness in all human offices and duties and added that a
monk as well should keep in mind obedience which is not
human in character but the commandment and example of
Christ of Phil. ii. 8.[71] Even on the jubilee day of the coronation of Nicolas I he spoke of obedience in the sense of
Philippians.[72] Certainly he knew how many of this world
were shocked by the humble aspect of the Lord, not only whilst
He was on earth. But, as a continual exhortation, he would
repeat : " Let meekness, simplicity, condescension to those

[65] *Ibid.*, t. II, p. 203, on contact of faith with Christ, 1825. This
thought reminds us of Gogol.

[66] *Letters of the Metropolitan Filaret,* published in the Report for 1888
of St. Petersburg Imperial Public Library (SPB. 1891), letter N. 41 to
Mme E. S. Naumova, p. 50.

[67] Filaret, t. II, p. 18, on the incorrupted relics in memory of St. Sergius
of Radonezh, 1821.

[68] *Ibid.*, t. I, p. 111, on the third week after Pentecost, 1820.

[69] *Ibid.*, t. II, on spiritual poverty, 1824.

[70] *Ibid.*, t. II, pp. 90 and 99, on the Prince Dimitry.

[71] *Ibid.*, t. III, p. 393, on the birthday of her majesty the Empress
Alexandra Theodorovna.

[72] *Ibid.*, t. IV, p. 35, on 22nd August, 1836, tenth year since the coronation of the Emperor Nicolas I.

lower than yourselves, condescension which would put you on an equal level with the lowest among them, let quietness in humiliation, patience which no offence could overwhelm, let all this become your mind as it was of Christ Jesus." [73]

If we remember the crowds which listened to the sermons of the famous Metropolitan and which were composed of all classes of society, we can see that the Church was never behind secular thought with regard to the image of the humiliated Christ. In an accessible form, Filaret presented to his listeners both the moral, devotional and dogmatic scheme of the humiliation. But, when he spoke of the condescension and of the complete human experience of Christ, he pointed out also that no salvation could follow it were there not behind the Incarnation " the divine nature (Phil. ii. 6) and the creative power." [74] The obedience of the Lord, culminating in the death on the cross, was followed by His resurrection and glorification, so that the whole creation bows the knee at the name of Jesus. But now man and creation also are associated with this life of glory, if only through hope. We recognize in this sketch the victorious message of the Gospels, the language of the epistles, in particular of that to the Philippians and the emphasis, familiar to Orthodox thought, on the resurrection and " deification " of man.

It seems typical that a book of the *Select Sermons of twelve Hierarchs of the Russian Church* should include, besides some of Filaret's sermons of kenotic inspiration, one more of this same type : that of Innokenty, Archbishop of Kherson and Tavrida (Borissov, 1800–55), a very popular figure of his time. It deals with the period between Easter and Ascension. The bishop, whom G. Florovsky describes as one who had not a creative mind but who " could enticingly put a question, attract the attention of his reader or listener," [75] was in fact putting a question in this particular sermon. Was not this period of forty days " a certain preparation of Christ

[73] Filaret, t. III, pp. 65–70, on Christmas Day, 1826.
[74] t. IV, p. 396, at the consecration of the church in memory of the Lord's Prayer at Gethsemane, 1845.
[75] G. Florovsky, p. 197, on Innokenty, pp. 196–9.

to hold the fullness of divine glory"? It is true, in Christ divinity is hypostatically united with His humanity. But it is united and it acts without violating the laws of humanity. That is why on earth it reveals itself gradually and is completely hidden at times, as in St. Luke ii. 52, in St. Mark xiii. 32. Therefore there is nothing incongruous with the dignity of the Godman if, according to His humanity, during forty days after His resurrection He would gradually approach the summit of divine glory where He had to mount in His ascension.[76]

Another influential man of the epoch wrote a commentary to the Epistle to Philippians. Theophan (Govorov, 1815-94), successively Bishop of Tambov and Vladimir, the *Hermit* who chose retirement and seclusion in order to consecrate himself to study, writings and translations, interpreted the Epistle morally, as an exhortation to follow the mind of Christ. At the same time he often referred to St. John Chrysostom, who saw in Phil. ii. excellent material against many heresies. The humiliation was spoken about in connection with the glory of Christ : " whosoever shall humble himself shall be exalted " (St. Matt. xxiii. 12, St. Luke xxiv. 26), "suffered . . . to enter into His glory" (Heb. ii. 9), " Jesus, suffering of death, crowned with glory and honour." The peculiar feature of this commentary is a certain asceticism. There is a certain monastic note in it, and humility with obedience are presented chiefly in relation to man's spiritual life. But there is also emphasis on glorification and deification which reminds us not so much of Filaret as of the Fathers of the *Philokalia* which the bishop was translating and systematizing.[77]

Let us pass now to a man whose tragic and strange destiny

---

[76] *Select Sermons of twelve Hierarchs of the Russian Church* (M. 1861), p. 273.
[77] The *Dobrotolubije* came out between 1876-90 in five volumes. Theophan rearranged the material compared with the Greek edition and introduced some Syrian Fathers. The epoch was a revival of interest in the ascetic and mystical literature. Monks of Optina worked also at the translation and so did the Moscow Theological Academy. The general stream presented in the book is well reflected in Mme M. Lot-Borodine, *La doctrine de la déification dans l'Eglise Grecque jusqu'au XIe siècle* (Paris, 1933), *Revue de l'histoire des réligions*, tt. CVI, 2, 3 ; CVII, n. 1.

seems even more expressive of the line of abasement than his writings. Many generations in the secular world passed without even knowing his name. Some of the Church regarded him as an unhealthy dreamer if not as an apostate; for some of his students he remained the true inspirer of their spiritual lives; some in later period saw in him the victim and sufferer for the idea of freedom.[78]

Son of a village deacon, Alexis M. Bukharev (the Archimandrite Theodor, 1822–71) knew a childhood of poverty, was brought up in Tver Seminary and in Moscow Theological Academy. His studies finished, he was persuaded to take Orders. The Academy considered it a failure if some of the pupils did not become monks. For some it was also the step to a promising career impossible for a member of the secular clergy. In this case it was obedience to the elders and the desire to consecrate his life to the service of Christ as fully as possible. Professed in 1846 with the name Theodor, the young man stayed at the Academy lecturing successively on biblical history, Greek and the Scriptures. He was liked by the Metropolitan Filaret. In 1852 Bukharev became professor. In his secluded life as monk and scholar he followed with interest the cultural events of the secular world. It was new, as Filaret was against even the possession of secular literature in the libraries of theological schools. Bukharev wrote to and about Gogol, he grieved over the anti-religious attitude of Belinsky, and in following years noticed the picture of Ivanov [79] and the works of Turgenev, Chernyshevsky and

[78] Among his defenders are Tareev, Bulgakov, Berdyaeff; the faithful pupils are P. Znamensky, A. A. Lebedev, V. Lavrovsky. The magazine *Pilgrim* (Strannik), the first number of which in 1860 had a paper by Theodor, kept a sympathetic attitude: see Nos. June—August 1909. G. Florovsky calls the Archimandrite " an apostate, breaker of his vows " and grants some indulgence only on behalf of his " dreaminess " and " sincerity " as well as of the general unhealthy and unorthodox " spirit of the epoch of Alexander I," p. 193, on Bukharev, pp. 344–9. We follow for the biography of Bukharev P. V. Znamensky, *The history of the Kazan Theological Academy in the years 1842–70* (Kazan, 1891), pp. 124–80. An interesting study " A. M. Bukharev on relation between Orthodoxy and modern world " was given by A. V. Karpov († 1937) in *Put*, nn. 22, 23 (Paris, 1930).

[79] The picture of A. A. Ivanov " Christ appearing to men " (Christ approaching Jordan where John already baptizes the Jews) was an event of his epoch. The artist worked in Rome and was befriended by Gogol.

Dostoevsky. In 1854 Bukharev was transferred to Kazan as professor of dogmatics. The harsh atmosphere of the place, where discipline was based on fear and punishment, was a hard experience for the goodhearted and dreamy man. He tried " to take upon himself the form of a student and considered the very faults of them as his own." [80] As we see, the very wording of this witness of one of his students reminds us of Phil. ii. Bukharev " was ill two or three days after some misdeed of a student." [81] Few round him were apt to see what was meant by the " spirit of sonship " and of freedom for which he stood. In 1855 he stayed in Raif-desert (a monastery) and expressed the desire to remain there. His resignation was not accepted. In the Academy, Bukharev was often mocked as a sort of innocent. He went to St. Petersburg, worked for different periodicals, and prepared a book on the Apocalypse. In 1858 he was nominated for the committee of the ecclesiastical censorship, and naïvely he expected to be more in contact with life : he wanted to link the life of the world with the accepted and acknowledged forms of a " good religious " life. He was misunderstood ; his desire to sanctify each act of life seemed bold and suspicious to many, among them his colleague Victor I. Askochensky (1813–79), editor of the " Home Conversation " (*Domashniaja Beseda*).[82] In 1862 Theodor learned that his work on the book of Revelation had not passed the censor. The Metropolitan Filaret was convinced of the good will of Theodor but considered that his language induced confusion of thought. It is quite true that Bukharev's style is heavy and confused with, at the same time, something childlike and convincingly sincere in it. The Archi-

See *Letters of Gogol* and also in *Selected pages from the correspondence with friends,* ed. Berlin, 1922, pp. 421–35 ; see also *Khomyakov,* t. III, pp. 349–53. (The picture was acquired by the Hermitage, St. Petersburg.)

[80] The sad twenty-fifth anniversary, 1896, *Orthodox Interlocutor,* p. 24.

[81] P. Znamensky, *History of the Kazan Academy,* p. 177.

[82] *Ibid., Theological polemics in 1860* (Kazan, 1902). The embittered, sceptical mind and the sad life of Askochensky are revealed in his *Diary;* see the *Historical Messenger,* 1882. The controversy was noticed in a few words and in favour of Bukharev by the exiled Herzen, *Works,* t. VI, pp. 97, 135. " The ecclesiastical and secular denunciations, the ' censoroquisition ' and literary tutors."

mandrite Theodor believed that his literary work was his true way of serving God and his fellow men. The crisis provoked by the impossibility of printing his book could be only explained by the deep conviction expressed by Bukharev as early as 1848 (*Letters to Gogol*) that the Church and secular life should unite in the common task of the sanctification of life as a whole. The Archimandrite decided to recover the freedom of action and asked to be reduced to the state of layman. The case was without precedent; the authorities tried to dissuade him, and actually a year passed between his letter asking for resignation of the monastic vows and the actual deposition (July 1863). Bukharev made it clear that he was not protesting against either Church or monasticism; he accepted all the legal consequences of his step. (Deprivation of civic right, losing of academic degrees and of all money or property connected with his previous occupations; prohibition of residence in the two capitals and in all the dioceses where he was known as a monk.) The scandal and humiliation were increased by the fact that, when in the world, Bukharev decided to contract a marriage. His wife proved his faithful pupil.[83] It was rather obvious that Bukharev would not find any place in the secular life. His occasional publications did not reach the reader. He lived a life of extreme poverty and comforted his alarmed friends by saying that none of the Apostles had perished from starvation.

Whatever our opinion about the personal drama of Bukharev it should be examined in the light of his writings. Two aspects of the Christian message impressed him : redemption of the world as a whole and the humiliation of Christ. Life had to be sanctified, " enchurched," embraced in all its forms by the spirit of Christ. The mode of this sanctification must be that chosen by the Lord who humbled Himself. In his work on the Revelation he wrote : " Our Russian task is to serve the purification of thought, of knowledge, of literature, of the whole civilization of the world," but we should act and be ourselves " in the spirit of condescension

---

[83] V. Rozanov, *In the world of the unprecise and undecided* (SPB. 1901).

of this Bride of the Lamb," Rev. xxi. 9.[84]   The world should reflect " the New Jerusalem *coming down* from heaven." [85] The orthodoxy of Bukharev's writings was never contested ; the ecclesiastical periodicals published his works after he resumed his monastic dignity. For himself, monastic obedience was that due to Christ directly " otherwise it would be a slavish humiliation of spirit."   It was to be expressed in patience similar to Christ's charity which made Him bear all as " if He were guilty Himself before His Father for the sinful omissions of the world." [86]   He did not think that, by being discharged from his promise to follow a certain rule of life, he was breaking his promise of direct obedience to Christ. Nevertheless it was natural to expect that his act would be qualified by some as Protestantism. Some mentioned in connection with his life the name of Luther. Bukharev replied in his *Apology* :

> " It is not Lutheranism to ask in accordance with the regulations of the Orthodox Church and to receive from her exemption from a good spiritual yoke.   And this without ceasing to recognize, to announce and even to defend its angelic loftiness and holiness; moreover, to bear witness to one's complete dependence upon the Orthodox Church by the acceptance of the legal ecclesiastical penance. . . . It is unjust to seek such guilt (Lutheranism) in an Orthodox who had suffered all that is said above, unjust even if you want to accuse him of moral fall." [87]

As for the marriage, did not some of the hermits of old practise even more audacious charity by entering houses of harlots ? Could not one come out of an "angelical abode, the monastery, and go (in the spirit of Christ's humiliation) into the world so as to appear there as a sinner under penance. . . . Why ? Now, first of all in order to live practically and, as much as it

[84] Bukharev, *On the book of Revelation,* ed. of the Sergiev Possad (M. 1916), p. 21.   The book is interpreted in the light of the Church history and of the history of Russia up to the time of Alexander I and Napoleon. It has some dreamy and nationalistic flavour and is the most laborious but the less valuable of Bukharev's writings.

[85] *Ibid.,* p. 641.

[86] *Ibid., On modern spiritual needs of life and thought, especially in Russia* (M. 1865), pp. 581–2.

[87] *Ibid., My Apology* (M. 1866), p. 17.

is possible to me in my weakness, to carry out with patience and to the end, as some say scornfully, my ' principle ' of following the Lamb of God and of revealing His light to all the classes of the world." [88]   Marriage being one of the domains where fear and despotism formed so often the chief basis, Bukharev was anxious to teach that " the matrimonial union should also reflect that side of Christ's union with His Church, according to which Christ through His Incarnation sacrificed Himself to the point, so to say, of identification with the Church composed of mankind (Phil. ii. 5), but is also raising her up to the revelation of all His divine fullness (Ephes. i. 23, iii. 19, i. 11)." [89]   And he wanted to show what place a woman may take in the world when, daughter of Eve, she shares in the nature of the Mother of God. [90]

" The innocent " professor of Kazan Theological Academy made it clear that his behaviour was inspired by the desire of self-abasement. He mentioned a priest who was in the eyes of many " not in his whole senses " yet a true spiritual director. [91] Foolishness for Christ's sake was greatly dear to Bukharev. He definitely spoke of it as of a valuable spiritual way. [92] He explained in the following words his understanding of it. " The true fools in Christ follow the words of 1 Cor. iv. 9, 10 : they become a spectacle to angels and to men. . . . The passage 'death worketh in us, life—in you ' refers to the same also. As fellow workers of the loving Christ's spirit, the holy men of God bear, by the grace of Christ, human sinful weaknesses and humiliations, as if they themselves were liable to spiritual foolishness. According to such heroism of faith and love, the grace of God does not abandon men who (*freely*) give themselves to these dishonouring weaknesses and silliness ; but meekly and patiently He brings them on the path of truth and clear understanding. [Ordinary] men pass gradually from their childish mind into the *life* of sane intelligence because

---

[88] Bukharev, *My Apology*, p. 19.

[89] *Ibid., On modern spiritual needs*, etc., footnote on p. 595 ; cf. pp. 69, 486, 493.

[90] *Ibid., The Revelation*, p. 19.

[91] G. Florovsky, p. 347—it was the " innocent " priest Peter Tomanitsky from Uglich.

[92] Bukharev, *My Apology*, pp. 74, 75.

those others, in their gracious love, offer themselves to the
hard *death* of frank madness in the eyes of men. Such is the
mystery or significance of foolishness for Christ's sake." [93]
May not this passage be an explanation of his own strange
destiny?

Moral and devotional elements prevail in Bukharev's
writings. But there is Christology also, and that was expressed
in the language of kenotic thinkers. M. M. Tareev, it is true,
reproached later this knowledge of the kenosis for " not
surpassing the elementary information of manuals " [94] and
for lack of philosophical basis. In fact, Bukharev cared less
for philosophy than for the living reality of kenosis. " Let
each dogma, each truth and each institution of Orthodoxy
be known to us and kept by us not only in their form and
letter but always in [Christ's] own spirit, namely in the spirit
of His descending from heaven on earth and, on earth, into
conditions not only of the Church but also of family and
citizenship—in the spirit of that love of His in which He
appeared Himself to be the Lamb of God taking the sin of the
world." [95]

Let us see more closely how he represents this Christ's
coming down. In his book on Job he wrote : " The heavenly
Father uttered His hypostatic or personal Word, and all came
into being; but uttering His thought and His will about the
existence of creation, He, at the same time, was determining
for His own personal Word or Son to take upon Him the
burden of all—already foreseen—sinful disorders of the
world. God the Word was mightily creating according to the
thought of His Father, but already He was dooming Himself
to the immeasurable self-sacrifice in order to keep this new-
created world in the meaning and designation given to it—
even in spite of the foreseen infidelity of the world to its meaning and designation. And the Holy Ghost was confirming
in existence the new creatures, inspiring them in such direction

[93] A. M. Bukharev, *On modern spiritual needs,* etc., p. 550. " The
important lesson taught to modern intelligence by foolishness in the name
of Christ."

[94] M. M. Tareev, *Foundations of Christianity,* t. IV, p. 325.

[95] A. M. Bukharev, *On modern spiritual needs,* etc., p. 596, on the novel
of Chernyshevsky.

and spirit of creative love [not quite clear what B. means here by ' creative '], that even then, from the very building of the world, in the divine love and thought, the *Lamb of God* would seem to be *slain* already on behalf of the world in the process of creation. Thus, the act of creation is to be thought of not only as an act of omnipotence for which it is only too easy to call creatures into existence out of nothing. It is also to be thought of as such a motion, or act, or manifestation of Deity in which the consubstantial refulgence of the Father— God the Word with the Holy Ghost dwelling in Him— whilst creating the world, was already emptying Himself by the definition of the whole Blessed Trinity and by His own personal readiness and love of the world; [He was] coming down in the creaturely existence through the Incarnation and that, up to the offering of His flesh in sacrifice for the world which He was creating." [96]

A similar allusion to the self-emptying of the Pre-existent One appears even in the letters to Gogol.[97]

Bukharev feels not only the self-emptying of the Son; he also loves His true humanity and His humble human existence. The earthly life of Jesus is for him a constant source of loving meditation. He goes away from all " theoretical " thoughts and calls one both to worship and to follow this life. His notes on the twelve main feasts of the Church were qualified as naïve; so they are with regard to the actual life which surrounded him. But devotionally there is plenty to think about. The manger is for him not only remembrance of the Incarnation, but also it inspires him to consider each poor person as the bearer of Christ. Here Bukharev is fully in the Russian tradition, and to receive a beggar means for him also a great honour—spiritual reception of Christ. Nothing else, according to him, could better help us to live in true humility, because though angels themselves are hardly worthy to approach Christ, " He, the King of glory who humbled Himself taking the *form of a servant,* deigned to be received by you in your deed." [98] The beggar or any suffering brother

[96] Archim. Theodor, *Job the longsufferer* (M. 1864), pp. 150, 152.
[97] *Ibid., Three letters to Gogol on occasion of Dead Souls,* written in 1848 (M. 1860), p. 162.
[98] Archim. Theodor, *Orthodoxy in relation to the modern world* (SPB. 1860), p. 13. The twelve feasts.

becomes our true benefactor. This thought, though inarticulate, runs through Russian life : it is the mystery of the spiritual Body.

Bukharev protested when " lofty " names alone were applied to Christ. He pointed out that His true image is better shown in " everyday language : a workman, a carpenter. . . . There is no scandal [in such language. Moreover] He accepted Himself the scandal of the cross." [99] On the contrary, it could help people to approach Him. It could help in political discussion as well. And he addresses the workmen as men whose lot was " so greatly blessed by the condescension to it of the Lord. It is not in vain that He was called a carpenter." [100] He insisted on this image of the unique Workman. Certainly such approach is far from solving any class or economic problem. Bukharev was not concerned with it, and it would be strange to ask a man of his epoch and environment to deal with such questions. He was much more afraid of the hostile attitude of many towards the men who struggled for justice in this field and, accusing the Church of inactivity, joined the ranks of unbelievers. Bukharev exhorted the faithful not to reject them but " to descend sacrificially down to their level, so that before the heavenly Father the believer could become in Christ as though equal to the unbelievers or the erring ones and, in this way, to support them during the period of their ignorance or fault, by the grace of the merciful condescension of God." [101]

The same spirit has to be manifested in all our activities, especially in teaching, namely in religious teaching; and, to denounce evil, we should also use the mode and disposition expressed in Phil. ii. 6 as well as we should remember the essential denial of evil which is in the cross of the One who suffered for all " beginning from Adam and finishing with Antichrist." [102]

The moral and the theological thinking of Bukharev are closely interwoven. The one Christ is both divine and human.

[99] A. M. Bukharev, *On modern spiritual needs,* etc., pp. 343, 344, 345.
[100] *Ibid.,* pp. 48, 343.
[101] *Ibid.,* p. 486 (concerning populists and workmen).
[102] *Ibid.,* p. 621.

Each act of His has eternal value. The reality of His temptation is emphasized, though Bukharev has no original interpretation of it.[103] (False messiahship, ostentatious miracles,
worship of the prince of this world.)

More interesting is his approach to the problem of knowledge in Christ. Christ is not against knowledge in the form of
science or learning: He was Himself a baby and a child, He
developed in proportion to His age. As man, He used
ordinary human ways of observation and questioning.[104] At
the same time, like Job, who in many ways was His prophetic
image, Jesus Christ could not deny either His righteousness or
His knowledge of God (St. John viii. 55). Bukharev saw in
the humble humanity of Christ "fullness of grace and
truth." [105] Whilst on earth, Christ subjected Himself to the
conditions of the existing world and of nature. "It appears
that by His human intelligence the Lord was penetrating His
own thought which belonged to His all-creative and almighty
divinity, united in one ' Me ' with His humanity." V. Soloviev
has the same idea of the self-revelation of the Logos. Now
for Bukharev—and here is his constant trait—all aspects of
earthly existence of the Lord must have an eternal, redemptive
meaning. With regard to knowledge and thought, he points
out that " the Lamb bore also the guilt of our erring thought
. . . emptying Himself for us not only up to the unconscious
state, according to His humanity, in the womb of His holy
Mother; up to the subjection to conditions of progressive
advance in wisdom [He, Wisdom Himself!]—up to human
ignorance of objects . . . up to death, up to consciousness of
some inscrutable abandonment by His consubstantial Father.
. . . And to such a spiritual nothing, deeper even than a
nothing, was emptying Himself the Lord who knew Himself
to be the foundation of the universal existence. It is just as
if we said that in Him, in His annihilation for all sins met in

---

[103] Archim. Theodor, *Orthodoxy in relation to the modern world,*
p. 148.
[104] A. M. Bukharev, *On modern needs,* etc., p. 265 ; cf. note 3.
[105] Archim. Theodor, *Job the longsufferer,* p. 63 ; cf. also *Orthodoxy
in relation,* etc., pp. 43–5.

spiritual mystery the *being* and the *non-being,* entering in one another in the unity of his Ego." [106]

Similar insistence was in the book on the Apocalypse: " Christ made human intelligence His own and He died for the sins of knowledge no less than for all other human sins." [107]

It is not necessary to ascribe to Bukharev a systematic kenotic doctrine. But, when M. M. Tareev reproaches him for having not pointed out Christ's subjection to the laws of human nature,[108] one has to remember many a reference to it in Bukharev's writings. And each time he underlines the self-emptying of the Lamb and the continuing action of His grace condescending " to the needs and infirmities of our earthly life, even of the physical life." [109]   In fact, the whole system of Bukharev holds together just because he believes in the redemption of the universe through the coming down of the Lord and His Incarnation.

The same is felt in his triumphant feeling of man's participation in Christ's glory: " He brought us into the delights of the fullness of divine life ";[110] and elsewhere : " the Lord Himself condescended to become an offering [victim] and a servant on behalf of men, that they may become communicants of His filial, free and active Spirit." [111]

The Spirit is acting in the life of the Church, but " the Omnipresent comes down to our limitations through His gracious indwelling in the temple not in order that we limit our service to Him by the churches only, but just that we, using the grace of the temple, may elevate ourselves to the constant feeling of His omnipresence and to His service in all places and in each occupation." [112]   This grace flowing over, embracing all life, means for Bukharev the education of men to the continual ministry so that " each Orthodox may enter

---

[106] Archim. Theodor, *Orthodoxy in relation,* etc., pp. 45, 46. Enchurchment of life.
[107] *On the book of Revelation,* p. 67.
[108] M. M. Tareev, *Foundations of Christianity,* t. IV, p. 325.
[109] Archim. Theodor, *Orthodoxy in relation,* etc., p. 12 ; cf. A. M. Bukharev, *On modern spiritual needs,* etc., p. 34.
[110] Archim. Theodor, *ibid.,* p. 34.   Enchurchment of life.
[111] A. M. Bukharev, *On modern spiritual needs,* etc., p. 597.
[112] *Ibid.,* p. 86 (speaking on prayer in the Church).

into the life of priesthood "—not of ecclesiastical functions, of course.[113] And because Christ came on earth, all " holy things " are to be, as it were, re-established, " put on earth." [114] One can only feel surprised when M. M. Tareev finds such penetration of life by the religious element pregnant " of the logical danger of papism " :[115] nothing is farther from Bukharev. On the contrary, it was a true contribution that Bukharev should have a vision of the whole life sanctified and organically living within the Church.[116]

The theological contribution of Bukharev was not understood by Tareev though he praised the man and the integrity of his ideas sealed by his life. V. Soloviev never mentioned him at all, though it seems unlikely that being himself a student of the Moscow Academy, he did not hear of the tragic archimandrite. S. N. Bulgakov had for him sympathetic words but omitted to refer to him in his theology. As for the secular world, for the sake of which Bukharev left his monastery, it did not hear his voice and did not realize that he was suffering in order to redeem and to unite with Christ the secular thought and art so often suspected by the clergy as an enemy. Besides this move towards the unity between the ecclesiastical and the secular worlds, Bukharev deserves our attention as one who discerned behind the golden icons of Christ the Almighty holding the world, the humiliated Son of God. None of the Russian writers on kenosis had questioned the divinity of Christ. There was in the country an opposite tendency of falling into other-worldliness in doctrine and in everyday life. If in the sixteenth century the foolishness of Basil the innocent counterbalanced the future growth of the idea of " the third Rome," it was important that in the nineteenth century the thought of the self-emptying and humiliation of Christ should emphasize Christ's true humanity and bring closer to us the reality of the Gospels and of the Creed.

[113] Archim. Theodor, *Orthodoxy in relation,* etc., p. 214. The Gospels read during the " tsarskie molebni "—prayer services. Cf. also *On the book of Revelation,* p. 85.
[114] *Ibid., Orthodoxy,* etc., p. 67.
[115] Tareev, *Foundations,* etc., t. IV, p. 333.
[116] G. Florovsky recognizes Bukharev's merit in this desire " to enchurch " life, p. 347.

CHAPTER V

DOCTRINAL WRITINGS ON THE KENOSIS

WE have already seen that the idea of the self-emptying of Christ was not totally absent from the Russian theological thinkers. With the writers of the *fin de siècle* it finds its metaphysical expression in the philosopher and poet, V. Soloviev, it is treated mainly from the Gospel portrait by another layman, Professor M. M. Tareev, and finally it is expounded from the standpoint of the Trinitarian dogma by S. N. Bulgakov, priest at the time when he wrote his theological treatises but who had before this the training and activity of a lay scholar. It is interesting for us to notice these biographical features, as they prove once more how closely were interwoven in Russia secular and religious thought or, even more exactly, how religious thought was helped by the work of laymen. " Russian religious philosophy in fact works out the subjects raised by Russian literature." [1] In this case not only philosophy but theology seems to give its final expression to an intuition felt by the writers of fiction. We shall see that the thinkers whom we shall study, even when working in the field of technical theology, still recognize their link with the artistic production of the nineteenth century and their debt to it. At the same time, all of them not only have a good knowledge of the Western philosophical and theological thought (as did many among those whom we studied previously) but they used Western sources and, in particular, they considered the doctrine of kenosis as a contribution of the Protestant world even though they themselves had a different approach to this doctrine.

This last remark does not concern Vladimir Soloviev. He did not mention the kenotic writers and his attention was

---

[1] N. Berdyaeff, *The Russian religious thought of the nineteenth century,* p. 335.

attracted by Rome rather than by the Protestant world.[2] It is not altogether without hesitation that we deal with him in this chapter. He cannot be regarded as a theologian in the technical sense of the word, though already a philosopher, and besides his manifold reading he consecrated a year to systematic study in theology and even spent this year as a student of the Moscow Theological Academy. We allowed ourselves to range him among the theologians because his system has definite references to Phil. ii. 5—11 and also because of the undoubted influence he had on S. N. Bulgakov. It is true that Soloviev, whom we have already mentioned as poet and as publicist, was so complex a personality that he should be hardly classified in any definite group. His rich and attractive person, his solid erudition, his intuition as a poet, his mastery of philosophic thought and the big systematic works left by him give him a place apart among his contemporaries. We can give here only very scanty information about the different fields he worked in so as to make it clearer what place and proportion is given by him to the thought on kenosis.

V. Soloviev went through a period of atheism almost as a boy. Spinoza's philosophy brought him back to God. From the age of nineteen onwards Soloviev becomes a believing Christian. Unity is the key-word for all his thought and life and it is important never to forget it when reading his works. Even the titles of his first works: *The Crisis of Western Philosophy* (1875), *Three Powers* and *Philosophical Principles of Integral Knowledge* (between 1874-7) express already this craving for integral philosophy. In this he was the true follower of Ivan Kireevsky, who had no opportunity to work out his ideas which found resonance and a brilliant development in Soloviev's idea of "free theosophy"—synthesis of mystical, scientific and philosophical knowledge. The topical

[2] It is out of place here to enter into the relation of Soloviev to Rome or to Protestantism. We must only make it clear that his thought was nourished by German philosophy and German mysticism. Rome, as an organization, corresponded to his idea of unity but had no intellectual influence on him. He spoke of his "religion of the Holy Spirit" and said to a friend, "I am regarded as a Catholic, but I am much more of a Protestant." C. V. Mochulsky, *V. Soloviev, Life and teaching* (Paris, 1936), pp. 209, 217.

writings of this period are also connected with the Slavophil movement; Soloviev breaks with the Slavophils only in 1881 Division of a life and work into periods is always somehow artificial; but, for the sake of convenience, one usually divides the activities of Soloviev.[3] The early period of philosophy (the above mentioned and the famous *Lectures on Godmanhood,* 1877–81); the religious and ecclesiastical problems (including *Spiritual Foundations of Life,* 1882–4 and *The History and Future of Theocracy,* 1885–7); politics, national problem, universal problem (*L'Idée Russe,* 1888, *La Russie et l'Eglise Universelle,* 1889, etc); period of poetic production; return to philosophy (*The Justification of the Good,* 1897–9); problems of ethics and æsthetics and, finally, problems of eschatology (*Three Conversations on War, Progress and the End of Human History* and *The Story of Antichrist,* 1899–1900). From 1875 onwards Soloviev lectured in Moscow and Petersburg Universities, with interruptions, intervals and finally complete prohibition of lecturing in 1881. In between took place journeys in Western Europe, contact with the Roman Catholic world and mystical visions to which we shall refer later on. A man who consecrated his life to the study of ecclesiastical and religious problems, Soloviev was not a very practising Orthodox. He attended, for instance, the Easter-night service of the Orthodox Church in Baden-Baden in 1887 and, for the first time in his life, he stayed until the end of this service. In 1896 he joined secretly the Church of Rome: he always defended the formal point of view according to which there was never any schism between Rome and Russia. When dying, he confessed to an Orthodox priest, received from him the last Sacrament and in this manner, fantastic for some, prophetic for others, he ended his days having as it were united in his person the two divided Churches.

Apologist of learning, culture and beauty, Soloviev in his personal life showed some " kenotic " features. For himself, he has chosen a life of poverty. He worked very hard, day and night, and distributed all his earnings. His generosity

[3] We follow here C. Mochulsky's scheme.

was almost legendary. He never inquired whether the person was in real need and helped even when he was convinced of fraud. Pity, compassion, which occupied such place in his writings, was not a mere theory with him. Another personal trait, which we have met already in many a Russian writer of the nineteenth century, was his attitude towards the penalty of death. In 1881, after the murder of Alexander II, in a largely attended public speech Soloviev expressed the hope that the new Tsar would forgive the assassins of his father. This speech was a parallel to Tolstoy's letter, though for Soloviev it had a different meaning. He was a convinced monarchist; according to him the Tsar should be a perfect Christian in order to embody, in accordance with the Pontiff and the Prophet, the ideal of theocracy.

The name of Soloviev is usually associated with his ideas about Sophia. We only mention this intuition of his outside our competence and our direct subject. We can only ask whether the three visions of Sophia which determined the life and thought of Soloviev could not account for the kenotic element in his writings as well. Sophia revealing herself might have been for him the revelation of the divine world in its condescension, in its movement down towards men and the world. We know how Soloviev insisted on the representation of the divine world coming down, acting upon man, waking in him a response—desire of knowledge and creation. For him the whole life, man and nature, was involved in this process of condescension of the ideal world towards the natural and the Incarnation therein whilst, in its turn, the natural world was regarded as attracted by the ideal world and tending towards unity with it. Sophia, belonging to the divine world as idea about the universe (idea for Soloviev is reality), becomes thus, in God, an ideal humanity, a plurality brought to unity; she is at the same time the soul of the universe, and even in the fallen world she remains ideal mankind. Sophia was often defined by Soloviev as the image of the Eternal Feminine; in other cases he did not insist upon this ambiguous definition and, instead of ascribing to Sophia separate existence he identified her, as Wisdom, with the Logos. In this case, he would say that the Word, or Logos, or Sophia " represents the integral divine organism, both universal and individual." [4]

How then does Soloviev picture this relationship between the descending divine or ideal and the natural world? We must not expect to find here the terms of the Scriptures. Soloviev will speak of the Trinity and emphasize the triune character of almost all the phenomena of life and thought; but he will rather speak of the " divine principle " than of God the Father. We do not want to suggest by this that his God was not the God of Jesus Christ. His God is a personal God; he thought of the Absolute Principle as a Being, thus overcoming pantheism and re-emphasizing his idea of unity. We must understand in this way his vocabulary and remember that, to a great extent, Plato and the Apologists with the doctrine of the Logos could be counted among his spiritual ancestors. Let us notice by the way the interesting manner in which Soloviev illustrates the idea of the Holy Trinity. He takes the analogy from man in the process of self-cognition. There are three intermittent moments : we as integral subject, we as revealing ourselves and we as consciousness of a self reflecting upon our subject and its self-revelation in the unity of this process. In the One Absolute Being, instead of the three successive experiences, there are three eternal experiences or three eternal subjects (hypostases).

Soloviev spoke of the relation of the divine and the natural world in terms of " godmanhood " or " god-manly process." He means by it (and with him other Russian thinkers) not only Christ in His two natures, not even redeemed mankind as a whole united to Christ. The term surpasses the regions of anthropology; it means the divinization of the whole cosmos as well. Godmanhood, as it were, " is not only the end of all evolution but also the very law of this evolution." [5] It consists of three elements : nature as material of life and consciousness, divine principle as the aim and the content to be

---

[4] V. Soloviev, *Works,* 10 vols. (SPB. 1896), second ed., t. III, p. 94, Lectures on Godmanhood.
[5] C. V. Mochulsky, *Soloviev,* p. 135.

discovered and human personality as the subject of life and consciousness.[6]

The cosmic and historic process of penetration of all by the divine element reveals itself as *self-denial*. The cosmic reason meets and fights the chaotic state of nature or the world's soul. It seeks elements capable of response. In nature, such element is beauty. Among mankind it is love which, in its intuition, reveals to an individual the true ideal (real) image of the other person. In human society it is art which tends to represent an object in the light of the future world and in its final form or state. The whole process can develop only in freedom. The unity between the descending divine world and the creation striving towards it can be only the result of free response. On the physical plane, the principle of unity is expressed in magnetic force, in light and in organic life. In natural humanity it works through the unity of race, illuminating men with the light of reason, penetrating them and finally producing a spiritual man. Soloviev gives here an important definition of the true spiritual man. It is, according to him, a person (a) in whom could be united the divine and the natural principles; (b) in whom one could actually know the presence of both these natures and (c) in whom the human will would freely participate with the divine principle so as to make the concordance or harmony of the two natures within this spiritual, "godmanly" person a truly free act. In the plane of reality all this was embodied in the Person of Christ.

Before speaking of the historical Christ, Soloviev relates the premundane act of kenosis. The divine Logos "by the free act of His divine will or love renounces the manifestation of His divine dignity (divine glory); He abandons the peace of eternity, He engages in battle with the principle of evil and He becomes liable to all the agitations of the cosmic process. He appears in chains of external existence, in limitations of space and time; He then appears to the natural man, acting upon Him in diverse finite forms of the cosmic life which hide

---

[6] Some translations use the term "theandric." We avoid it because the meaning given to "godmanhood" by Russian thinkers is larger, and also because we think this term might be confusing in relation to the Person of Christ being associated with definite Christological discussions.

rather than they reveal the true substance of God." Men on
their side strive towards new perceptions of the divine world
and show it by their dissatisfaction with life in its imperfect
temporal forms. The self-denial as presented in this first
contact is not yet complete : for Deity, the limitations which,
in the historical or cosmical order, enshrine theophanies are
but exterior limitations, whereas in the natural man craving
for perfection is an instinctive rather than a deliberate process.
The kenosis becomes complete only in the Person of Godman.
In him—to quote Soloviev's not very happy term—the divine
principle " actually descends, humbles itself, takes the form of
a servant. . . . The divine principle is no longer hidden, as in
previous incomplete theophanies, by the limitations of a passive
human consciousness : it [or rather, he, the Logos] accepts
these limitations : not that it wholly enters into the limits of
natural consciousness, which is impossible, but it actually *feels*
these limitations as *being its own at the present moment*. This
self-limitation of divinity in Christ sets His humanity free; it
allows to His natural will a free renunciation in favour of the
divine principle, not as exterior force (such renunciation would
not be a free one) but as an inward good. Christ as God freely
renounces the divine glory and thus, as man, He receives the
possibility of achieving divine glory." [7]

Two kenotic moments are noticed by Soloviev in the Christ
of the Gospel's narrative : the temptation of Christ and His
obedience.

The temptation of Christ is the very consequence of the
union in Him of the two natures. The consciousness of His
divine nature and that of the limitations of a natural
existence might have induced Him to make His divine power
a means for the achievement of something demanded by the
state of limitation. For instance, He could make material
welfare the aim and divine power a means to obtain it (bread,
temptation of the flesh). The divine power could also help in
the affirmation of the human personality (" if Thou art the
Son "—sin of the reason, pride). Finally, when these lower
temptations were eliminated there rose the last, the strongest

[7] Soloviev, *Lectures on Godmanhood*, t. III, pp. 167–71.

and worst of all : that of using divine power as violence, even in the name of establishing good.   To use divine power for such an aim would be an actual recognition of evil as the main power of the world or, in other words, it would be worship of the principle of evil.[8]

The spiritual victory of Christ had to be completed and expressed in His natural, bodily life as well.   He gained this victory through the hardships of His earthly life and, most particularly, when on the cross, having taken upon Himself all human weakness, sin, suffering and death, Christ did no more call God, as He usually did, " Father " but He cried together with all the groaning creation, " My God, My God."

The death on the cross was the last and most perfect expression of the obedience of the Son of God.   The kenotic terms were used by Soloviev not only in relation to the pre-existent Logos and to the Christ of history but also to Christ after His ascension.   His obedience and humiliation are made clear in that " all His destiny is from above, not from below." He said in St. Matt. xxviii. 16—20 that all power is given to Him—it was not robbed by Him (Phil. ii. 6—8).[9]   The power understood as force based on right, Christ receives because all right belongs to Him.   Right is confirmed by merit, and " Alone the Godman who has life in Himself and yet gives His soul for the world, satisfies the conditions of true merit. His obedience has absolute value because for Him [right] is not an acquisition but humiliation and sacrifice " (Phil. ii. 6, 7).[10]

Let us examine now how the kenotic idea is applied by Soloviev to the Church which for him is the expression of Godmanhood and which he regards as the Body of Christ; " body " being for him not a metaphor but a metaphysical formula.

[8] It may be of interest to notice that the problem of temptation is raised by Soloviev and by Dostoevsky. It seems to us superfluous to guess whether it was Dostoevsky who influenced the young philosopher or vice versa.   But they went together on a pilgrimage to Optina in 1879 when Dostoevsky was already making notes for the Karamazovs. See *Materials on Dostoevsky,* ed. by N. S. Dolinin, Academy U.S.S.R. (Leningrad, 1935).

[9] Soloviev, *History and future of theocracy* (1887), t. IV, p. 608.

[10] *Ibid.,* p. 619.

The earthly existence of the Church corresponds, according to Soloviev, to the earthly life of Jesus Christ. The " revelation and glory of the sons of God " becomes the task of the godmanly unity, the free theocracy, the Church Universal growing into the fullness of the stature of Christ. Soloviev did not escape the schemes of his countrymen : he generalized also on the East-and-West problem, especially in the period of his friendship with the Slavophils. He would say that the West with its emphasis on empirical knowledge and its economic socialism was under the temptation of the flesh. Historically, Rome has sinned by violence and Protestantism by the pride of reason. The East preserved the truth of Christ, but the Eastern Church failed to create a Christian culture and thus allowed the permeation of dualism. The West, at its best, represents the human element; the East, at its best, is bearer of the divine idea. Faithful to his idea of the godmanly process of unity, Soloviev expressed the hope that the two branches of the Church should unite and give birth to true spiritual mankind. The utopia of Free Theocracy is constructed as follows : the fullness of time must be fulfilled in the life of the Church through three different phases which must not replace but complete each other. The future of the Church is already existent and expressed in *Prophets*. " Her past is represented by *Priesthood*, by spiritual fathers united in one father, the universal High Priest [the Pope]. . . . The present of the Church is in her people, her state, her *Kingdom* " [Russian monarchy].[11] The branches of the Church should follow the descendant of the kingly race of David who came to be baptized from John. Himself sinless, He did not subject Himself to John as prophet of repentance, but as the descendant of the seed of Aaron, as representative of true Old Testament high-priesthood.[12] The historical inconsistency of this construction is obvious. More important for us is the kenotic principle laid as foundation of the future reunion of the Churches : it is expressed in terms of obedience and humility.

[11] Soloviev, *History and future of theocracy*, pp. 258, 259.
[12] There was a tradition in the Church of Russia according to which Zacharias was regarded to have been a High Priest.

" The principle of obedience to God-established authority defines the Church as a real form of society. It is the first beginning of new mankind. . . . Obedience or renunciation of one's will is not yet moral perfection but without it one cannot reach perfection; it is the first condition of perfection and the beginning of true religion." [13]   The importance of obedience was shown by the prescriptions of the Old Covenant; now, far from being abolished, it is confirmed and connected with principles of grace and free charity. " Obedience is demanded by the living authority" of the Incarnate who emptied Himself and humbled Himself according to Phil. ii. 5—9. [14]   The practical conclusion of this system of thought which Soloviev came to was his recognition of the primacy of Rome.

But even his Romanizing ecclesiology had a kenotic note. In *La Russie et l'Eglise Universelle* he spoke of the humility of the Pope and developed the anagram " Roma-Amor." For him, the Pope was necessary as expression of perfect humility, as true servant of the servants of God, whose love and charity attain its maximum. The heir of the universal love of Christ, the Pope should embrace everyone in his care, whilst other bishops have charge of their own flock only. The Roman primacy would be not the primacy of dominion but that of humble service, a truly kenotic primacy. It may be even that the " social " character which he appreciated in the Church of Rome was pictured by him as the expression of this spirit of service. [15]

In his ethics, Soloviev gave a large room to the feeling and practice of pity. In the triad of shame, pity or the sympathetic feeling and the feeling of reverence or of piety, compassion had to take a prominent part as a quality exercised in relation to one's fellow-men. It should take the form of true condescension in the sense of " voluntary suffering " with and for others. It would not mean a loss of one's personality

---

[13] Soloviev, *Theocracy*, p. 608.
[14] *Ibid*.
[15] Soloviev's emphasis on " social Christianity " of the West reminds one of similar ideas of Chaadaev. But Soloviev read him only after his own evolution towards Rome. See *Letters* (SPB. 1911), t. III, p. 29 to the Rev. Martinov in 1878. Newman is also mentioned in this letter.

in complete identification of ourselves with others, which is impossible and would be a denial not only of our own personality but also of that of the other person who suffers.[16] Compassion, as the whole of life, is rooted in the essential unity of the universe and it was expressed to its utmost in Christ.   Soloviev, who was interested in the cosmic, social, collective aspect of life more than in the individual one, spoke of the State also as of an " organized compassion."

The Spiritual Foundations of life carried on the analogy of the earthly life of Jesus with that of mankind.   Originally created in the divine image, fallen humanity had now to " re-establish its life among natural phenomena and to regain through labour and suffering what remained in the plane of eternity : its inner union with God and with nature." [17] Christ, the active principle of this unity, helps mankind to find its way back.   Subjecting Himself to the laws of external existence He, the centre of eternity, becomes the centre of history.   Here Soloviev repeated his kenotic assertions from the Lectures on Godmanhood.   Among temptations of mankind he particularly notices that of pride—pride of reason.   Though Truth as such is illimitable, our reason insisting on its own assertions is limited and even becomes separated from Truth.   " It can and must *become conscious* of its limitations and humble itself before the unlimited Divine Reason so as to be able, turning from itself towards the Truth, to become transparent for the divine light." [18]

Truth bows down ; it needs men as object of its revelation. " The causes of everything are in heaven, here on earth is their reflection."   Our earthly Ego, only a shadow of our heavenly existence, strives after false independence and separateness ; it reverses the natural order and revolts against Truth.   This is why Truth appears in this realm of rebellious shadows so as to humble them by the power of its own humility.   " He took the form of a servant, He was like man." This appearance of God-man re-establishes monarchy in heaven and earth. The distinction between the world from above and that from below is thus

[16] Soloviev, *The Justification of the Good*, t. VIII, pp. 85–101.
[17] *Ibid., Spiritual Foundations of Life, Works*, t. III, p. 366.
[18] *Ibid.*, p. 330.

overcome. It remains to mankind to strive after the final victory where there will be no more authority and power but all and everything will shine with evident and living Truth.[19]

This system allows M. Tareev to criticize it saying that for Soloviev " the Kingdom of God is a philosophico-humanitarian notion or else humanitarian and universalistic."[20] The remark has some justification, but one should not forget that the final criterion proposed by Soloviev in his ethics, for both society and individual, was the question : Would I have done it in the presence of Christ?

We repeat that, though Soloviev was not a systematic theologian, he interested us because he spoke of the self-emptying of the divine Logos; he showed the reality of the full human nature of Christ. Christ being the centre of cosmical, historical and redeeming process, His kenosis becomes thus the basic act of this " godmanly process." His humility, obedience and meekness are proposed as examples for individual morality. Obedience is given even a larger space and is shown to be the true nature of all power and authority. It is applied to organization of human society and, most particularly, it finds its expression in the Church in the character of true priesthood and in the principle of ecclesiastical authority. Knowing what an important part was given by Soloviev to the problem of the Church, one realizes how important it was that he took as his reference no other text than Phil. ii.

It is difficult to find a field of thought in the following years which was not influenced or inspired by Soloviev. The Psychological Society becomes in 1907 " Religio-Philosophical Society of V. Soloviev." The development of problems of Christian humanitarianism and Christian anthropology goes back to him. The cosmological problem and the teaching about Sophia found a great following not only in theologians as P. A. Florensky and S. N. Bulgakov but most emphatically in the poets of the twentieth century. His assertion of earthly

---

[19] Soloviev, *History and future of theocracy*, p. 622.
[20] M. M. Tareev, *Foundations of Christianity*, t. IV, p. 361. Speaking of Soloviev in connection with freedom or criticizing his ideas of the Kingdom of God or of the Church, Tareev keeps silent about the kenotic hints in Soloviev.

phenomena as reflection of the divine realities, together with Goethe's " *alles Vergänliche ist nur ein Gleichniss* " and the French Symbolists gave rise to the Symbolist movement, a true revival of Russian poetry. It was Soloviev who discovered in Tyutchev the " poet of chaos "—chaos redeemed and trans-figured for both of them through Christ. We know that Tyutchev's Christ was " the King of heaven in the form of a servant." We think it appropriate to finish this sketch of Soloviev's by pointing to this link which he forms as poet and critic, between the secular world of the nineteenth century and the poetic and theological revival of the twentieth century.

M. M. Tareev (1866—1934) was the Professor of Moral Theology at the Moscow Theological Academy. Though we enter with him the twentieth century, the technical difficulties do not vanish. *Temptation of the Godman,* his thesis pub-lished in 1892, does not exist in libraries available to us. It is true the subject is repeated and reworked in the *Foundations of Christianity* (1908–10). According to the author, all the unnecessary " school " element is removed, and the four volumes as they stand now express completely his whole system. There is no full biography of Tareev and no informa-tion about him after 1917, the date of his last publication. Nobody knows the destiny of his finished manuscript on the *History of Russian Theological Thought.* We learn from a few scattered articles that in 1908 Tareev's orthodoxy was suspected and he had to face an ecclesiastical commission. His answers were found satisfactory, but the atmosphere of suspicion was never completely dispersed. In *Philosophy of Life* (1916), Tareev deals at length with his opponents and largely quotes them. It makes clear that the doctrine of kenosis was not among the subjects of controversy. The examination had in view Tareev's opinions on the Resurrec-tion, on tradition and on the Church. This book brings in a sore personal note: " Could I, lonely, rejected and defence-less, expect anything other [than suspicion] when I ventured to accuse society of moral atrophy? . . . My sight diminishes. My strength decreases. Heavy is God's plough for tired

hands. But firm as in the days of youth resounds in the soul
the order from above—not to care for my soul, not to treasure
my reputation." [21]

Tareev is very important for our investigation. First, he
gives to the doctrine of kenosis the place of honour and builds
all his system round the humiliation of Christ. The earthly
Jesus was especially dear to him. It was not the interest of an
historian. The works of historians and textual criticism were
used by Tareev, an up-to-date scholar, as a necessary scientific
apparatus. But it was " the fact of Christ," if one could say
so, which attracted him to the utmost. Brought up on
orthodox dogmas, he was ready to start his quest from dogmatic Christology; but he believed in the need of a philosophy
of Christological dogma which should throw light upon " the
idea of self-emptying which subjected Christ to the laws and
conditions of human existence." [22]

Another feature interesting for us lies in Tareev's attitude
towards the secular and particularly artistic thought of Russia.
He insisted on the significance of this free expression of
national religious ideal and recommended the ecclesiastical
erudite to pay attention to it : " The alliance of theology with
literature," he said, " must bear good fruit." [23]

Logically, among many artistic works which attracted his
attention he chose as the most representative, typical and best
expressing " the Russian Christ," the poem of Tyutchev which
was so often referred to by different thinkers of the Russian
nineteenth century : " Tyutchev was right when he spoke of
the King of heaven walking through Russia in the form of a
servant." [24] Almost like a Slavophil, Tareev believed in the
Christian character of his nation. He gladly recognized many
achievements of the West, both Catholic and Protestant, in
the domain of science and social life. As for Russia, however
uncivilized and " elementary " her life (in the sense of

---

[21] M. Tareev, *Philosophy of Life* (M. 1916), pp. 301, 302 ; on the
controversy, pp. 149–302.
[22] *Ibid., Foundations of Christianity,* 4 vols. (M. 1910), t. I, p. 7,
Christ.
[23] *Ibid.,* t. II, p. 13, the Gospels.
[24] *Ibid.,* t. III, p. 318, Ecclesiastical history of Christian nations.

powerful, natural and chaotic), she needs chiefly and chiefly carried out " an unseen, indefatigable work, an inner, meek action." [25]   Neither the rationalistic West nor Byzantium (" intellectualism," " gnosticism ") would help her to achieve her task but an innate Russian faith " in a God's man, suffering and humiliated, together with the conviction that Christian beatitude is independent of conditions of external welfare and visible perfection." [26]

The brilliant theological literature of the West, with its valuable results in the fields of philology, exegesis, history, etc. is the opposite of what there is in Russia.   " Poor and insignificant is our literature (in the fields mentioned); but on the contrary the problem of the very nature of Christianity is faced in all its depth." [27]   Tareev illustrates this bold statement not from the writings of the theologians (he mentions Bukharev alone) but from novelists and poets.   He does not bring in " kenotic " characters.   It is impossible that he had not detected them.   The most reasonable explanation is that he aimed to find out not the " kenotic " but the " free and harmonious " Russian Christian type.   He sees it in Zossima and his pupil Aliosha.   With great reverence and devotion he speaks of the secular literature of his country, " work of truthful, pensive genius, kindled with compassion for all the toiling and humble." [28]   He reproaches Soloviev for ascribing to the Church what was done by literature and a few statesmen : the abolition of serfdom.

Tareev was typical of the moralist school.   He would almost reject both Christian history and the doctrinal statements.   It is surprising that he, himself a thinker, failed to see the true place of doctrine and was ready to consider it " a burden " or a screen hiding the reality of the Gospels.   The actual conditions in which he had to work make it more understandable.[29]

[25] M. Tareev, *Foundations*, etc., t. IV, p. 143.
[26] *Ibid.*, t. III, pp. 317, 318, Ecclesiastical history of Christian nations.
[27] *Ibid.*, t. IV, p. 195, Christian problem and Russian religious thought.
[28] *Ibid.*, *Foundations*, etc., t. IV, p. 7, Types of religious and moral life.
[29] V. Soloviev, *Letters*, ed. E. L. Radlov (SPB. 1911), t. III, p. 19, to the Rev. Martinov, 31/1/1887 : " The expression Godman Christ is crossed out by the ecclesiastical censor ; he puts instead ' the Son of God.' "

Tareev recognized for tradition an importance of fact, not of principle. The dogmas, important in the life of the Church, seem to him less important for Christianity itself. He called men " back from the fathers " to the Gospels. In spite of his intention, this " return " was not so much the return towards the Gospels as an investigation into the inner logic, laws and spirit of a " philosophy of evangelical history." Paradoxically, this very man gave the first doctrinal exposition of the kenosis with reference to patristic thought. This was necessary in order to decline a possible accusation of modernism. The repeated endeavours of Tareev to affirm his orthodoxy prove that his intention was not to break with the Church, however poor his conception of the Church.

The Church was almost reduced by Tareev to a something answering to the practical purposes and needs of people : " ecclesiastical administration, the creed and rites of worship." [30]   He does not seem to distinguish between rites and sacraments. The organic conception of the Church is alien to him. He only admits that personal Christianity and the Church meet in the religious and ethical basis of the Church and also that not a personal religion but the Church " sanctifies nature and the world," as a cultural and historical factor.[31]   His view was a denial of the exterior authority of the Church, who could teach or oppose " only by the witness of martyrdom, by disgrace of exile and slander. . . . She cannot conquer the world in the Christian spirit unless by the victory of meekness. . . . The true society of the disciples of Christ is the society of the servants of the world." [32]

This view of the Church corresponded logically to the method of Tareev which he regarded as his original contribution. Religion was, according to him " an inward value and could be discerned only immanently, through affinity in the creation itself," religious or artistic.[33]   This method shows

It is forbidden to speak of the theophanies of the Old Testament ; it is forbidden to quote biblical texts otherwise than in the translation of the Synod, etc., etc." Partial as Soloviev could often be, he hardly exaggerates in this particular instance.

[30] M. M. Tareev, *Foundations,* etc., t. IV, p. 104, Flesh and spirit.
[31] *Ibid.,* t. III, p. 130, Church, nature and the world.
[32] *Ibid.,* t. II, p. 30, the Kingdom.
[33] *Ibid.,* t. II, p. 13, the Gospels.

also why he gave such a large place to the works of art : an
artistic intuition may at times gain a deeper insight than any
authoritative statements or beliefs based on such statements.
Tareev believed in a spiritual science as " teaching about
Christian experience as historical fact and personal feeling." [34]
He gave large space to intuition. In the writings of his last
period he goes so far as to say that " the only interpreter of
the intimate content of Christ's teaching is the believer
himself." [35]   Had he ever considered that such method can,
and does, create too many Christs, projections of human per-
sonalities and not necessarily of the highest type? Mysticism
was disliked by him no less than intellectualism. But, by
applying his subjective method to religious and ethical
philosophy, he expected to create a " mysticism of consciousness . . . a particuar direction of spiritual thought, a particular type of philosophy which has almost no past and to
which belongs the future." [36] This would be a " philosophy of
the heart " which he unjustifiably generalizes as the Russian
philosophy. Tareev wrote abundantly on the subject, eager
that his method should gain recognition. One feels, though
he does not express it definitely, that he thinks of religion in
terms of value.

Tareev did not hesitate to divide existence into two spheres :
that of religious experience and that of empirical life. He did
it purposely and even saw in this his vocation as writer and
theologian : " Consciously, I drew a border line between
evangelical purity in spiritually-absolute personal religion and
the conditionally-social life." [37]   The Gospels, according to
him, were meant for elect persons and not for the definition
of forms of life. The attempt " to put Christianity at the service of practical interests of life means a temptation to
blasphemy." [38]   A Christian could not be indifferent to the
needs and sufferings of his fellow-men but it does not belong

---

[34] M. M. Tareev, *Philosophy of Life* (M. 1916), p. 68.
[35] *Ibid.*, p. 100.
[36] *Ibid.*, *Christian Philosophy* (M. 1917), pp. 47, 126 (New theology).
[37] *Ibid.*, *Foundations*, etc., t. IV, p. 389, Theory of Christian freedom.
[38] *Ibid.*, *Philosophy of Life*, p. 124.

to him to elaborate systems of social salvation. We shall see this point worked out in the ethical system of Tareev.

Tareev, as we have already mentioned, gave an historico-doctrinal account of kenosis. He examined the early fathers, up to John Damascene. This part of his work is not original: he follows A. B. Bruce's *The humiliation of Christ,* adding to the survey the names of Sophronius of Jerusalem and of Agathon of Rome. In the first edition of his thesis he referred also to modern kenotic writers. Once more, we regret not having found this book.

Kenosis in the speculative Christology was for Tareev of meagre interest. He was not a dogmatist. In fact, after having asserted that the dogmas " hide " the Gospels, he politely went back to explain that " in its essence dogmatic Christology brings our thought back to the fact of the Gospels and leads our hearts to the living Christ. Such a meaning has for us the apostolico-patristic thought about the self-emptying of Christ, found in germ in the Christology of the Church but not included in dogmatic formulas." [39]

Tareev does not doubt the divinity of Christ. Roughly speaking, the Russian kenotic thought as a whole could be compared to that of the Western theologians as the Alexandrian school in relation to the Antiochene. In fact, even Tareev's chief authority is St. Cyril of Alexandria who, according to our author, suffered only from inexactitude of technical vocabulary. Nothing is said about St. Cyril's division of Christ's acts into those of God and those of man. At the same time, a silent footnote sends the reader to Bruce's p. 55—the very page where St. Cyril's views are qualified as " doketic in the intellectual region. . . ." However, it was to Tareev's true merit that he tried to revive patristic thought and to bring it home. An important problem was raised and answered in the language of modern thought. Tareev was the first to expound systematically both the self-emptying of the Son of God and the humiliation of Christ.

The kenosis begins, according to Tareev, long before the Incarnation. There was in Bukharev already a foreboding of

[39] M. M. Tareev, *Foundations,* etc., t. I, p. 7, Christ.

this thought: creation as a kenotic act. Let us hear how Tareev puts it: "Having created the world, God revealed His life in conditions of creaturely limitations and, in particular having created man, He revealed His almightiness and omniscience under a form of conditional consciousness and of gradual development: all this presupposes His self-limitation. Limiting Himself in His love for man, God reveals His glory not only in Himself but for the other and through the other and thus gains this other, the man . . . makes him bearer of His glory." [40] There must be a response on the part of man, self-denial of man who should feel God's glory as his own.

This first kenotic act is not to be confounded with the Incarnation and the earthly humility of Jesus. "We distinguish the self-limitation of God as a condition of creation, and the generation of the Son of God as a *condition* of Godmanly temptation, from self-limitation as redemptive act (" podvig ") of the earthly life of Christ. What in the self-limitation of God was a passionless act of divine love—was in the Godmanly act (" podvig ") of the Incarnate Son of God an act (" delo ") of struggle and victory. God in His love to man eternally desires his salvation, and consequently eternally desires His self-limitation for the sake of man. The Son of God personally—as one with the Father—desires also both the salvation of man and the self-limitation of God: My meat is to do the will . . ." [41] It will be explained later on what is meant by temptation.

The true divine life is called in the Holy Scriptures the divine glory, and Christ possessed it in His Father and revealed it to men; but the way, the mode in which the revelation of divine life was manifest in Him, was His self-emptying. Whether one thinks of the doctrinal " how " of the Incarnation or whether one meditates on the historical life and character of Jesus, one meets self-emptying and humiliation. The whole scheme of kenosis, humiliation and glorification of Christ is represented by Tareev in terms faithful to the Gospels:

[40] M. M. Tareev, *Foundations*, etc., t. III, p. 164, First temptation of men.
[41] *Ibid., Foundations*, etc., t. III, pp. 229, 230, Temptation of Christ.

" Christ brought to men eternal life because He Himself was from above, St. John viii. 23. He was the Son of God, and in Him was revealed the life as it was with the Father, 1 John i. 2; St. John xiv. 7; 2 Tim. i. 10. Yet this life was not revealed in Christ in its divine form, but in human form (servant). The revelation in Him of His divine life was the act of His condescension, Phil. ii. 5—9. He had to live this divine life in conditions of human existence in order to give to men the spirit and to make them also sons of God; he had to take their flesh liable to suffering, Heb. ii. 10; and, that they might be born for spiritual life, He had to love them humanly, friendlily and sacrificially, St. John xiii. 34; xv. 12—14; to make them believe, He had to be the author and finisher of faith, Heb. xii. 2; to give them hope, He had to learn obedience through suffering and to be heard, Heb. v. 7, 8. Contrary to Adam who desired to become god, Gen. iii. 5, Christ, instead of joy, suffered the cross, Heb. xii. 2. Being the image of God, He did not cling to His divine glory, but He humbled Himself taking the image of a servant, becoming like man and humbling Himself He became obedient unto death, even the death of the cross, Phil. ii. 6—8. He was not seeking His own but the glory of God, St. John viii. 50; with the obedience of divine sonship He fulfilled all truth about man, St. Matt. iii. 15. In Him there was the mood or the mind or feelings which God demands from men. To the question whether the aim proposed by God to man was ever achieved, we Christians reply wholeheartedly: it is achieved in Christ, Son of God. All cosmic life, all human history has meaning, because there lived on earth Jesus Christ. And, as in His person man fulfilled what was demanded from Him by divine truth [*pravda* means justice and truth] God exalted Him and gave Him a name above all, Phil. ii. 9—11. Through Him, God gave to all men eternal life because as the Father has life in Himself, so He hath given to the Son, St. John v. 25, 26. He gave Him power over all flesh, St. John xvii. 2." The reference to Rom. v. 15—17 links the humiliation of Christ with the justification and salvation of men.[42]

[42] Tareev, Khomyakov, Bulgakov accept the same interpretation of

Soteriology, according to Tareev, is " included in the consciousness of Christ and flows out of it " : " the blessedness of
the Son of God becomes historical blessedness in the self-denial
and suffering of the Son of man ; the eternal glory of the Son
of God becomes a real [empirical] glory in the humiliation of
the Son of man," who was alone to know the religious task
involved in His acts and who brought men from the natural
world under the banner of the heavenly Father.[43] This conception differs, of course, from the Old Testament idea of
redemption and from the scholastic idea of satisfaction.

Let us see now the kenosis in evangelical history. Turning
to the earthly figure of the Lord we shall follow Tareev's order
in the exposition of the earthly story of humiliation. The historical frame is that of modern exegetes : " The acceptable
year of the Lord," the crisis and the last period of ministry.
But the whole development of the life of Jesus is examined in
the light of His consciousness. Though completely a man, He
is " not of this world," St. John xvii. 16. Lonely among men,
from childhood He is turned towards *His* Father. His consciousness of God coincides with His self-cognition not only in
acts of obedience but in real unity, St. John x. 30; xiv. 10.
Yet at the same time He distinguished Himself from the
Father as the one sent by Him, St. John viii. 16—29; xvi. 32.
Two different worlds or natures are expressed in the language
of two relations : Son of God and Son of man. The central
idea of humiliation is emphasized by the fact that Christ calls
Himself mostly " the Son of man," whilst the disciples exalt

verse 6. Khomyakov says (t. II, p. 144) : " Being the image of God He
did not think to ascribe to Himself equality with God, but He awaited
from God His destiny and glory." The interpretation given by
Khomyakov was " that the humility of Christ went so far that He even
renounced His right to consider Himself equal to God ; in other words,
in the depth of His consciousness of Himself, Jesus Christ felt Himself
in such state of exinanition that He subjected His will completely to the
will of the Father, after which he would consider the thought of equality
with the Father as a robbery." Khomyakov regarded other interpretation
of this passage " incongruous with the spirit of the epistle of St. Paul,"
as the whole epistle is an appeal to humility. Zavitnevich, *Khomyakov*
(Kiev, 1902), pp. 1389–91. For Tareev (t. I, p. 22) Christ " not only did
not commit robbery, but even did not think of it," " did not regard it as
booty." This resembles Bruce, p. 364, who reminds us that many Greek
Fathers interpreted the verse in this sense.

[43] M. M. Tareev, *Foundations,* etc., t. III, p. 91, Aim and sense of life.

Him as Christ. " The seed of woman, the Son of man is a man conscious of his limitations and therefore reposing all his hopes in God." [44]   " In His inner personal life Christ is the Son of God, whilst He ministers to men as the Son of man." [45] He Himself considered His humiliation as the love of His Father to the world, St. John iii. 16—which only underlines the voluntary character of His self-emptying. The life of Jesus is marked by " (a) continual consciousness of the will of God and (b) the consciousness of His complete fulfilment of divine will." [46]   This is, in other words, His sinlessness. The consciousness of sonship was always in Him, though " it increased in clearness and in content in relation to His spiritual growth." [47]   Tareev is not concerned with the question of modifications in human knowledge of Jesus. Recognizing His true and full humanity he logically recognizes human ignorance in Him. More important is the growth of the Godman in relation to His Father. In His growing sense of sacrifice He learned and experienced God who is love. He knew also His role and place in history : He came to fulfil the prophets. Prophecy is not external to Him, but is accomplished in Him : the suffering servant is no more an image, but a living experience.

The baptism of Jesus is interpreted as a symbolical act. It is judgment, because God approached men, and it is condescension. The waters of Jordan are, as it were, full of the sin of those baptized by John. Coming down into the river Jesus takes already, in this symbolical action, the sins of men. " So," " in this way " He had to fulfil the truth.

The temptation of Jesus is regarded by Tareev as essentially religious, " godmanly " temptation. The centre of gravity is in the problem of sonship. Put in this way, the whole question gains in insight and allows us to avoid petty discussions as to how sinlessness and temptation can be reconciled. Tareev himself considered this theory as his original contribution. There can be attraction by evil or test in sorrow. Resistance

[44] M. M. Tareev, *Foundations,* etc., t. I, p. 160, Christ.
[45] *Ibid.,* t. II, p. 293, Gospels.
[46] *Ibid.,* t. I, p. 169.
[47] *Ibid.,* t. I, p. 169.

to evil attractions brings man to moral perfection is a moral act; victory over sorrows caused by passions teaches one humility and faith—it is a religious act. The sinless Christ could not be attracted by evil; His temptation was that of *faith* and *obedience*.[48] Temptation, as described by the evangelists, was rejected by Christ's (a) humble obedience to natural laws of human life with its human limitations, (b) by His refusal to seek an evident and special divine protection,[49] and (c) by refusal to serve the malignant spirit of national pride in sense of false Messiahship.[50] But the whole temptation was even deeper than it seems. It was mainly an attack against the consciousness of His sonship. In the victory of Jesus there was a " true human act of faith in the divine sonship "—and that of a man who all His life long refused to display divine power. The mystery of the wilderness has a double aspect. Jesus " was tempted as the Incarnate only-begotten Son, clearly conscious of His sonship, as the witness of divine love sent by God on earth. In His condescension He entered the sphere of human temptations and accepted His temptation that He might become a merciful high priest. . . . But having taken our weaknesses, He was tempted like us, in infirmity of our nature. . . . The Son of God might be tempted by desiring to show His particular relation to God and to the world ; the Son of man—the very same Son of God deprived of His glory—might have been in doubts about His sonship." " The *if* means : either show thy extraordinary relation to God and men, or thou art not the Son of God."[51]

As man, Christ chose the divine will instead of bread ; whilst the Lord *manifested patience,* willing to wait that human ways and laws should be fulfilled in their natural course. As for rejection of power proposed to Him by the Evil One " by faith in the inward dignity of man veiled in his humiliation and moral filth, Christ conquered all the temptations,

---

[48] M. M. Tareev, *Foundations,* etc., t. III, p. 256.
[49] Here, resemblance to Soloviev.
[50] *Ibid.,* t. I, p. 194, Temptation in the wilderness.
[51] *Ibid.,* t. III, p. 263, Temptation of Christ.

especially the third." [52]   The divine and the natural world
were thus reconciled in Christ's consciousness (the central
soteriological moment for Tareev as we have said).

Humiliation and sonship, these are two motives running
through all the earthly story of Jesus.   His teaching and
deeds are the revelation of divine life ; in their historical form
they are the material or the mode in which He carries out His
vocation.   The miracles have for Tareev not an apologetic
value in the ordinary sense, but on the contrary are one more
proof of his kenotic outlook :   " reflecting symbolically the
idea of the Gospels, they are a transition from inner self-
emptying [of Christ] to His outward suffering.   Symbolizing
for the believers spiritual blessedness, they provoked His
enemies who brought Him to death.[53]   Evidently the coinci-
dence of approaching and presaged suffering and of messianic
claims is not left out by Tareev.   The transfiguration is for
Jesus the true experience of divine greatness—and it will make
even more real the hours of Gethsemane.   Meanwhile the
disciples are taught not only as they were taught in the Sermon
on the Mount, but by His example of service and lowliness.
They are exhorted to condescending love, to the spirit of childhood, to poverty and disinterestedness even in spiritual life :
" do not rejoice that the spirits obey you."   They are to pass
through dishonour and to drink the cup without expecting
any glory and feeling themselves no more than unworthy
servants.   Not only have they to wash each other's feet but,
even more humbly, they have to allow the others—the Other
—to do so for them.   All this is inadmissible to the Jewish
mind ; the betrayal of Judas and the hatred of the crowd
are rooted in their disappointed hopes.   The death of Jesus
was logically unavoidable " because death alone extinguishes
last hopes of external glory, crushes all the dreams about
divine election, all hopes of divine benevolence." [54]   The
obedient acceptance of death expresses one's faith in the ulti-
mate reality and value of spiritual life.   " The soul of the Son
of God outwardly abandoned by God was left to itself and, by

[52] M. M. Tareev, *Foundations,* etc., t. III, p. 281.
[53] *Ibid.,* t. I, p. 151, Humiliation of Christ.
[54] *Ibid.,* t. II, p. 313, the Saviour.

the force of the inner creative principle of divine sonship in human life, it became for and in mankind the beginning of new spiritual life." [55] The cross on which Jesus of Nazareth rendered His spirit is visualized by Tareev as the sum of four ends : " the extreme humiliation of the Son of God and His complete outward abandonment by God; disbelief of men waiting for miracles opposed by salutary belief in the humiliated Son of God and spiritually of His eternal life." [56] Not without certain reason one suspected Tareev of reducing the resurrection to this triumph of eternal life which " receives historical flesh and blood in the hearts of the believers." [57]

We know now how Tareev understands kenosis in speculative Christology and in evangelical history. But what place does he assign to this doctrine in his moral theology?

The Sermon on the Mount is the centre of his system. Righteousness and justice of the Old Covenant seem to him to be superseded by love which extends to the form of non-resistance. This love carried with it such apparent contradictions as positive meaning of suffering, of foolishness for Christ's sake or else of a perfect spiritual love compatible with hatred of one's kindred. An important place is occupied in Tareev's scheme by foolishness for Christ's sake. He regards it, of course, as an individual vocation which could not be proposed as a rule of spiritual or moral life. He looks upon it as did Bukharev: as upon " death and corruption of the outward man " in the sense of 2 Cor. iv. 10, 2 Tim. ii. 11, 12, Phil. iii. 10. He also sees in it a form of freedom from conventions of the world which is even acknowledged as such by society in cases of monks or innocents, though not always approvingly. " Innocency is indeed a madness in the eyes of common sense. But, if even expressed in the form of sewing of one's own shoes or wearing a peasant coat, it is a necessary condition of spiritual freedom." [58] Spiritual poverty, tears, meekness, hunger and thirst after righteous-

---

[55] M. M. Tareev, *Foundations,* etc., t. I, p. 321, the third period of ministry.
[56] *Ibid.,* t. I, p. 336.
[57] *Ibid.,* t. I. p. 346, the Resurrection.
[58] *Ibid.,* t. III, p. 107, on spiritual life. The shoes and the coat are obviously an allusion to Tolstoy.

ness, readiness to endure death. . . . These commandments
are absolute. What in the act of creation was expressed by
" fiat " is paralleled in the Sermon on the Mount by " Be ye."
The matter obeyed the command of the Creator; now there
is no more appeal to natural life, but to the holy one. A
Christian, through Christ, is in the centre of creation, God
works through him, and he himself, if he truly follows the
Master, sees his vocation in his disposition to be sacrificed for
all. There is no hope of reward—Christ calls for the narrow
path and promises to His disciples persecution, humiliation
and death—the " twelve thrones " stay only as a distant image
of spiritual bliss, and are not given by Christ Himself but
rather come from the Father. As to the power of forgiving
sins, it is given to those who neither judge nor condemn.[59]

Eternal life, godmanhood, such are the terms used to desig-
nate the bliss of future life. They are not synonyms of the
Kingdom. Tareev, to the reader's surprise, affirms that one
could give an account of the Gospels without referring to the
Kingdom. (He only mentions the entrance into Jerusalem—
meek and peaceful, true reflection of the Lord's character.)
For our author, the image of the Kingdom of God suggests
" more real values of the experience of sonship, of spiritual
righteousness and of eternal life." [60]

The fundamental contradiction of life : craving for union
with the divine and craving for personal happiness—
unachievable as well—shows to man his nullity. It opens his
mind, makes him ready to receive a message from the One
greater than himself. Man's humble condition is thus a way
to discover the divine world and its greatness. Man, recognizing his poor condition, through patient forbearance of his
limitations advances in knowledge and experience of the
spiritual world, changing from glory to glory (2 Cor. iii. 18).
The sense of cosmic and human life is to reflect and to render
glory to God in and through the humiliations and limitations
of earthly life. There is essential difference between the ideals
of natural perfection and the inner, spiritual absolute. Here

[59] Here Tareev is much nearer to " priesthood of all orthodox " dreamt
of by Bukharev than to Soloviev's ideas.
[60] M. M. Tareev, *Foundations,* etc., t. II, p. 336.

is the centre of eternal temptation : to reapportion the values, to mix human and divine. Reconciliation of these contradictory worlds, recognition of oneself as God's instrument, such is the victory over religious " godmanly " temptation which, in mankind, repeats and reflects the temptation of sonship.

Faith in God when it overcomes temptation is called by Tareev " hope." Faith is for him not an act of mind, but of will. " It belongs to the heart, though it begins in the thought." [61]

His own belief is stated as follows : " (a) In Jesus Christ as Son of God and the persecuted and humiliated Son of man, (b) in the divine love revealed in Him—belief in the One who sent Him, and (c) in our own sonship as sonship of each of the little ones." [62]   Love implies choice between God and the world ; " given " by God it becomes in this act of choice a free act of man. It is a forbearing, patient, humble and essentially believing love. " To believe in the sonship of humiliated man " such is the first condition on the way to eternal life. Weakness and suffering from nature, free faith of man, recognition of his nullity and of divine love, endurance and self-denial—all this is answered by the condescension of divine love bestowing upon man the dignity of sonship. [63] Henceforth, the force of nature is replaced by the central role of man ; the evangelical universalism breaks the frontiers within human societies, and Christian eschatology projects the authority of spiritual life over the limits of time, history and cosmic development.

The intention to organize temporal life on absolute principles is Tareev's chief objection against socialism to which he consecrated an historical survey of strictly informative and scientific character. [64]   Civilization, wealth, the state, all good on the natural plane, become less innocent in contact with the higher truth. " The development of science and the arts, the flourishing of industry and trade, all this is possible only when

[61] M. M. Tareev, *Foundations,* t. III, p. 119, Faith, hope, charity.
[62] *Ibid.,* t. III, p. 122, Love, faith, hope.
[63] *Ibid.,* t. III, p. 260, cf. t. II, p. 345.
[64] *Socialism* (M. 1912).

there is wealth. But when a man is called by God, the evil of riches is then revealed. . . . According to the teaching of Christ, good tidings to the poor composed the content of His gospel and the aim of His ministry, together with the healing of the sick and the bringing of peace to the brokenhearted." [65] Poverty or wealth are neutral in themselves, but wealth can be used according to Christianity only in one way : by complete distribution of it, not by exercises of charity. The absolute of Christ's commandments throws a new light on such positive relations as marriage and the family and, with regard to state or nation, it creates not indifference but that spirit of sacrifice which led Christ to His cross. His followers who want to carry out their convictions meet " the duty of voluntary death." It is obvious that accepting death for himself a Christian can only deny violence—whether in form of war or of penalty of death—an evil denounced by Tareev with vigorous logic and inspiration.[66] Above all, there must be freedom of choice, freedom of willing sacrifice.

The secular life—body, nature, history—must be set free as well and left to its own development. This would allow the religious world to be preserved in its fullness and purity. This idea of Tareev aroused lively controversy and gave occasion to some of accusing him of heathenism and even immorality. Such accusations are obviously harsh and wrong; but had Tareev an organic view of the Church he could overcome the difficulty. It is the more astonishing, as he in his turn criticized Bukharev's " monastic " outlook. If even the world was for Bukharev a sinful world, he saw it on the way to salvation through the Incarnate, sacrificial Lamb. Tareev, who considers the world and natural life neutral or even good, almost excludes it from the realm of grace. His clear-cut method shows both extremes of the Russian kenotic mind : its evangelical pureness and desire to cling faithfully to Christ's ways and commandments and also its social dangers.

There are certainly points which one can criticize in

---

[65] M. M. Tareev, *Foundations,* etc., t. II, pp. 263, 265, Eternal life.
[66] *Ibid.,* t. II, p. 217 ; cf. pp. 207, 212, 214, 216, and t. III, p. 306.

Tareev's general theological position. His idea of the Church is inadequate. His distrust of patristic thought and of dogma were justly qualified by G. Florovsky as "the objections of a man in the street." [67] But with regard to the doctrine of kenosis he made a real effort to present the living Christ, divine yet human. Instead of the heavy authoritative statements of official catechisms there was a keen thought and real devotion to Christ, devotion which should have, according to Tareev, the character of a personal love. His clear thought and the simple elegance of his style make his system understandable even for a non-theologian. It is also noteworthy that he deliberately tried to link his own system and all the theological thought with Russian literature. He thus tried to bridge the two worlds which, though united in their very depth, were so tragically separated by the reality of Russian life. To finish, we would like to show the appreciation of his work given by a Western scholar : " Durchweg trittzutage, wie Tareev bestrebt ist, das eigentliche Wesen des Christentums in seine Tiefe zu erfassen und es in selbständiger Weise als ein einheitliches Ganze vorzuführen. Dies geschieht in fesselnder Sprache und oft glanzender Darstellung. Seine Schrift ist ein Beweiss wie nicht nur auf exegetischem und historischem Gebiet sondern auch auf sistematischem die russische Theologie darnach ringt, hinter der Theologie der andern Kirchen nicht zurückzubleiben." [68]

On the side of the Orthodox, the doctrine of kenosis as expressed by Tareev found quite a favourable reception. His work was appreciated as "a real contribution to our literature, poor in the field of history and philosophy of dogmas, which deserves the serious attention of its readers." It was noticed that the author avoids the Nestorian tendencies of the extreme kenotic writers of the West; " Everywhere the author eliminates such extremes, with the inflexibility of an historically-orthodox conviction. But, defending the kenosis, he should make it more clear that he understands it differently from well known kenotic theorists. In a sense it is a termino-

[67] Florovsky, The Ways, etc., p. 444.
[68] N. Bonwetsch, Theologische Literaturzeitung, 1909, n. 3.

logical misunderstanding." [69] This last remark seems to us a just one and, in a way, it could be applied to all the Russian writers on the kenosis, though on the other hand, their approach may be also qualified as an Orthodox attempt to treat the subject, in order to work out doctrinally the fact of human nature in Christ.

We should mention that N. N. Glubokovsky does not approve of kenotic theories, and even Bishop Theophan's assertion of the self-emptying of Christ seems to him an exaggeration. He insists that all the emphasis is and should be, as it is in the epistle to Philippians, only on the moral aspect of this soteriological self-humiliation of Christ. But N. N. Glubokovsky refers to the problem only in footnotes of his great book on St. Paul [70] and he has nevertheless to acknowledge that it is impossible to take the " He emptied Himself " for a metaphor.

The literary production of S. N. Bulgakov—extending to economics, philosophy, theology—is too manifold to be adequately examined here. We shall take it only in its relation to the doctrine of kenosis. But we should like to note that by the various aspects of his own life and his work, S. Bulgakov represents a bridge between the literary-secular world and the theological world. A few words about his personal evolution, about his double career, first as layman and philosopher-economist then as priest and theologian may help to situate him on the historical plan.

Sergej N. Bulgakov, born in 1871, started his career as an economist. His first works (between 1896–1901) including his thesis for St. Petersburg University on Capitalism and Agriculture are completely outside our field. Professor, successively, of Kiev and Moscow Universities, at the beginning of the century he becomes with N. A. Berdyaeff (born in 1874) coeditor of the periodical *New Way (Novi Put)* and

[69] *Christian Reading* (SPB. 1901), t. CCXII, part II, pp. 614–18 ; see also the good press on Tareev in *Christian Reading,* 1900, ix. pp. 461–4 and the *Ecclesiastical Messenger,* 1892, n. 48, p. 761.
[70] N. N. Glubokovsky, *Evangelization of St. Apostle Paul* (SPB. 1910), footnotes to pp. 281–313, especially pp. 282, 285, 286, 288, 291, 296, 300, 308.

Problems of Life (Voprosi Zhizni). The writings of this period appear in 1903 under the title *From Marxism to Idealism.* The dialectic-materialist theory of progress is rejected as not wholly scientific. The quest for man, his freedom and rights, the absolute dignity of his personality comes now to the forefront. The importance of individual facts in history speaks against the materialistic interpretation of it. Out of this criticism will grow the teaching about man, and it will lead the author to the perfect man—the Godman. With regard to society, Bulgakov revalues the *Economic ideals* and *Social ideals* (1903). Humanism with Christ and Church as both organization and organism, now take their place in Bulgakov's system. Like V. Soloviev, he wants to overcome pantheism, cosmotheism and "man-godhood" (the supermen of Dostoevsky understood in the light of Nietzsche). The *Two Cities* (collection of articles between 1904–10) refers to Christianity as history and metahistory. Social, economic and historical life are now related to "the divine Logos." Instead of economic systems there is now the vision of Providence and Wisdom. The year 1909 is marked by the publication of *Vekhi* (landmarks): all the authors who contributed to this symposium (Berdyaeff, P. Struve, Trubetzkoj, etc.) stood out against the materialism of the Russian intelligentsia and atheism " uncivilized and uncritical, taken for granted from Belinsky onwards." [71] *Vekhi* marked a date in the history of Russian intelligentsia and, long before the events of 1917, it was a spiritual overcoming of the atheistic revolution (politically and socially the members of the group belonged and remained rather with the left wing). As a member of the Second Duma Bulgakov protested against both terroristic actions of the left and the penalty death on the part of the government. In 1917 Bulgakov published an important treatise of religious—more precisely of neoplatonic and Christian— philosophy, *The Unfading Light.* The same year he was ordained priest. He took part in the Council of Moscow of 1918 which reorganized the Russian Church. Expelled from Russia by the Soviet Government, he became professor

[71] S. N. Bulgakov, *Periodical Vekhi* (M. 1909), p. 30, Heroism and asceticism *(podvizhnichestvo).*

at the University of Prague and, later on, vice-rector of the Russian Institute of Orthodox Theology in Paris, a position he still holds. During the period of emigration he edited many works, among which we should mention *Chapters on the Trinity, Die Tragoedie der Philosophie* (in German; dogmas are here presented as the only possible answer to the *aporia* of metaphysics), *On the Church* (principles of Orthodox, as opposed to Roman and Protestant ecclesiology), *Peter and John* (on the Roman claims), *The burning Bush* (on the Virgin Mary), *De l'Orthodoxie* (a book of popularization in French, translated into English), *The Ladder of Jacob* (on angels conceived in some way as the Platonic Ideas), *The veneration of icons.* The most significant works of S. N. Bulgakov in relation to our subject are *The Lamb of God* (a full treatise of Christology, Paris 1935), to a lesser degree *The Comforter* (On the Holy Ghost, 1936). S. N. Bulgakov published this year a small book in English *The Wisdom of God.*

Bulgakov's production covers nearly the whole field of theology. Before expounding his views about kenosis, we should give a short general characterization of his thought. Bulgakov could be called a theocentrist. In the controversy which we shall mention later on, Metropolitan Sergius of Moscow wrote about him : " in general, his teaching recalls the Gnostics, whose basic problem was the teaching concerning Wisdom, the Logos or the medium between God and the created world." To this Professor Bulgakov replied that " he had no taste for the semi-pagan syncretistic systems of the Gnostics and has never felt their influence." But there is a Christian gnosis to which Bulgakov stands very close. He has been undoubtedly inspired by the great Alexandrians and by the Cappadocian Fathers, behind whom we find Plato. He himself acknowledges his debt to Jacob Boehme and the English Platonists. More than to anybody else, he is indebted to V. Soloviev. He is an admirer of P. Florensky, whose book *The column and Foundation of Truth* (M. 1912) was, at the very eve of the Russian revolution, the cleverest and strangest embodiment of Orthodox neo-platonism in a halo of decadent aestheticism. Bulgakov's insistence on the problems of theology does not exclude from his mind a deep interest for the problem of God's approach to man. He never lost contact with the problems of human life, as shown by the fact that he never lost contact with the world of secular literature. Since 1901, he has given brilliant papers on Ivan Karamazov as a philosophical type, on the inner drama of Herzen, on Chekhov, on Tolstoy. In 1906 he prefaced the Jubilee edition of Dostoevsky. He gave also a lecture and wrote an essay on Pushkin's centenary. In Russian life and literature, he saw the thirst of the Russian soul for the Person of Christ and the Russian way of picturing Him.[72] In 1908 already he said " We enter again the epoch of Christological discussions." [73]   It was difficult to revert to the epoch of Christological discussions without meeting again the problem of kenosis.

Bulgakov is a vigorous supporter of the idea of kenosis. He writes that the Protestant kenotic doctrine has given a new life to the theology of the West, while the theology of Byzantium has become dead on this particular point and that his own purpose is to bring an Orthodox answer to the kenotic problems.[74] Like all the Russians he would not accept any theory jeopardizing the divinity of Christ. But he is convinced that the kenotic theory may be taken as the development and explanation of the Chalcedonian definition. A prominent feature in Bulgakov's teaching on kenosis is the way in which this teaching seems intermingled with the author's special ideas about God's Wisdom. The kenotic theories of Bulgakov cannot be rightly grasped if one does not understand the nature and place of Sophia or Divine Wisdom in his system. Bulgakov is accounted for being and agrees to be, most of all, a Sophiologist. The newness of his contribution to the Orthodox theology consists in his sophiology, i.e. in a coherent and very systematic speculation about the Wisdom of God. This sophiology has become in Orthodox theological circles an object of vivid controversy, not exempt from personal and,

---

[72] Cf. our p. 69.
[73] S. N. Bulgakov, *Two cities*, 2 vols. (M. 1911), t. II, p. 155, Religion of man-godhood in Feuerbach.
[74] Answer to the Metropolitan Sergius.

even worse, political motives.[75]   Bulgakov claims for his
sophiology scriptural and traditional grounds (the Book of
Wisdom, Russian iconography, Russian prayers to the Wisdom
of God, some passages of St. Irenaeus, St. Athanasius,
St. Maxim the Confessor, St. John of Damascus, pseudo
Dionysius, Gregory Palamas).   How far such a claim may be
founded does not concern us here.   But something must be
said about Bulgakov's conception of Wisdom.

What is exactly, for Bulgakov, the Holy Sophia?   Soloviev
claimed to have several apparitions of Sophia; he saw in her
not a moral attribute of God, not even an impersonal force, but
a real and conscious Person or Supraperson, who was at the
same time the soul of the world and the eternal feminine
principle.   In Bulgakov's conception Sophia is not an attribute
or an abstraction.   She is a real entity or rather a real being.
There are two aspects of Sophia: Sophia uncreated and
Sophia created.   Sophia uncreated is the Holy Wisdom existing inside the Trinitarian life.   As such Sophia is the Idea of
ideas, the prototype of all things in the divine thought.   She
is not God but she belongs to Him and dwells in Him.   Sophia
is the common life of the Three Persons.   In her is revealed
God's nature.   In her does the Logos reveal Himself as
Wisdom.   In her does the Holy Spirit reveal Himself as glory.
She is God's body or garment.   She is the object, the content

---

[75] On the controversy see *The Christian East,* vol. XVI, nos. 1, 2, Jan.-
July 1936, pp. 48–59.   The most striking is that the " index " signed by
the Metropolitan of Moscow is based " on information received " and, to
refute the unsound doctrine, qualified as poetry rather than theology, the
whole of the system was not examined " in order not to be hypnotized by
it."   The procedure is alien to the rules of the Orthodox Church and can
be only explained by the confusion and complications due to political
circumstances.

By the way, the same review (p. 40) publishes the discourse of the same
Metropolitan Sergius pronounced by him in 1901 when he was consecrated bishop.   He speaks there of the pastoral duty and office as a following
of Christ who " left His divine glory and heaven and the ministry of
angels, and being made in the form of a servant He served us and saved
us "—language and emphasis of the Epistle to the Philippians again.
(Sergius Starogradsky, born in 1867, M.D. of the Moscow Theological
Academy; the Rector of Petrograd Theological Academy, the Metropolitan of Nizhni Novgorod and the guardian of the Patriarchal see of
the Russian Church in Moscow after the imprisonment in 1922 of the
Patriarch Tykhon and of Peter, Metropolitan of Krutitsi († 1937), the
successor and guardian of the see appointed by him.

of the Godhead.   As for Sophia created, she is the outpouring
of Sophia uncreated; we should not say outside God (for
Bulgakov, who rejects resolutely pantheism, admits the fact
and the term " panentheism "), but outside God's immanent
life, into the external world ontologically distinct from God.
Even before the creation, even in God's bosom, Sophia is
ready to radiate out of Him as His beauty or glory.   The
created Sophia—the world and man considered as a whole,
as a metaphysical unity, has something " in common " with
God.   It is Sophia created who, in the inanimate world, praises
and blesses the Lord.   She is not conscious as a person might
be, but she is able to give an unhypostatic and answering love
to God.   Though she is not a person, she is, if we may risk the
term, " personable " or, to use Bulgakov's words, she is not a
hypostatis, but she is a " hypostasibility," being able to assume
an indefinite number of persons or hypostases.   The Church
and the Virgin Mary, for instance, are sometimes spoken of by
Bulgakov as being such personifications of Sophia.   Though
Bulgakov does not emphasize Sophia's feminine character in
the same way as did Soloviev, she retains, according to his
conception, a character of passivity, which constitutes the
metaphysical essence of the feminine principle (feminine, says
Bulgakov, but not female).

What is Sophia's relation to kenosis?   If we admit, as
Bulgakov does, of a kenosis within the Holy Trinity, Sophia,
being the common life of the Three Persons, is intimately connected with it.   Kenosis among the three hypostases consists of
certain self-emptyings, self-givings, self-sacrifices and here
Sophia is the " what," the very material of those renounce-
ments and exchanges.   Because she is the essential possession
of the Three Persons she alone can be their mutual gift.   If
we turn to kenosis outside God Himself, the sophianic origin
of the world makes it possible to receive God, to communicate
with the divine Logos, to provide a flesh for the Incarnation;
thus Sophia is the basis and necessary condition of Christ's
self-emptying.   In both cases Sophia is, one could say, the
substance of kenosis—let us take this term in its strict etymo-
logical meaning :   what underlies kenosis.

This short outline of Bulgakov's concept of St. Sophia seems to be sufficient for our purpose. We shall enter into the details of Bulgakov's kenotic theories without reverting to the notion of Holy Wisdom. It would bring into our subject, as we think, unnecessary complications. Moreover, we can conceive Bulgakov's ideas on kenosis independently of any Sophianic theology. But, even though we do not feel the need of recurring to the notion of Sophia in the following pages, we must always bear in mind that, for the author himself, every process of kenosis is based upon and realized in Sophia.

The originality of Bulgakov's approach to the kenotic problems—leaving aside their Sophianic aspect—consists in the extension of the notion of kenosis outside the process of Incarnation. He introduces the kenosis not only in the act of creation, but within the life of the Holy Trinity. The premundane kenosis consists of the mutual love of the divine hypostases. This love surpasses all individuation and brings the Three into One, in spite of the real existence of three personal centres.

The Fatherhood is the image of love which does not desire to possess within and for Himself; it reveals His love in the spiritual begetting of the Son, the Father's living image. This life-giving power is the ecstasy of coming out of Himself, a certain self-emptying which, at the same time, is a self-realization.

" The Sonship is already an eternal kenosis " in that the second hypostasis, " the Word seems to become wordless (in Himself) and makes Himself the Word of the Father. He becomes poor and sacrificially silent in the bosom of His Father. . . . If, on the side of the Father, there is self-negation in begetting of the Son, the Son is thoroughly emptying Himself when He accepts the passive state of the One who is begotten." [76] It is not only a pretemporal fact but also an act for both the divine hypostases. This mutual sacrifice is not a tragedy because it is overcome by the bliss and joy of this accepted mutual sacrifice.

[76] S. Bulgakov, *The Lamb of God* (Paris, 1935), pp. 122, 200, 468. We prefer personally to use, with regard to the relation with the Holy Trinity, the traditional expression used by St. John Damascene: perihorisis.

Now, the triumphant cognition and witness in God of Himself and His only-begotten Son is the procession of the Holy Ghost, " proceeding from the Father on the Son . . . *Ideally* God defines His nature in the begetting of the Son as the Father uttering His eternal word. But the *reality* of His nature is tested through the Holy Ghost. As in God there is no self-definition of non-hypostatic character, it means that the cognition by God of His nature is an hypostatic act—the procession of the Spirit." [77] The passive character of the procession is in harmony with the sacrificial kenotic love.

We have now some idea of the kenosis within God Himself. Let us turn to the kenosis manifested through the process of creation.

The divine Three, in the fullness of their love, do not need any other form of life. But " God is love. To extend is the property of love." [78] The divine love seeks to be realized not only within Deity—and this is the foundation of the creative act. We must carefully notice here the distinction which Professor Bulgakov makes between the divine world in its fullness, the Holy Trinity as absolute and this Absolute existing for the other, for the " not me " (the world). Essentially, the Holy Trinity is the Absolute. But, descending towards the object outside Him—to the creation, result and aim of divine love—the Absolute becomes God. The notion of *God* includes the created world and the divine relation to it ; it is the economic life of the Holy Trinity. This is important to remember with regard to further development of the idea of the Incarnation.

How is creation a kenosis? God in His immanence is not lessened by the creative act ; but He " surpasses the regions of His immanence and comes out into the world." [79] The new categories of space and time come now into being. The act of creation, though as an act of divine self-definition it belongs to eternity, receives, as turned towards the world, a temporal

[77] S. Bulgakov, *The Lamb of God*, p. 123.
[78] *Ibid.*, p. 142.
[79] Though unknown to each other S. N. Bulgakov and F. H. Brabant express similar views. Cf. A. Rawlinson, *Essays on Trinity and Incarnation* (1908), pp. 325–60, esp. pp. 355 and 356.

M

aspect. The world as something which is becoming belongs to time, time itself being a becoming. The "six days" indicate this transition from the eternal to temporal. Pouring itself out in the act of creation, the divine love in its kenosis establishes time for God and makes God Himself live in time. In this sense He is also becoming for the world, together with the world. He is revealed now to the world, not in His omnipotence, but in His providential care.[80] The continual bestowal of grace is also a form of divine condescension. The freedom given to man leaves room "for a certain risk of unsuccess." [81] The Father consents to wait until His creation will respond to His love.

This creative kenosis is shared by the Son also. As " the Word about the world " [82] He is already sent into this world. Not only is He already perfectly obedient to the Father, but He comes down serving the self-revealing God and He "becomes the content of this revelation. He gives Himself to the Father and, emptying Himself, He gives what is His own to the world." The Son is, for S. N. Bulgakov, the *Lamb* offered already and offering Himself in the act of creation : the other aspect emphasized is the beginning of divine sacrifice in that the Father not only condescends towards the creation but also sends His Son. (Perhaps here the term Logos would be better and would make clearer the distinction between this creative kenosis and the Incarnation.)

The Holy Ghost shares also in the creative kenosis. The third hypostasis gives life to the Father's " let there be." It means that the Holy Ghost enters thus in the state of becoming. The Spirit becomes, if one may say so, the becoming of the world, the actualization of its content. He is sent from the first, when He is moving upon the face of the waters and will remain sent until the last when " God will be all in all." The life of the world itself is the Holy Ghost, the Giver of life. The third hypostasis reposes on the Son who is the Logos of the world; but, in the process of becoming, the world cannot comprehend the fullness of the Logos, neither can it embrace

---

[80] Thought expressed also by Tareev.
[81] *The Lamb,* p. 169.
[82] *Ibid.,* p. 151.

the Comforter and Giver of life. This becoming, this passing from and between fullness and incompleteness is the activity of the Holy Ghost, His kenosis in the world.

Kenosis within God's life and in the act of creation having been thus defined, it remains to see the meaning of kenosis in the Incarnation.

The act of creation, as we have seen, was understood not as due to necessity but to the impossibility that God should not love. Now we face the Incarnation as a fact eternally foreseen by God (1 Pet. i. 20). The Incarnation, says our author, cannot be a mere outcome of sin. It actually did happen as the act of redemption; but before Adam existed, there was already in the divine world an image " of the perfect man Jesus." Christ is more than the second Adam; he is the first.[83] The coming of the Son is not only a providential act resulting from the fall of man, but an original good will of God which existed " before the creation of the world as its basis and aim." [84] The Incarnation of the Son is not merely a *means* of redemption but its highest achievement; the last goal is " to unite all the heavenly and the earthly world under one head, Christ." Hence, " the soteriological task is included in the eschatological as a means into the aim; the redemption is the way to our glorification." [85]

We shall not follow Bulgakov in his very elaborate treatment of the Christological question, for there is much which, interesting as it may be, does not refer directly to kenosis. We shall strictly select from his Christology what belongs to the self-emptying of Christ.

There was a moment when the Logos, leaving heaven, became a creature. Phil. ii. 5—11 is interpreted as concerning both the self-emptying of the eternal Logos and the earthly humble life of Jesus. " The divine nature of the Logos as the basis of the hypostatic being and the source of life remains unchanged and undiminished in Christ. The humiliation affects not the nature (*ousia*) but the divine form or image

[83] *The Lamb*, p. 192.
[84] H. M. Relton, *Study in Christology* (S.P.C.K. 1917), holds a similar view.
[85] *The Lamb*, p. 193.

(*morphe*) which is laid aside by Christ at His Incarnation. He deposes His divine glory which He will receive again at His ascension. Christ, potentially, is glorious; but He renounces the divine joy." [86]   He remains with the nature of Deity yet without its glory. The second hypostasis seems to abandon His own will, emptying Himself and bringing His life into complete subjection to the Father. He disappears, giving room to the Father: His words are no more His own but the Father's, and He is so utterly transparent and free from any ego that whosoever has seen Him, has seen the Father. Thus, keeping His divinity and not being affected by the kenosis as the second hypostasis, Christ is nevertheless separated from the divine life which will only gradually come back to Him in the process of the human life, death and victory over it.[87]   Whilst Incarnate there is in Christ a certain " Christological subordination " which by no means implies any immanent subordinationism. The dogma of the Orthodox Church concerning the procession of the Holy Ghost from the Father eliminates one of the difficulties unavoidable for a Western kenotic writer.

If we turn now to the earthly figure of Jesus, as it is pictured in the Gospel narratives, we see that the empirical image of Christ is that of limitation : He belongs to a definite epoch, nation, land. Yet the individuality of Christ does not know any limitation. His all-embracing manhood surpasses all His temporal characteristics. He appeals to all. It is so because the human hypostasis of Jesus, " son of the carpenter," is the hypostasis of the Logos, and at the same time He is truly man, the true descendant of Adam. How did the divine nature of the Logos not swallow the weaker one, the human? S. N. Bulgakov would not think of it in terms of Paul of Samosata or Arius; there is no shade of thought of divine inspiration or adoption. But he would not agree with St. Cyril of Alexandria in regarding humanity as a veil. It is not the flesh which is

---

[86] *The Lamb,* p. 252.
[87] This statement marks a strong opposition to the extreme kenotic views.

the veil of Deity but the fact of the kenosis spread, as we have seen, on the divine Logos at the Incarnation.[88]

How did the self-emptying of Christ affect His own filial consciousness? The consciousness of being divine and only-begotten is growing in Him with the growth of His temporal and human consciousness. His divinity is revealed to Him as His Sonship. " My Father's house " are the first words which we know of His. Praying, He always uses the words " my Father." His personal consciousness as God's Logos is now bound to His consciousness as the Son made flesh; this divine consciousness of Himself becomes proportional to the human consciousness and is never allowed to prevail over it.

Kenosis in Christ affects also His knowledge of things. In order to solve rightly the problem of Christ's knowledge we must realize how, in Christ, the state of becoming does not exclude, but proceeds from, the state of fullness. Once His divine attributes laid aside, Christ took upon Himself the limitations of humanity. He was now in the state of becoming. But the becoming does not mean merely that things are passing away, that all flows and disappears. On the contrary, " all comes out of the depth of being and comes back into it— in other words, becoming is a certain form of the fullness and not its absence." [89] Thus the transcendent depth of the divine consciousness of the Logos contains all; but in His godman-hood it is hidden and shows itself only partly and by moments. As the Logos, Christ keeps the beatific vision. Yet the human, earthly ministry of Christ did not coincide with His omni-science; consequently, this omniscience was limited in the Godman. It is vitally important to acknowledge that Christ might not know the time of the second coming or of some events : the measure of His godmanhood was not yet fulfilled and the divine nature was not wholly revealed in the human. The child Jesus, bearer of the divine Logos, was in a state which may be compared to every mystery of babyhood with all its hidden riches.

[88] S. N. Bulgakov protests against the juxtaposition of divine and human in the one Christ. Cf. Ch. Gore, *The Reconstruction of Belief* (1926), p. 523: " We must repudiate that mode of speech which prevailed at the time of Chalcedon and later."

[89] *The Lamb,* p. 333.

It even seems that for Jesus human knowledge—

> " culture in its present or past did not exist. He never discovered any mystery of the world known to Him alone and on the discovery of which labours human thought ; it seems as if cosmic and historical existence did not interest the One who was the Logos of the world. . . . His task was that of the divinization of human nature itself, its rising, the bestowal of the grace of sonship upon redeemed manhood. It would be the task of man to rediscover the true content and meaning of their humanity." [90]

Limiting His activity to the religious field, Christ leads His followers to the full discovery of divine life and inspiration.

Even Christ's manner of teaching is to be considered in the light of kenosis. Without the self-exinanition of the Logos, the revelation concerning the Son might have been the direct revelation of His nature. But the self-cognition of Christ is now subjected to a certain mode of life. It has to be expressed in human language and addressed to men. The Godman humbled Himself to the state of prophet.

So far, we have seen the effects of kenosis upon Christ's intellect. Still more patent is the effect of kenosis upon Christ's will. This last becomes completely surrendered to the Father. The attitude of Christ appears as an attitude of obedience. If in His first recorded words Jesus speaks of His Father, the first *act* of His known to us in that He followed Joseph and Mary and was subjected to them until the time of another stronger call which drew Him out of His silence into a new world. There also He went not to reign but to minister. We remember here what was already said about His premundane obedience and what S. N. Bulgakov called a " Christological subordination." It seems almost superfluous to dwell upon this point : it would practically mean the repetition of the whole Gospel's record. " Know ye not that I came to fulfil my Father's will ? " And Jesus lives a life of obedience until death. This state of obedience does not exclude inner

---

[90] *The Lamb*, p. 278. Cf. Ch. Gore, *The Reconstruction of Belief,* pp. 488, 489 : " On matters not within the scope of His Mission, He appears as giving no positive teaching at all."

conflicts and trials. The human will of Christ belonging to the true human nature may be subject to temptation. There is a struggle, there is a tension in the human nature, enlightened and inspired by His divinity. But the struggle ends with the victory over the temptation. This continuous surrender of Christ's will must be understood by us in connection with His priestly and sacrificial self-offering on which the Epistle to the Hebrews lays such stress.

It is not only the inner life of Christ which bears the mark of kenosis but His life in the eyes of man; the events of His ministry show Him liable to the weakness of human nature, with the exclusion of sin. He was tired, thirsty and hungry. He knew human sorrow about the dying friend or the spiritual deafness of His disciples and the stiffneckedness of the people. " The one who could call to His help all the angels appears abandoned and defenceless before Pilate." [91]

This last name introduces us into a sphere of Christ's ministry which is the climax of kenosis: i.e. Christ's redemptive work through His passion and death.

Becoming flesh, the Logos comes into a sinful flesh—at least a flesh weakened by the consequences of original sin. He himself is free from sin, but through His true manhood the sinful flesh becomes His own. " The Just who came to take away the sins of the world is thus very far from His Father." [92] " The prayer in Gethsemane, apart from its other meanings, reveals also the depth of kenosis, as it were a certain ignorance of Christ concerning God's way in His destiny: ' If it is possible.' . . . The omniscience of the Logos takes in Jesus the humble form of obedience. How is it to be reconciled with the personality of the One who claimed His equality with the Father? Only the sin of the world taken by the Incarnate seems to explain such a possibility." [93] It seems that the divine side is so extinguished in Christ at this moment that it leaves His humanity alone to experience, while abandoned by God, all the power, the darkness and the sorrow of the sin of the world.

[91] *The Lamb*, p. 317.
[92] *Ibid.*, p. 384.
[93] Bukharev insisted upon Christ's sacrificial taking upon Himself of the sin of human ignorance.

The Gospels show the Father Himself extending the cup to His Son. He sends His Son, which is already an act of sacrificial kenosis of the Father—different however from that of the Son. By this decision He remains, so to say, without His Son. In the sense in which we distinguished between the immanent and the economic kenosis, the Son lives no more in union with the Father, as the Father is no more with the Son—because the Father sent and the Son was sent by His Father on the cross. " As the acceptance and the willingness of Christ to be sacrificed is also due to the help of the Holy Ghost (Heb. ix. 14—through the Eternal Spirit He offered Himself to God without spot)—the joy of their relationship extinguishes also in the night of Gethsemane. The Holy Ghost, who always reposes on the Son, seems also to have abandoned Him." [94] The abandonment of the Son in an act of the Father expressing His *acceptance* of this death of His Son is in a sense the Father's participation in the sacrifice. Of course, it is not the death of the Father but an image of spiritual participation in the sacrifice of life. The immanent Trinity is above and beyond the world; the economic Trinity is related to the world. " In the redemption we have a composite mode of mutual relationship in which the hypostasis of the Son is united to the world and suffers in it, while the other hypostases, remaining alien to this direct act, are spiritually compassable with the Son through their union of love." [95]

The death of Christ, bodily consumed on the cross, is at the same time the spiritual agony of the immortal life. The extinction of the Logos is so deep that the abyss of death truly receives the Godman. " This endlessly profound kenosis is equal only to the depth of the divine love." [96] The whole Godman in His unity and complexity is dying on the cross. The humanity dies and, together with it, the divine nature comes down approaching its last limitation. Therefore it seems to S. Bulgakov impossible to exclude even Christ's divinity from participation in death. Together with the Incarnation the death of the Godman is the greatest act of His self-emptying.

[94] *The Lamb*, p. 383.   [95] *Ibid.*, p. 401.
[96] *Ibid.*, p. 343.

The laying of Jesus in the grave belongs to kenosis. It is a particular moment in the humiliation of the Son in which, in a way, the Father is also taking a part. He receives the soul of Jesus. The divine mystery, inaccessible to human understanding, is hidden in this receiving by the Father of His Son in His deathly exinanition and in the keeping of His soul until the resurrection. The " descending into hell " is also the continuation of the sacrificial aspect of Christ's ministry. It is still the high priest and the prophet redeeming the souls of the departed and bringing to them the good tidings.

Kenosis is not absent from the glorification of Christ, i.e. from His resurrection, ascension and sitting at the right hand of the Father. In His high-priestly prayer the Lord asks the Father to glorify Him with the glory which He possessed before all worlds—He prays for the end of the kenosis. It is still a ministry of the high priest whose offering was acceptable to God. There is no self-glorification but glorification by God (Phil. ii. 11). In this sense it is still ministry and not kingly triumph. It is still an aspect of kenosis " though it seems paradoxical to unite such notions as : kenotic glorification, glory in humiliation." [97] Here is the thought particular to S. N. Bulgakov : he accepts the usual characterization of Christ's ministry as prophetic, priestly and kingly, but in fact he leaves no room for the kingly ministry even to the ascended Christ. On earth, Christ felt His Father to be His breath, His daily bread. His prayer never ceased. Now, when " all power is given into Him " He is still eternally interceding just as for ever He remains the Godman.

The kenosis of Christ is still going on. As far as there is evil in the world, the Lamb is still slain. Christ is still humbling Himself and waiting for the decision of man's freedom. Nature is " groaning and expecting " this last victory when the last enemy will be conquered—death. The reality of the kenosis is compatible even with the present heavenly state of Christ. " Christ suffers and is crucified in the world, because the sacrifice of Golgotha is still repeated

[97] *The Lamb,* p. 410.

in the world until He comes (in the Eucharist, 1 Cor. xi. 26).[98]
The Lord in His glorified manhood is sitting on the right hand
of the Father, but in the earthly manhood of which He is the
new Adam, in His body the Church which is still in the state
of Church militant, Christ dwells not only in His glorification
but in His kenosis also." [99]   In the glorified Christ the kenosis
of the Logos who emptied Himself is finished but there is still
the humiliation of the manhood of Christ.   It is no more the
personal humanity of Jesus, now glorified and ascended, but
mankind, all this earthly humanity united with that of the
Redeemer.   We finish with our author's own words :

> " As far as Christ Himself is concerned, He is com-
> pletely glorified.   But, even ascended and King, He is still
> expecting the fulfilment and the coming of the " last
> day."   The true God Christ, reigning in us and over us,
> is enthroned to gain His eternal kingdom."

In hope to be united with Him and to see His final triumph,
" we pray to the Father : Thy kingdom come, and we call
to the Son : Come, Lord Jesus." [100]

Such are the main lines of the doctrine of kenosis according
to Bulgakov.   One could also find, in his works, some hints
about the application of the kenotic theory to practical human
life.   In his early writings Bulgakov already opposed the ideal
of the hero and of the saint ; repentance, renunciation of one's
will were claimed to be the first steps to take.   He repeated
insistently all through his life Dostoevsky's demand for
" spiritual denial, for sacrifice of the proud ego " of the
intelligentsia.[101]   It is a return to the Christian and Russian
ideal of obedience, humility, repentance.   All life should
become " the holy obedience," because, like Bukharev,

---

[98] At the same time the last mass does not signify for S. N. Bulgakov
the end of Christ's mediation in heaven because for him it has not the
redemptive meaning alone but is related to the kingly aspect of the Lord
as well as to the glorification of man.

[99] *The Lamb*, p. 436.   Let us notice here that in this conception of the
poor, humiliated and suffering humanity as the body of Christ S. N.
Bulgakov does not differ from the general stream of Russian thought.
The spiritual songs in the folk-lore, the writings of St. Tykhon, so
powerful a writer as Tolstoy, or a third-rate narrator Levitov, all unite
to recognize in the abased humanity the humiliated Christ.

[100] *Ibid.*, p. 468.

[101] *Heroism and asceticism* (*Vekhi*, 1909), pp. 55-6.

Bulgakov sees in the Incarnation the foundation of culture in its fullness.

It might be interesting to make a brief comparison between Bulgakov's and Tareev's approach to the kenotic problem. We are first of all struck by the external features in the treatment of the subject. Tareev, disliking patristic thought, felt compelled to refer to it as to an authoritative basis. S. N. Bulgakov is much more daring in his criticism of the Fathers just because he is devoted to their memory and because his main idea is to understand and to develop the treasure left by them. Conscious of their historical and philosophical background, he is not afraid of pointing the monophysite tendency of St. Cyril or to acknowledge the debt of Chalcedon to Apollinarius. But this is a mere superficial contrast between both authors. If we say that Tareev refuses to place himself on the ground of dogmatic theology, whilst Bulgakov is primordially a dogmatist, we go deeper in their mutual contrast. But the chief difference is still elsewhere. Tareev like Bukharev is a Christocentrist. One could hardly say the same of Bulgakov. His complete treatment of the Christological problem, his emphasis on the kenotic aspect, may create an illusion if the reader does not keep in mind the whole content of Bulgakov's theology. Before everything he is a theorist of the Holy Sophia. Important as the self-emptying of Christ is in his writings, when replaced in the ensemble of his speculation it is rather a part of sophiological synthesis. The glorious radiance of the Holy Sophia, the illumination and transfiguration of the world, in brief the theosis, occupy more central a place in his thought than the humiliation of Christ. Tareev has been deeply seized by the human, earthly figure of Jesus as portrayed in the Gospels. Like many Orthodox, even more so being such a gifted dogmatist, Bulgakov contemplates rather the eternal Logos, the second hypostasis of the Blessed Trinity. He has spoken without indulgence of " jesuanism," of a certain attachment to the person of Jesus, too much coloured by a preoccupation with psychology and history. He has no leaning to this side. But no less than Tareev he is faithful to the Gospel's portrait and the scriptural references. His approach to the doctrine of kenosis makes it even clearer than in the case of the other writers that insistence on the kenosis is here the basis for the acceptance of Christ's true humanity. And, if so, it is clear why this doctrine claims to be within the scope of the Chalcedonian definition. But even if one rejects the kenotic ideas, it remains that S. N. Bulgakov has been the first to introduce a complete and deeply worked out in detail doctrine of kenosis.

CHAPTER VI

CONCLUSION

THE following summary may serve to put the material of the preceding chapters into its proper perspective. We knew that the Russian folk-lore and the early written documents exalted personages endowed with meekness and humility, who have accepted the attitude of obedience, voluntary poverty and " non-resistance " in cases of violence. The popular memory cherished also the names of those who chose the way of voluntary self-abasement in the form of "foolishness for Christ's sake." There were also a few documents where the humiliation of Christ was spoken of directly in relation to His Incarnation.

This current became less evident with the beginning of the imitative " European " period of Russian history. Yet it never completely disappeared, and found its expression in the life and writings of St. Tykhon Zadonsky.

This early tradition was rediscovered in the nineteenth century in connection with the discussions raised by the Slavophils and the Westernisers. Eager to define the character of their nation and its historical task, the Slavophils paid tribute to the early tradition and they thought it possible to speak of their land as a Christian land. The history and the folk-lore of their people convinced them that the image dear to their folk was that of the humiliated Christ. They proposed this image as a basis for the following of the mind of Christ, not only in personal life, but in the life of their nation as well. Their opponents the Westernisers, though they disagreed over the interpretation of Russia's immediate task and her destiny, used nevertheless a similar language as soon as they tried to express some typical features of their nation. In these controversies it became clear that the main interests of the Slavophils were not in the field of history but in the religious sphere. There was no room for Christological problems, but the question of the Church as approached by the Slavophils was dealt with on the lines of the "kenotic" virtues and ideals. Artistic interpretation of the relationship between Christ and the Russian land was given by Tyutchev, who depicted Christ as "the King of heaven in the form of a servant," walking through Russia. The Slavophils spoke of their country in terms of "holiness" and exhorted Russia to become "the most Christian country."

Turning next to fiction, we realized that the novelists also were anxious to decide the problem of holiness. They spoke of it in relation to individuals rather than in a general sense. It was not necessarily Russia of which they thought, but a man in his search for a righteous life. With some writers it was their personal concern, and in such cases we thought it relevant to mention their biographies. We noticed that long-suffering, meekness, patience, obedience, acceptance of death were presented as positive and active traits of a character. Perfection sought by the writers of nineteenth century Russia was presented not in terms of morals or of philosophy but in the language of the Gospels. The novelists called their readers, not to progress or happiness, but rather to that blessedness which was promised to the meek and humble who do not oppose violence by violence and who follow the example of the Son of man, obedient unto death.

Besides literature, there was one more important and influential factor in nineteenth century Russia—the radical movement. Some of the leaders of the movements claimed to be positivists. But there were others for whom their activity had a religious meaning. Both were inspired by the desire for service and for self-sacrifice. This movement in its origin was not only a protest against injustice but also a personal effort of perfection and almost of expiation. The young men and women of the 'seventies who joined the ranks of the revolutionaries put into practice their ideas of poverty, of social self-abasement, of voluntary suffering. We had thus to classify the movement as one of "kenotic" inspiration.

The investigation into this particular emphasis on perfection or, even more definitely, on the following of the humiliated Christ gave us the desire to examine whether it was a current of thought or devotion peculiar to the secular world alone or whether it was somehow related to the life and teaching of the Church. In spite of the historical alienation of the educated classes from the Church, there was still a contact intimate and close enough to be of influence. Besides the direct preaching of the Gospel the Church spoke to the nation through the liturgy; the influence of the monasteries, with their spiritual directors and the memory of the early saints who followed the example of the humiliated Christ, was certainly instrumental in the keeping up of this tradition. But continual reference to the past of the Church did not satisfy us. We tried to investigate whether there was a pronounced teaching or at least exhortation to enter into the spirit of the humiliation of Christ.

The writings of St. Tykhon which were studied in the ecclesiastical schools on the topic of moral theology revealed to us that not only was there an exhortation to be of the mind of Christ but that it was founded on Philippians ii. The voluntary self-abasement of Christ, both in His premundane life as the Son of God and in His earthly life, were shown to be the true basis of Christianity. The same teaching, expressed with more doctrinal definiteness, was proposed to his listeners by the famous preacher of the nineteenth century, the Metropolitan Filaret of Moscow. He, also, never omitted to relate the text of Philippians to the fact of the Incarnation. His sermons on Christmas Day, both as moral and doctrinal teaching, were a constant reminder of the humiliation of Christ. We found also in the Russian Church of the nineteenth century the writings of Bukharev, with his constant appeal to follow the " humiliated Lamb," and his own strange and sorrowful destiny which could be explained from his desire for personal self-abasement on the lines of foolishness for Christ's sake.

There was no attempt to rewrite a systematic Christological treatise. By the end of the nineteenth century, M. M. Tareev felt the need to express " the faith of the fathers " in the language of modern thought. He started from patristic thought in which he was especially attracted by the allusions (though not elaborated) to the humiliation of Christ. For Tareev, the kenotic theory was the only possible approach and the only possible explanation of the Gospel Portrait. But it is important for us to remember that Tareev's devotional and intellectual background lay not in patristic thought but much more in Russian secular literature of the nineteenth century. He emphatically acknowledged his link with it and gave it the place of honour in the religious sphere. He also pointed to what was—or was believed by the writers to be—the popular devotion to a " God's man, humiliated and suffering."

The link between theological and secular thought was even more obvious in V. S. Soloviev, himself belonging to the secular world. As poet and as political thinker he spoke of Russia in " kenotic " terms. And when, as a philosopher or as a theologian, he meditated upon the " process of Godman-hood," he found the basis of the relationship between God and the world in the fact of the self-emptying of the divine Logos, and referred his speculation to Phil. ii. 5—11.

Finally, we studied the treatise of dogmatic Christology by S. N. Bulgakov. There we found a complete and thorough exposition of the doctrine of kenosis. Knowing how intimately S. N. Bulgakov was related to the world of secular thought and literature, we consider that his thought also was influenced in some measure by what he called " a purely Russian manner of the artistic interpretation of Christ's image."

The whole purpose of the exposition of the previous chapters has been to show that, however different the epoch, the language, the manner of presentation, all the writings which we have examined were only diverse manners of expressing one and the same image, namely that of the humiliation of Christ. The technical language of the theologians seemed to us to be, in this instance, the theological interpretation and definition of what was dimly felt by the secular writers.

Whilst examining our material we found our attention called to another feature which was closely connected with the idea of the humiliated Christ—namely, an intuition of direct presence of His Body still accessible to people under the form of all who suffer. The material illustrating the " kenotic " aspect was convincingly abundant. Yet, even risking the contradiction of our own thesis, we would like to link the " kenotic " idea with this idea of Christ's Body. This half-uttered intuition seemed to us of importance. It allows us to affirm, in the sphere of secular and artistic thought, what we regard as the only plausible reason for the doctrine of kenosis in the sphere of technical Christology. Namely, we regard the " kenotic " devotion as expressed through the material examined on these pages, as devotion to the humanity of Christ. Russia had no devotional stream comparable to that of the Western worship of the humanity of the Lord. The passion of Christ was most vividly felt, but the Church offered to popular devotion nothing except the sober reading of the Gospel narrative of His passion (the " twelve Gospels " and the shroud or winding sheet, image representing the buried Christ). Christ was repeatedly and mainly spoken of in terms of His divinity. The thought of many of the writers examined by us remained faithful with regard to the divinity of the Lord. But the writings of " kenotic " character completed the image of Christ known through the Gospels and the Creed by adding devotion to His humanity as well. Perhaps even the adoration of Christ in the form of a servant, or speaking through a beggar, influenced the further development of the idea of the Body, and produced the organic conception of the " *sobornost* " of the Church. But this last point goes beyond our direct subject.

Perhaps a word or two might be added with regard to secular literature after the epoch when we left it. Kenotic Christological thought found its expression in the twentieth century. Meanwhile, the secular world was deeply interested in religious problems. It is impossible to give here any picture of it. We would like to notice only that the " Religio-Philosophical Meetings " of 1901 gathered together poets and novelists as well as clergy. It was a conscious attempt to bring these two worlds together. The outstanding writers of the epoch are characterized by both religious and literary interests and works. It may be enough to mention such outstanding

N

examples as V. V. Rozanov (1856—1919), D. S. Merezh-kovsky (b. 1866), L. I. Shestov (b. 1866), N. A. Berdyaeff (b. 1874). The poets shared in the religious quest. Russian Symbolism was a religious movement no less than it was a revival of the art of poetry. Vyacheslav Ivanov (b. 1866), Andrey Bely (1880—1935), Alexander Blok (1880—1921) were greatly indebted to Soloviev. They shared with the writers of the nineteenth century a mystical love of their country. Without drawing any conclusions about the religious or the " kenotic " current in post-revolutionary Russia, we thought it of interest to mention a few lines of modern poets which refer to Christ.

Tyutchev was appreciated by this generation more than he had been ever before. We cannot help remembering him when we read in Maximilian Voloshin (1877—1933) a poem called " Holy Russia " (1917). Refusing to be a princess, she " delivered herself to the robber and to the felon, set fire to her farms and crops, destroyed her ancient abode, and went out into the world humiliated and a beggar, and the slave of the vilest slave. . . . Shall I dare cast a stone at thee? . . . Shall I not go on my knee before thee in mire? blessing the trace of thy bare foot, thou wretched, homeless drunken Russia—thou fool in Christ." Or else, he spoke of the grain of wheat, reminding all that its death expressed a spiritual law. " Dissolve, Russia, and come to new life as the Kingdom of the Spirit " (*Transubstantiation*).[1] It may be perhaps of interest to mention also, without any political reference, a poem of Sergej Esenin (1895—committed suicide 1925)—or at least ascribed to him. It is the poem alluded to by André Gide as one secretly recited to him by a young Russian.[2] The poem is an answer to an antireligious poem of Demian Bedny. The poet asks the antireligious colleague; why had men put Christ to death? Was it because He, with a group of fisher-men from the poor villages recognized as Caesar's only the power of gold, whilst " light and shadow " were full of the worship of Caesar all around them? Was it because He pitied

---

[1] Both fragments translated by D. Mirsky, *Contemporary Russian Literature* (1926), pp. 209, 210.

[2] André Gide, *Retouches au voyage en U.R.S.S.* (Paris, 1937).

all and blessed all, " loving sorrowfully small children and the dirty prostitutes "? Himself refusing to pray in each church or to believe in miracles, Esenin nevertheless felt ashamed after having read " this lie about Christ." " Son of a carpenter, the Christ was put to death. But when once men asked : who art thou? He answered : I am the Son of Man. And did not say : the Son of God am I." After having expressed his indignation at this attack against Christ, in energetic and at times almost indecent terms, Esenin concludes : and the Russian peasant having read this paper " more desperately still will cling to Christ." [3] The atmosphere of Tyutchev seems unexpectedly revived in a poem which is utterly different from Tyutchev in style and in content—we mean the greatly-discussed and multifariously-interpreted masterpiece of Blok, *The Twelve* (1918).[4] The soldiers of the Red Army, in their symbolical number, go throughout the country. " Freedom, freedom, hey, hey, without a cross." They shoot the bourgeois or a girl who happened to be unfaithful. They go " firing a shot for Holy Russia." A little noise disturbs them, and a half-vision moves in front of them. As they can see nobody distinctly and they receive no answer, they fire in the dark. And

> " So they go with sovereign tread . . .
> Behind them a hungry cur.
> And at their head, with the blood-stained banner,
> Invisible in the raging snow,
> Unwounded midst the bullets' flight,
> With gentle gait above the storm,
> Scattered o'er with pearls of snow,
> With a white aureole of roses,
> At their head goes Jesus Christ."

[3] From periodical *New Russia (Novaja Rossija)*, Paris, 11th July, 1937, n. 31.
[4] Transl. C. E. Bechhofer, 1920.

INDEX

* (F = fiction).

PRINTED IN GREAT BRITAIN
BY THE FAITH PRESS, LTD.
LEIGHTON BUZZARD